Fired, Laid Off, Out of a Job

Fired, Laid Off, Out of a Job

A Manual for Understanding, Coping, Surviving

B. KEITH SIMERSON AND MICHAEL D. McCORMICK

Westport, Connecticut
London

Library of Congress Cataloging-in-Publication Data

Simerson, Byron K.
  Fired, laid off, out of a job : a manual for understanding, coping, surviving / by
  B. Keith Simerson and Michael D. McCormick.
    p. cm.
  Includes bibliographical references and index.
  ISBN 1-56720-634-4 (alk. paper)
    1. Unemployment. 2. Unemployed. 3. Job hunting. I. McCormick, Michael D., 1953- II.
  Title.
  HD5707.5.S557 2003
  650.14—dc21   2002044966

British Library Cataloguing in Publication Data is available.

Library of Congress Catalog Card Number: 2002044966

ISBN: 1-56720-634-4

First published in 2003

Praeger Publishers, 88 Post Road West, Westport, CT 06881
An imprint of Greenwood Publishing Group, Inc.
www.praeger.com

Printed in the United States of America

The paper used in this book complies with the
Permanent Paper Standard issued by the National
Information Standards Organization (Z39.48–1984).

10 9 8 7 6 5 4 3 2 1

I dedicate this book to Darlie, my wife, and our three sons, Jarrett, Brent, and Andrew. Their inspiration and encouragement was a much-needed source of support.

I also dedicate this book to my parents, Boyd and Coleen Simerson, who through words and actions are a constant reminder of what it means to be truly "successful."

I am grateful for the guidance and support of Kristin English, who served as our reader and advisor while this project was underway.

—B.K.S.

I dedicate this book to Nancy, my wife, and our children, Jenny, Patrick, Joe, Kevin, Brian and Kelly, who keep life in perspective.

I also dedicate this book to my late mother, Loretto McCormick, whose wise advice to those who faced a forced career transition was: "This is not a boot out the door, it's a boost to a higher level." Truer words were not spoken.

—M.D.M.

Contents

Tables

Preface

My career has spanned both the public and private sector. I have been affiliated with several professional services firms, the petrochemical industry, the health care field, and the criminal justice profession.

While job cuts were not inherent in any of these industries or professions, their potentiality led to my being trained to serve as an out-counselor. Their presence is real: I have previously been responsible for out-counseling an entire management consulting department and have, along with thousands of my colleagues, been out-counseled on two separate occasions.

Such knowledge and experience have given me a unique perspective—I know what typically is expected of an out-counselor during the out-counseling session. I also know what it is like to be informed "you no longer have a position with the company."

In addition to this particular perspective, I also have certain tools in my personal toolkit that—if shared—may help others prepare for such an event. I have, therefore, written this book. It was initially intended to be for readers who have been laid off from their jobs or who discover today their services are no longer required.

Fortunately, this book was expanded to benefit those readers who are at risk of losing their jobs. That list includes everyone—each of us is at risk of being laid off! For many reasons, mostly outside our personal control, we may learn tomorrow (in person, by memorandum, or by voice mail) that our position is being terminated.

This book takes the form of a toolkit, rather than a voluminous book spanning several hundreds of pages. It is concisely written—to maximize information and to minimize space—and bullet points highlight key messages. Although designed for use as a toolkit, this book is detailed yet comprehensive enough to serve as your one-stop shop for such information.

This book is not a job-hunting book. First, it is a safety manual. We provide detailed information about how to plan for a successful career, along with information about "bulletproofing" your job once you have entered it. Second, it is a blueprint for survival. We provide detailed information about how to win in today's corporate wars (marked by layoffs, downsizings, and wholesale, across-the-board dismissals). Such dismissals, previously termed "firings," are so prevalent as to now be called "corporate rightsizing." All occur within an environment in which CEOs continue earning millions and receiving huge bonuses (in the form of stock options, cash, and executive benefits).

You will find this book to be useful, regardless of where you are in your career cycle. Chapters provide information about your rights and responsibilities as an employee, as well as the privileges, rights, and responsibilities of your employer. Whether you are initially entering today's workforce or are a veteran, you will learn what it really means to be in today's business environment and why you must continually take steps to bulletproof your career. This information will prove equally useful to the college student attempting to enter the competitive job market, the recent entrant attempting to assimilate into the workforce, the veteran employee attempting to assess and alter his or her career plan.

This book will help you plan your career, to position yourself for success. It provides strategies and tactics you can use to "win" the organization/position you desire. It also answers the countless questions you have (and addresses the numerous challenges you face) while attempting to negotiate "land mines" scattered throughout the terrain otherwise known as corporate America. Such a place is not for the weak-hearted. We tackle tough issues head-on, addressing issues such as:

- Steps you can take to reduce the likelihood of your being terminated;
- If you are terminated, when and how to negotiate your dismissal;
- How to examine and negotiate your termination package;
- What to do, if your employer decides to play "hard ball";
- How to select an attorney, after properly determining that you need one;
- What to expect from an attorney, and what an attorney expects from you;
- How to prove your dismissal was inappropriate, or worse, illegal;
- What attorneys must do to establish grounds for a lawsuit; and
- How to move from a bad job situation to one likely to work out better.

In summary, this book is meant to serve as a comprehensive guide for those being laid off. If you find yourself meeting with your organization's out-counselor, it will help you do what is in your best interest and reduce the likelihood of your making a serious mistake during the severance process. It raises legal issues that must be taken into consideration during such trying circumstances. It provides concrete information in the form of sample separation letters and job offer letters (which must be carefully reviewed when you are laid off). It also contains useful worksheets and templates (along with selection criteria, guidelines for use, and helpful examples). Reproduction masters are included in the Appendix.

Equally helpful, this book tells you what to watch for as you participate in the separation process and as you review its deliverables and stipulations. This will help you interpret the soundness of the agreement or program you are being, or have been, offered.

Finally, this guide will help you shift focus as a result of being laid off. It places emphasis on your personal transition and gives numerous pointers for re-entering the job market as an applicant.

Consistent with this book's being written as a toolkit, we provide a detailed listing of counseling, job search, and advisory resources available to the reader.

To achieve its intended purpose (serving as a toolkit, while providing comprehensive and detailed information to individuals at risk of being laid off, about to be laid off, or in the process of being laid off), this book must address several key topics. In addition to being adequately covered, these topics must be addressed in the most appropriate manner. Such need magnified the need for a contributing author. While trained to serve as an out-counselor and previously involved in human resources matters, I considered it imperative that an individual possessing deep skills and expertise in employment law help write this book.

I therefore asked a close friend and colleague, Michael McCormick, to serve as a co-author. Michael not only brings expert knowledge and understanding of employment law to this project, but he also draws upon his years of experience working with employees and employers to investigate and resolve many of the issues raised in this book.

A final note to those of you who have been laid off or who are at risk of being laid off: Being discharged is a very emotional event; it raises a multitude of fears. (We will lose our house. Our parents will not understand. Our children will suffer because of this. Our neighbors will be shocked.) Some of these fears are real—others are simply imagined. This book will help you more clearly understand the event itself, think through all the relevant issues, capitalize on available resources, and take appropriate action.

—B. K. S.

When B. K. asked whether I would be interested in writing this book
with him, I was intrigued by the idea, but uncertain of my contribution. I
had known B. K. for some time, and knew that he had broad experience as
an executive in human resources, but did not appreciate the depth of his
knowledge and insight until we began writing. We discussed the concept
in greater detail, and I realized we could construct a toolkit of means of
handling the difficult issue of losing your job and of approaching a post-
layoff job search from many perspectives—professionally, emotionally,
financially and legally. I became very excited about the project. A principal
focus of this book will be to protect yourself—if you do not, no one will.
That goes for employees and employers, in different ways.

This book is not simply for laid-off or fired employees. It is a valuable
resource for employers as well. Just as (former) employees should be
aware of their rights and options, employers should be aware of the ramifications of their actions. Both employees and employers must protect
themselves in these turbulent economic times. Understanding the hiring
and firing processes from both the employer's and the employee's perspective is essential to understanding your rights and options.

For over twenty-three years in my legal practice, I have represented
clients in a variety of types of commercial litigation and alternative dispute
resolution matters. One of the areas of practice in which I have concen-
trated is employment law. With that employment law experience coupled
with many more years of litigation experience, I welcomed this opportunity to work with B. K. to share my perspective concerning (1) what
employees who face losing their jobs (or have lost their jobs) should do to
help ensure both the vindication of their rights as well as a successful reen-
try in the workforce and (2) what employers facing the difficult decision to
discipline, lay off, or discharge an employee should do to protect themselves and fend off being sued. Because the majority of my practice has
been representing businesses and corporate clients, I welcomed the opportunity to bring that point of view to the analysis of what both employees
and employers should do in the event of layoffs, reductions in force and
employment terminations in these turbulent economic times.

We have tried to integrate B. K.'s wealth of experience in human
resources management and my trial and employment law experience to
help employees facing a difficult situation. To those who recently lost their
jobs, my hope is to help you realize (1) you are not alone—there are literally thousands of employees who have faced and have overcome an
unplanned career transition; (2) despite your involuntary transition, you
have rights you can protect; and (3) you have many career strategies to
consider and implement to help ensure your job security in the future.

Of course, providing legal advice is not our goal. We cannot provide
you legal advice without a full and complete understanding of your facts.
We can, however, point out issues for you to consider that affect your

rights. We also can propose strategies to protect those rights. The tools in our toolkit do just that. Load your toolkit and get to work on your career.

There will be situations where you will need help. You may need to seek the assistance of experts, whether they are medical, legal, or career consultants. Again, we will help you identify those situations.

For example, remember the employee handbook you received on your first day of work, read quickly, and put in the back of the bottom drawer of your desk? Did you ever consider that the handbook might provide you contract rights that protect you from being laid off or discharged without any compensation or benefits? Did you ever consider that the handbook protected you from being disciplined, laid off, or fired? These are examples of issues I will raise with you throughout our book. They are issues you may decide require legal advice.

How to obtain legal advice was another issue B. K. and I felt we should discuss with you. Many of us never retained an attorney for anything other than a house closing or a will. When should you retain an attorney? How do you go about finding and hiring an attorney for something like a layoff or employment termination? After you hire an attorney, what can you expect? What will the attorney do for you? We will help you answer those questions and demystify the process.

My most fundamental hope is to provide you hope—and tools to construct your future. In recent years (make that recent months), thousands of people have lost their jobs to layoffs, reductions in force, and other reasons completely unrelated to them as persons or their job performance. When you realize this, you realize that thousands have undergone the same process you are experiencing, and survived. This book will help you survive one of the most stressful situations in your life.

Of course it is important to safeguard your legal rights in this difficult time. Just as important is using the tools we propose in this book to move on. Advance your career. Remember always: "This is not a boot out the door, it's a boost to a higher level."

—M. D. M.

CHAPTER 1

We Are All at Risk

TIMES HAVE CHANGED—BE PREPARED FOR IT

Baby boomers were raised in a world whose bedrock economic principles were trust, diligence, loyalty, and prosperity. We trusted that if we were diligent and loyal employees, we would prosper hand-in-hand with our employer while moving up the corporate and socioeconomic ladders. We graduated from school, went to work for a company, and expected to remain there until retirement.

In the modern world of disposable commodities, this paradigm has changed. Regardless of the depth of our trust, the endurance of our diligence, or the extent of our loyalty, we can no longer assume we will work continuously or prosperously for any employer (much less for one employer) until retirement. The American ideal was supposed to be that if we did good work and were loyal employees, our employer would return that loyalty. In today's workplace, the expectation of employees seems to be: "I will contribute to my employer's financial success—but only if I'm paid what I'm worth." Even in today's changed world, however, employees seem to share a fundamental belief that one good turn deserves another. In the business setting, we believe that if we do a good job for the company, the company should "watch out for us." That ideal may have been lost in recent turbulent times.

Just as employees seem to share a fundamental belief in fairness, so do employers. The expectation of employers in these tough economic times seems to be, "We will compensate you fairly in return for your loyal and diligent efforts." Our turbulent economy, the competitive business environment, and the need for employers to meet the economic expectations of shareholders or partners have changed our workplace. This change is not necessarily bad, so long as the guiding tenet of the decision makers is to treat employees honestly and with dignity and respect. Unfortunately, the business world is apt to sacrifice these standards in the name of economic reality or profits. We cannot, indeed must not, assume that the former benevolent philosophy guides corporate decisions. Self-preservation must replace the former idealistic principles of the employer-employee relationship.

No Job Is Secure

Given today's prevailing business philosophy that employees are replaceable, no one has job security. The corporate world sometimes refers to employees as "human assets." What an objectionable term! Characterizing employees as assets reflects a lack of respect for human dignity. People are not interchangeable and disposable, like supplies and equipment. Yet, that is how many corporate officials view their personnel. That attitude will come back to bite them in the end! (Pun intended.)

We may feel as though the job security we learned of in school and early in our careers no longer exists. In reality, however, security really never existed. The industrialists and robber barons of economic days past hardly had their employees' best interests in mind when making business decisions. Today, we notice the absence of any semblance of job security; employers now without hesitation take actions they previously may not have taken, and they do so more publicly and frequently.

At-Will Employment or At-Whim Employment?

The job security of all employees is at risk, to differing degrees. Many factors contribute to this risk-laden employment environment. First and foremost, many states adhere to the rule that employment is "at-will." Employment at-will means that employment can be terminated at any time, for a good reason, a bad reason, or for no reason at all—so long as the reason is not discriminatory. Absent an agreement to the contrary, such as a written employment contract or union collective bargaining agreement, employment for an indefinite term is deemed to be at-will. The at-will employment doctrine was adopted in this country late in the nineteenth century and was used to justify employers' unfettered right to hire and fire employees. From an employee's perspective, at-will employment is more than risky; it is illusory. At-will employees may be discharged for reasons completely unrelated to their performance. Stellar performers are just as at risk as slackers. Either can be discharged without cause and without explanation. From our perspective, "at-will" employment is little more than "at-whim" employment. We can be discharged at the whim of our employers.

Whether the discharge is for budgetary reasons, an economic downturn, or a change in corporate direction, at-will employees often are not told why they are being let go. Whether based on whim or economic necessity, at-will employment may be terminated at any time. At-will employees have little protection from arbitrary employment decisions.

Given its unfairness, courts have weakened the at-will employment doctrine by making exceptions to it where:

- An employee handbook or policy manual provides implied contract rights to the employee;
- The termination of employment is a result of discrimination or has a discriminatory effect; or
- The discharge is in retaliation for the employee exercising a right protected by public policy, such as filing a worker's compensation claim or reporting criminal activity.

In at-will employment states, an employee may challenge the presumption that his or her employment is at-will by proving that the employer made a promise of employment for a definite term or on certain conditions. Such a promise may be oral or written. Here are some examples. Occasionally, an employer may make a written offer of employment. Although it may not look like a formal contract, the written offer may become a contract if the employee accepts the terms of the offer and begins working in the position. An offer of employment may be for a definite period at a definite rate of compensation. Such an offer, when accepted, may become a contract, even if it is called an "offer." In that case, the written offer may give the employee rights that an at-will employee may not have. The "offer" may restrict the employer's right to discharge the employee or reduce his or her compensation during the term set out in the offer.

Occasionally, an employer requires employees to sign a written employment agreement. Written employment agreements generally do not exist except for managerial employees or employees with special skills or training. Like any contract, an employment agreement gives the parties certain rights. The employee may have a right to continued employment for a definite term, at a definite rate of compensation, and may not be terminated except for certain reasons. If the employer discharges the employee during the term of the employment agreement, the employee may be entitled to continued compensation during the unexpired term of the contract.

Some employment agreements are for a one-year term but are renewable automatically unless either the employer or the employee gives the other notice of nonrenewal. This is common in sales and marketing positions. Such an employment agreement may give the employee a right to continued employment unless the employer follows the nonrenewal procedure in the contract. If an employer discharges an employee during the contract year, the employee may be entitled to salary and benefits through the remainder of that year.

An employment agreement also may provide that the employer may not terminate the contract except "for cause." This will provide a level of protection an at-will employee does not enjoy. At-will employees may be discharged without cause.

The issue of what constitutes cause for termination of employment has generated much litigation. As a general rule, "cause" for termination is a violation of an employment policy, or misconduct such as committing a crime, engaging in discriminatory or harassing behavior, or insubordination. Disloyalty to your employer may also be cause for the termination of your employment. Employees must be loyal to their employer. While performing his or her job duties, the employee must act in the best interest of the employer, not in his or her personal best interest. Employees conducting business in competition with their employer or making a profit from the business of the employer may be discharged for disloyalty.

Being discharged for cause or misconduct may damage both your ability to obtain new employment and your ability to obtain unemployment insurance benefits. Under most state unemployment insurance laws, discharge for cause or misconduct is grounds for denying unemployment benefits.

Even if you did not have a written employment agreement, you may have contract rights protecting you from being disciplined or discharged unless the employer follows its own rules. Many employers have a written employee handbook or policy manual it expects employees to follow. Such a handbook or manual may form an implied contract between the employer and employee. If the employer requires employees to abide by the employee handbook or employment policies in return for initial or continued employment, and the handbook or policy provisions alter the at-will status of employment, the handbook or policy may give the employee contract rights and a level of protection not available to at-will employees.

Some courts have found that employment policies or handbooks create enforceable contract rights if the policy contains a clear promise that the employee reasonably believes is an offer of employment or continued employment subject to its terms. For example, the employee handbook or policy manual may require the employer to follow progressive discipline procedures before discharging an employee. That is not the case as to disciplining or discharging an at-will employee.

A typical progressive discipline policy will provide for a verbal warning or reprimand for a first infraction, a written warning and suspension with pay for a second, and suspension without pay or possible discharge for a third violation. Such a policy restricts the employer's ability to discharge an employee at any time for any (or no) reason. This employee is not truly at-will because the employee handbook or policy manual gives him or her rights an at-will employee does not have. In today's economic climate, however, some employers attempt to compress the progressive discipline process by taking the position that the termination of employment was for a serious infraction of employment policies, allowing the employer to cut to the chase and discharge the employee without progressive discipline.

Many employee handbooks and policy manuals contain a disclaimer that they do not constitute a contract and do not alter the at-will nature of the employment. In reality, however, whether the handbook or manual provides contract rights depends on the provisions of the handbook or manual, the nature of your employment relationship, and your state's employment laws. Many courts recognize the unfairness of an employer unilaterally imposing policies or other terms and conditions of employment, and then revising them midstream. These courts often find that, to be enforceable, such policies must be mutual, providing both you and your employer with rights and obligations. This mutuality is an indication of the existence of a contract.

Employment law in this area is very complex; you may have to consult an attorney familiar with your state's employment laws to determine whether your employer's employee handbook or policy manual provides you contract rights and recourse for any discipline or adverse employment action against you.

While your employment is increasingly at risk, you also have rights. Those rights continue to exist, even when your employer imposes discipline or terminates your employment. Although your employment may be "at-will," that does not really mean "at-whim."

Without a written or implied employment contract providing employment for a definite term or on specified conditions, we are at risk because our employment is at-will. This risk must be assessed in the context of the terms of the employment as defined in the offer of employment, any written employment contract, and any employee handbook or policy manual. If you are laid off or let go, you should review the documents you signed when you took the job to determine whether the termination of your employment violated any written agreement or employee handbook or employment policy that may give you rights at-will employees may not have.

Another risk you must assess when your employment is terminated is whether your former employer may prevent or restrict your future employment opportunities. For example, if you signed an agreement not to compete with your employer, the agreement may restrict the geographic location where you may seek new employment and the type of employment you can accept. Courts are reluctant to enforce noncompetition agreements because they restrict free trade. However, if you signed a covenant not to compete and received a benefit (such as initial employment, a raise, a promotion, or additional benefits) for doing so, courts will enforce the noncompetition agreement so long as it:

• Is of a relatively short duration (one or two years);
• Is limited in geographic scope (where the former employer conducts its business); and
• Restricts activity that actually is competition with the employer's business.

Another risk factor you have to consider when your employment is terminated is whether you can use information you attained during your employment. If you signed a confidentiality agreement, you may be obligated—even after you are discharged—to maintain the secrecy of your former employer's confidential information and trade secrets, such as training materials, production processes, formulas, and customer lists.

Although courts are reluctant to enforce noncompetition agreements, they are more likely to enforce confidentiality agreements because using a former employer's confidential information is a form of unfair competition. Confidentiality agreements usually protect information that the employer maintains as private, is access-restricted (on a need-to-know basis), and is not readily accessible using public sources. You should maintain the confidentiality of your former employer's confidential information even after your employment ends.

Even if you did not sign a confidentiality agreement, many states have laws protecting trade secrets from being misappropriated and used. In essence, it is simply inappropriate for you to share your former employer's proprietary information with your new employer.

I Was Riffed!

We have been talking about the many risks inherent in at-will employment. Even employees with contract rights under employment contracts, employee manuals or union contracts, are at risk. Uncertainty and loss of revenue resulting from the weak economy have caused employers to reduce their workforce. This occurs when companies merge and consolidate operations, reorganize voluntarily, or consider bankruptcy. Reductions in force (RIFs) pose a risk to all employees. Although employers do not have an unfettered right to reduce their workforce, RIFs, when managed and implemented properly, are legal.

Employment agreements, employment policies dealing with RIFs, civil service laws, union contracts, and discrimination laws affect an employer's right to reduce the workforce and how to implement one. Employees facing a RIF should consult their employee handbook, manual, union contract, or an employment law attorney to determine their rights.

From an employer's perspective, the criteria for selecting which employees to be included in the RIF are very important in avoiding claims. The criteria should be objective, not subjective. Subjective criteria are prone to abuse and to claims of discrimination. If an employee is not given concrete and objective reasons for being riffed, it may be assumed the decision, "must have been discrimination" due to race, sex, age, ethnic background, or other wrongful basis.

Some RIFs are implemented on the basis of seniority—the last employee hired is the first to be let go. More frequently, however, the employer chooses which employees are riffed. If the RIF is driven by economics and the employer is seeking to reduce its costs (by reducing the payroll), generally older and higher-compensated employees may be targeted. Such a decision-making practice, however, may violate federal law. The federal Age Discrimination in Employment Act of 1967 prohibits discrimination in employment decisions on the basis of age. This may mean that if workers over forty years of age are targeted, the employer may be liable to the affected employees.

Occasionally, job cuts are accomplished by offering severance benefits to employees who "voluntarily" resign and sign a release or waiver of claims. We have all seen situations where employers request such a "voluntary" resignation in return for take-it-or-leave-it severance benefits. Under such circumstances, we know that if we do not accept the severance offer and sign a release, we will be let go with nothing.

Certain "older" (over forty) workers also have rights under the federal Older Workers Benefits Protection Act, which amended the Age Discrimination in Employment Act. Even in cases of voluntary resignations, where the employer offers severance benefits and asks the employee to sign a waiver or release of claims, the waiver or release is not effective unless the waiver or release:

- Is part of an agreement between the employee and the employer and is written in a manner calculated to be understood by the employee (not legalese);

- Refers to rights under the Age Discrimination Employment Act and the Older Workers Benefits Protection Act;

- Does not apply to claims arising after signing the waiver or release;

- Is in exchange for value in addition to that to which the employee is already entitled (the employee gets something extra for releasing age-related claims); and

- The employee is advised in writing to consult an attorney before signing the waiver or release;

- The employee is given twenty-one days to consider the agreement; and

- The employee is given seven days after signing to change his or her mind.

In addition to the Age Discrimination in Employment Act and the Older Workers Benefits Protection Act, releases typically specifically mention the release of claims under the Civil Rights Act of 1866, the Civil Rights Act of 1964 (Title VII), the Civil Rights Act of 1991, the Employee Retirement Income Security Act of 1974, the Americans with Disabilities Act, the Rehabilitation Act of 1973, the Equal Pay Act, the False Claims Act, the Family and Medical Leave Act of 1993, and claims under state law. As you can see, signing a release without fully investigating your rights could result in losing rights you never considered. This is why we suggest that you consult an attorney before signing any severance agreement that contains a release.

Other federal laws also may affect your rights in the event of a RIF. Under the Worker Adjustment Retraining and Notification Act, in the event of a RIF by an employer with 100 or more employees, sixty days' notice must be given in the event of a mass layoff or a plant closing. A "mass layoff" is a layoff of at least 33 percent of the workforce, but not less than fifty employees (excluding part-time employees), at a single location. A "plant closing" is a shutdown of a single site of employment, or one or more operating units within the site, resulting in the loss of employment for fifty or more employees. Employers and employees alike should consult an attorney in the event of significant layoffs or plant closings by large employers.

Although employers implementing a RIF must follow these rules, RIFs should be implemented in an honest, even-handed, and nondiscriminatory manner. The decision of which employees are chosen to lose their positions should be made using criteria such as performance evaluations, job skills (or lack of them), and seniority. Ideally, employees will be given the opportunity to choose to participate in a RIF in exchange for severance benefits. A voluntary resignation is always preferable to a forced layoff.

If the employer's guiding principle in a workforce reduction is fundamental fairness and preserving the dignity of affected workers, the employer may be less prone to lawsuit by affected workers. The recommended protocol for handling a RIF is to be forthright with employees. They should be advised of the scope or depth of the layoffs, the criteria used in determining which employees will be laid off and their reemployment rights.

Employers who arrogantly advise employees of the RIF or layoff when they are on their way out the office door at the end of the workday are more likely to be invited to explain themselves in a courtroom or before the Equal Employment Opportunity Commission (EEOC). Ignoring the principles of fundamental fairness and human dignity is an invitation to litigation.

What Is Due Process? What Process Is Due?

Nonunion employees in the private sector are considered to be at-will unless they have an employment agreement or an employee handbook or policy manual that gives them implied contract rights. Unlike typical at-will employees, union members and government employees usually have employment security rights. The principal right they enjoy, which most at-will employees do not, is due process. The underlying tenet of due process is "notice" and an "opportunity to be heard." Civil servants (by law) and union members (by a collective bargaining agreement) usually are not subject to discipline or discharge without notice of the infraction and the possible adverse employment action, and without being given an opportunity to be heard on the issue of the reason for the employment action.

Some employee handbooks and policy manuals also provide due process rights, but that is the exception, not the rule. This is typically the result of employers asking employment attorneys preparing their employee handbook or policy manual not to provide anything (such as due process rights) that alters the at-will nature of the employment. Even so, employees should review their handbook or manual carefully for the procedures or due process to which they are entitled before being laid off or discharged.

If you are being laid off or discharged and are entitled to due process rights, the stage is set—until the final decision is made to terminate your employment—for you to make your case (perhaps with the assistance of an attorney) that your continued employment will benefit your employer. Now is not the time to be throwing darts. Even though you may be facing a very emotional and potentially financially disastrous time, logic and common sense (rather than anger) should guide you.

Faced with a possible layoff or discharge, you must market yourself to your employer. For example, if corporate restructuring or change in business direction is the reason for the employment action, show your employer how you will fit in and provide a benefit in the restructured workforce or business plan. Rarely will "fire me and I'll sue" convince an employer to retain you. We make suggestions for defending your career and promoting yourself during these turbulent times in chapter 3, "Bulletproofing Your Career."

How Employers and Employees Should Manage Layoffs and Discharges

Knowing your employer's perspective on handling layoffs and discharges will help you understand the process and to act accordingly. Many adverse employment decisions (demotions, layoffs, terminations, etc.) are communicated to employees in a setting seemingly designed to prompt litigation. The five-minute "exit interview" scenario we describe in chapter 5 is not all that unusual. A typical exit interview at which an employee is told that he or she is out of a job takes the minimum time possible. Why is that? Human nature tells us that no normal person enjoys breaking bad news. If an employer handles the difficult situation properly, however, treating the employee honestly and with dignity and respect, even the employee may understand the decision.

The five-minute exit interview is not appropriate. Such a seemingly hurried setting at which to communicate a life-changing (and economically threatening) decision is not only uncaring, but also downright dangerous. Violence in the workplace has been given much publicity in recent years. So much so, we have a colloquialism to characterize it—"going postal." Instead of the five-minute hurried exit interview, employers and employee alike are better served by being prepared for what may happen, which lets them defuse a possibly inflammatory setting by calmly and compassionately dealing with the uncomfortable event. We said it before and will say it again and again: Treat employees (even on their last day) honestly and with dignity and respect. Employees who are taken completely by surprise may react emotionally or, more dangerously, violently to the news that they are losing their livelihood. Employers should prepare for this possibility by assessing the risk that the employee (who perhaps in the past displayed anger, threatening, or violent tendencies) may become violent or disrupt the workplace. Employees who see the handwriting on the wall (for example, if economic conditions seem to be leading to job cutbacks) should prepare themselves for possible bad news as well. Planning ahead, assessing your career, anticipating what you may do to find employment, and how to manage economically during a period of unemployment may help you handle one of the most stressful events in your life—losing your job. Throughout the remainder of this book, we introduce strategies and tools you should consider using at such a challenging time.

In addition to anticipating possible problems, handling the difficult decision to demote, lay off, or discharge an employee requires the employer to do its homework. The employer must be prepared to respond to the employee's inevitable question, "Why me?"

No answer is going to satisfy the employee fully. An employer that does its homework before making a final decision, however, is less likely to be required to answer the "Why me?" question in a courtroom. If an employment decision is based on performance, the written record must support the decision. For example, before telling an employee that his or her performance does not meet the employer's requirements or expectations, management must carefully review the employment file. Any employee subjected to an adverse employment action will want to exercise the right to review his or her employment file to try to understand or find a reason for the adverse action. If the written record does not support the stated reason for the employment action, the employee will be justifiably confused and upset.

Many supervisors are reluctant to give candid annual performance evaluations, for fear of embarrassing or alienating employees who often are friends as well as colleagues. Positive performance evaluations, however, do not support the position that a decision to let an employee go was performance related. The employee may have been given awards, bonuses, or commendations for good performance. So why is he or she being rewarded by being let go? Honesty and candor in performance appraisals is an absolute necessity for both the employer and employee. From the employer's perspective, false positive evaluations may restrict necessary employment decisions. From the employee's perspective, performance evaluations that omit details of the employer's concerns prevent the employee from addressing them and improving his or her performance, and enhancing his or her job security.

As we have said, it is essential that management treat employees honestly and with dignity and respect. Employees seeing their friends and colleagues being discharged for seemingly irrational or dishonest reasons say to themselves, "There, but for the grace of God, go I." Employees in such situations do not view their employer the same ever again. To enhance the credibility of the overall process, employers must accurately evaluate employees and ensure that resulting documentation supports their decision if performance is the stated basis of an adverse employment action.

If an employer discharges an employee for misconduct, the employer must be prepared to support the allegation of misconduct. In some cases, such as allegations of sexual or other forms of harassment, federal law requires employers to conduct a prompt and thorough investigation. In all fairness, and under federal law, the alleged perpetrator has rights, too. The federal Fair Credit Reporting Act (despite its name) protects employees from certain investigations and reports of their personal affairs without their knowledge or consent. Employees who are accused of misconduct prompting the employer's investigation, and any employer who conducts such an investigation, must be aware of and comply with these laws.

If the employee's contract, the employee handbook, and the policy manual procedures have been followed, and the employer has decided to implement the adverse employment action, how is it done? We have said it before and will say it again, "Treat employees honestly and with dignity and respect." An employee should be told of his or her discharge in person, preferably not by the supervisor (who may have too personal an interest in the situation), but by a person who can relate the reasons for the action without personalizing it. It is advisable for the employer to have two representatives at the meeting, and the employee should request to have a representative there as well. The National Labor Relations Board has taken the position that even nonunion employees may request that a coworker be present during any interview as a result of which an adverse employment action may be taken.

At many exit interviews, the employer will provide the general reasons for the adverse action without details or specific instances of problems. Both the employer and the employee should avoid any debate of the merits of the decision. By the time the discharge meeting is scheduled, the decision has been made. No useful purpose is served by arguing a point or decision that is unalterable. Such debate only gives rise to the risk of saying something you will later regret. Employers, don't make damaging admissions that belie your position! Employees, don't burn any bridges!

All compensation, unused vacation or personal time due, severance benefits, insurance continuation, and retirement benefits should be explained and accompanied by a written explanation of all benefits at the exit interview. Communicating a layoff to an employee in a manner that allows the employee to leave with his or her dignity intact goes a long way toward avoiding claims of discrimination or wrongful discharge.

Why Me?

We have been discussing some very serious personal and legal issues about the risks we all experience in our employment. One way to minimize, or at least recognize, the inherent risk of losing our jobs is to examine the reasons employers frequently give for discharging employees or reducing the workforce. By understanding those reasons, we may be able to formulate strategies to avoid them from cropping up in our relationships with our employer. You cannot bulletproof your career unless you understand and formulate strategies to address the reasons why many people lose their employment.

Paul Simon wrote a famous song, "Fifty Ways to Leave Your Lover." Our play on that song title is "Twenty-Four Ways to Lose Your Livelihood." Based on our experience, management typically cites one or more of twenty-four reasons when discharging employees. These reasons fall into two general categories—misconduct-related (see Table 1.1) and performance-related (see Table 1.2).

These lists are not exhaustive. No doubt, "ingenious" employees and "devious" employers (depending on your perspective) will add more humorous and more fanciful reasons for being fired or firing. The point is that in these turbulent times, all employees must realize that the risk of losing their employment is increased, and all employers must realize that despite these turbulent times, the law and sound business ethics and prin-

Table 1.1
Misconduct-Related Reasons for Discharge

Actions Reflecting a Lack of Intelligence

- Providing false information on the employment application

- Falsifying your credentials or work history

- Leaving the workplace without authorization

- Engaging in a unilateral or unauthorized work slowdown, stoppage, or strike

Actions Reflecting a Lack of Character

- Improper or unauthorized use of the employer's property

- Improper use of the employer's equipment such as telephones or computers

- Disloyalty I—Doing personal business while on duty

- Disloyalty II—Making a profit personally from the employer's business

- Disloyalty III—Unauthorized release or use of the employer's confidential information

- Disloyalty IV—Making disparaging remarks publicly about the employer

- Stupidity I—Drinking alcohol on the job

- Stupidity II—Sleeping on the job

Actions Reflecting Criminal Conduct

- Conviction of a felony involving moral turpitude

- Use of illegal drugs

- Theft of the employer's property

- Threats of violence to supervisors or coworkers

- Fighting

- Sexual or other harassment

- Discrimination

Table 1.2
Performance-Related Reasons for Discharge

Failure to obtain or maintain required licenses

Excessive absenteeism

Abuse of sick leave

Failure to meet legitimate expectations of the employer

Failure to meet sales or production goals

---

ciples limit their discretion in making employment decisions. Employers, you must treat employees honestly and with dignity and respect! Employees, you must reciprocate!

WHEN "GOOD" IS NOT GOOD ENOUGH

When Being Good Is Not Enough: The "Up or Out" Philosophy

Professional services firms working within this turbulent and competitive environment must take steps to ensure a competitive workforce. While doing so may contribute to the firm's survival, it also may be at the expense of employees. This is especially true when management does not apply standards of fairness and respect or when, due to time constraints and other pressures, it shortcuts and therefore invalidates the process.

Accounting, law, consulting, and other professional services firms have traditionally ensured a competitive workforce by applying what is called an "up or out" philosophy. Such a policy, consisting of career tracking and steady progression toward becoming a partner or owner, is desirable from the employee's viewpoint—upon becoming a partner, one has an ownership interest in the firm's business, is allowed to vote on important issues (such as allocation of resources and investments), and if an equity partner, share in the firm's profits. Such a policy is desirable from the firm's perspective—only employees having a proven track record of hard work (billable hours), diligence, and judgment (sound decision making) are invited to become a partner.

Unfortunately, the "up or out" policy has its downside. Even when recognized as a formal career track within a firm, not all employees within the firm can be offered a partnership, because that is not economically feasible. The time frame for inviting an employee to become an owner or partner also has increased. What was once a time frame of five to seven years has now expanded to seven to nine years, and the concept of being a partner is no longer what it once was (firms now have equity and non-equity partners, junior and senior partners).

A critical aspect of the "up or out" policy is the way in which partners are selected. In the past, selection criteria were frequently subjective. Senior partners appointed partners on the basis of "gut feeling" or intuition, rather than on evidence or supporting facts. Today's selection process may be only slightly more sophisticated, however, and it may still involve only a few "discriminate" or objective factors. For example, employees contribute to a firm's success by: serving as a thought leader, putting forth unparalleled effort (workdays of twelve to fourteen hours), and consistently doing "good work" (in terms of quality and cost-benefit). Such a solid employee may not be a viable candidate for becoming partner, however, if he or she has not been allowed to expand upon current projects or engagements or to develop new clients. Often, effort and performance in all areas are discounted or completely nullified if the employee has not exhibited the potential for being a "rainmaker" or business developer.

The "up or out" principle contributes to an overly competitive environment; it does not recognize or reward the "solid" employee. Solid employees, year after year, contribute to the success of projects and engagements, and ultimately, the firm. Such employees, considered by many to be the backbone of professional services firms, are often discharged at the end of the five-, seven-, or nine-year "up or out" cycle.

The "up or out" principle "leverages" firm resources (having lower-paid employees doing a majority of the work, with the work being reviewed and endorsed by higher-paid senior managers, principals, or partners). This concept results in more and more junior-level employees (associates, seniors, and managers) being employed by the firm. This staffing model, no longer feasible in today's cost-conscience business environment, has led to layoffs of large numbers of junior-level employees within professional services firms.

When Doing Good Work Is Not Enough: Forced Ranking

As do professional service firms, public and privately held companies also must take steps to ensure a competitive workforce. While such steps may contribute to the organization's survival, they also may do so at the expense of the employees. As with professional services firms, this is especially true when management does not apply standards of fairness and respect or when (due to human nature) personal bias influences decisions and therefore invalidates the process.

Companies have traditionally ensured a competitive workforce by using performance management systems and performance evaluation processes. Both allow companies to identify their superior employees and thus compensate and treat them accordingly. Such systems and processes also allow companies to identify their average (and provide needed guidance) and below-average (and provide needed development opportunities) employees. Traditionally, below-average employees, whose performance went unchanged after being given the opportunity to improve, were put on a performance plan and eventually discharged from the organization.

Performance management systems and performance evaluation processes are desirable from the employee's viewpoint—they ensure compensation, recognition, and rewards based upon individual effort and accomplishment. Such efforts are desirable from the organization's perspective—the overall workforce is constantly improving, only employees putting forth required effort are retained, and only those putting forth exemplary effort are recognized and rewarded.

Unfortunately, practices to differentiate "exemplary" (for example, the top 10 percent to 20 percent) from "nonexemplary" performers (the remaining 80 percent to 90 percent) have their downsides. Such systems and processes may create unrest within the workforce. This is particularly true when success depends on team, rather than individual, effort. Another downside is that such practices become less effective over time. As nonexemplary performers are discharged and are replaced by exemplary performers, the bar is raised—it quickly becomes evident that exemplary performers soon must be recategorized (or labeled) as nonexemplarly.

Finally, many of today's practices are based on the normal distribution curve. Such norm-referenced grading cannot be applied fairly to particularly talented (in terms of not only their knowledge, skills, and abilities, but also the effort they put forth and the resulting accomplishments) groups or teams of individuals.

This reality is disturbing: if only a percentage of a high-performing group can be rated as exemplary, then a percentage of that high performing group will be rated as nonexemplary and ultimately be discharged; there is only so much room at the top. When such practices are in place, every member of the workforce is at risk of eventually being discharged.

Another aspect of these forced ranking practices adversely impacting one's job security is the way in which employees are judged. These evaluation processes are not sophisticated—some require managers simply to decide if Employee A is better than Employee B and if Employee B is better than Employee C. However, even the simplest grading systems are flawed when human subjectivity is introduced. As we described with professional services firms, the assessment can still involve a few "discriminate" factors. For example, an employee can contribute to a firm's success by serving as a thought leader, by putting forth unparalleled effort (twelve- to fourteen-hour days), and by consistently doing "good work" (in terms of quality and cost). Such a solid employee may not be rated in the top 10 percent of the group if he or she has not been given an opportunity to lead a start-up team or to expand upon a current product or service line. Oftentimes, effort and performance in all areas are nullified if the employee has not shown the "potential" for leading such efforts— although such potential can only be shown if one is given the opportunity to do so.

Perhaps fundamentally more disturbing is the way personal bias influences "forced ranking" assessments. Again, these systems and processes may, on the surface, appear to be very straightforward and sophisticated. However, managers may attribute good performance by "preferred" (translate as "liked") employees to the individual's knowledge, skills, abilities, or the amount of effort he or she put forth. These managers may attribute poor performance by "preferred" employees to bad luck, to bad timing, or to other members of the team. Conversely, these same managers may attribute good performance by "nonpreferred" (translate as "disliked") employees to good luck, good timing, or to other members of the team. These managers may consider poor performance by "nonpreferred" employees to the individual's knowledge, skills, abilities, or the amount of effort he or she was willing to put forth. The bottom line is this: in such an assessment system, factors outside the employee's control impact his or her ranking, and therefore impact his or her job security.

Whether the result of forced ranking or of some other assessment/evaluation process, layoffs associated with performance review scores or ratings are on the rise. Systems and processes forcing the entire workforce into a bell curve ultimately threatens everyone's job security. We all, therefore, are at risk.

All Is Not Lost Even in This Risk-Laden Workplace

Without doubt, today's turbulent economy and competitive business environment have dramatically affected the way we do business, manage our careers, and live our lives. Corporate management is under intense pressure to see that the company delivers value (money) to shareholders. Yesterday's assumptions and expectations about an enduring and benevolent employer-employee relationship may no longer be valid. Yet, principles of treating each other with dignity and respect are ingrained in our society. We therefore hope (and expect) the new rules governing the employer-employee relationship to be founded on the same trust, diligence, loyalty, and prosperity that drove our economic engine in the second half of the past century.

CONCLUSION

We must realize that no longer can we expect the job security we came to expect in years past. Our future employment no longer depends solely on our level of commitment, competence, and contributions. Today's business environment requires employees to be educated, committed, and informed. Understanding this new workplace rule will allow you to continue doing the right things for the right reasons, to take steps—to the extent possible—to control your own destiny, and to rebound quickly if actions beyond your control temporarily derail your career. In this chapter, we have been discussing the risk-laden workplace. We will now turn to issues about which both employers and employees must be aware.

CHAPTER 2

Employers, Beware; Employees, Be Aware: How to Fire Your Employer or Employee

In chapter 1, we pointed out that we all are at risk of losing our employment involuntarily. Employers are at risk, too—of losing you! We all have choices. We are not bound indefinitely to our employers. After all, the U.S. Constitution prohibits involuntary servitude. You are free to leave any job. The important issue we will discuss in this chapter is not whether you can leave your job, but the appropriate manner of ending the employer-employee relationship—and what can you expect when you end it.

We chose to discuss an employee's voluntary resignation together with an involuntary termination of employment because the principles governing the employer-employee relationship should apply equally to both. We say repeatedly in this book that employers should treat employees with dignity and respect at all times. So, too, should employees treat employers, even when "firing" them.

Another reason we chose to discuss termination of employment from the employer's and the employee's perspective in the same chapter is that the employer-employee relationship is a partnership. It is a partnership of mutual aid and benefit. For services rendered to further the employer's business objectives, the employee receives the rewards of compensation, personal satisfaction and career advancement. We cannot establish mutual goals and objectives, however, without mutual understanding.

To help you reach mutual understanding, we will discuss an employee voluntarily resigning (to help employers understand their employees' perspective) and an employer firing an employee (to help employees understand their employer's perspective). Our hope is that understanding each other's perspective will help us be better and more productive employers and employees. It's not quite as bad as "know your enemy," but understanding each other's perspective makes us better able to protect ourselves.

HOW TO FIRE YOUR EMPLOYER

"I'm out of here."

Not so fast! Before quitting your job, you should conduct a self-evaluation and self-assessment. Human nature makes us judgmental from a self-centered perspective. "If only my boss would. . . ." "I can't believe the Company would. . . ." Don't be so egocentric! Instead of always looking at others for answers or excuses, turn around and look in the mirror. Ask yourself:

- Am I really satisfied with my career choice? Should I change careers?
- Am I satisfied with my job performance? Why not? What can I do?
- Am I satisfied with my job security? Why lose it by leaving?
- Do I like my coworkers? Do I really want to leave them and start over?
- Should I go back to school to continue or complete my education?
- How will my family fare if I am out of work for longer than I expect?

Honest answers to these self-probing questions may surprise you. Maybe your job is not so bad after all. After looking inward, seek advice from others in the market. Talk to recruiters, outplacement specialists, and professional colleagues about the job market. The timing may not be right. You may be better off trying to make a bad situation more bearable than losing what you have.

As always, when planning your resignation, expect the unexpected. We will discuss "Bulletproofing Your Career" in chapter 3 to protect against a layoff. We suggest here that you protect yourself and your family before resigning. The first matter to consider is whether you really want to (or have to) resign. Is lack of job satisfaction behind your decision? If so, can you do something proactively, such as initiating a change in your job duties or position, to make your professional life more satisfying?

Perhaps the reason for your dissatisfaction is problems with your supervisor or coworkers. Can you do something to build a better relationship with them? Instead of jumping ship right away, consider talking to your supervisor or human resources manager about changing your job assignment or duties. Offer to take on additional duties. Show your employer that you can perform at a higher level. If this works and you become satisfied with your career advancement, by changing your career from within the organization, you have demonstrated to yourself, your coworkers, and your employer that you are a valuable part of the organization. You have earned the respect of others and built up your self-respect.

Work with your supervisor or manager to establish concrete goals and the means to achieve them. If you fail to achieve them, work with your supervisor or manager to determine why you did not meet your goals. If necessary, revise your action plan within the organization. Do not give up too quickly or quietly.

Repeatedly ask yourself: "Do I really want to leave?"

Before going down the road to resignation, do your personal and family homework, too. Ask yourself:

- "Is the grass really greener on the other side?" Do I expect too much?
- "Will there even be an 'other' side when I get there?" Will a job be there?
- "How will I manage personally and financially during a prolonged period of unemployment if my plans are derailed or delayed?"

After considering your personal situation and post-resignation options, you may decide to defer resignation. However, you may still have the Monday morning (or every day) blues, and you may dread going to work in the morning. The Monday morning blues are a sure sign of job dissatisfaction, and it will be hard for you to disguise it or prevent it from affecting your performance.

If that is the case, recharge your batteries and attempt to make your job more rewarding. Be proactive. You need to make your professional life bearable, and you need to advance your career. Upon careful consideration, you may find it easier to do so in your current position than by moving to an unknown, untested position within another firm. The grass may not be greener on the other side.

Why prepare for resignation? Why not just get up and go?

Self-preservation and protecting your rights require careful thought and planning. Many of us see the handwriting on the wall by being subjected to poor working conditions, unfavorable work assignments, or unjustified poor performance reviews. When you experience such conditions, get out your paper and pencil and start writing. Here is one way you might plan ahead.

Fast-forward to the day you testify to the jury about how your employer treated you unfairly or discriminatorily. Plan for that day by preparing to support your subjective feelings with concrete facts to prove your dissatisfaction. How are you going to prove your case, instead of looking merely like a disgruntled former employee (as your former employer's lawyer will describe you) complaining about the former employer? Do yourself and your trial lawyer a favor: keep a journal. We recommend that you prepare at least one journal page each day, just like a diary. Every day, when

Table 2.1
Journal Page

DATE	DETAILS
WHAT OCCURRED	
PEOPLE INVOLVED	
WITNESSES	
CONVERSATIONS	
DOCUMENTS	

you get home, write down what happened that day. Be sure to record names, dates, conversations, events, and witnesses.

Too much trouble, you say? You won't think so when you win your case against an unfair or abusive employer because you did your homework for five or ten minutes each day.

A sample journal page is presented in Table 2.1. You should use each journal page as an incident report. Use a different sheet for each incident. Use as many sheets as you need for each day. It is very important to prepare these journal entries daily, because our memories fade over time and your evidence will be lost if you do not make a contemporaneous record of your recollection. Your lawyer also will be impressed, because he or she understands that your past recollection recorded on paper is admissible evidence in court (as an exception to the "hearsay rule") even if you forget details.

In addition to documenting the bad, document the good. Document your work performance. Did you meet or exceed your employer's expectations? Did you receive any complaints, reprimands, or awards? You are far better off (and will not look like a disgruntled ex-employee) if you remain objective, recording both your victories and setbacks. You will enhance your credibility if you admit your weaknesses or failure to meet your employer's performance standards at the same time as reporting the faults of your employer, which may contribute to your decision to resign.

Do you feel you are expected to meet performance standards or quotas other employees need not meet? Are all employees in your job category treated similarly? All of these issues probably will arise in litigation. Write down everything, just like your employer probably will "paper your file" to build a case for firing you. Start building your case while you are living it.

You may ask: "Why should I build a case if I am going to resign? I'm leaving, not suing."

Just because you resigned, you did not give up the right to sue your former employer for discrimination, breach of contract, or retaliation. You also did not necessarily give up your right to unemployment compensation. You may feel as though your life is unbearable because of your working conditions, and resignation is your only livable option. If that is the case, you may have been "constructively discharged." Under this legal principle, an employer who improperly increases or changes your job duties, working conditions, or work rules has constructively discharged you, possibly entitling you to resign immediately, to obtain unemployment compensation as though you were laid off, and to bring an action against your employer. Here is an example from the courts:

Larry Tadlock was hired by the Federal Deposit Insurance Corporation (FDIC) in 1967, when he was twenty-six. For nearly thirty years, he received favorable performance evaluations and never received disciplinary action. He received many promotions and supervised many employees at the Little Rock regional office. In 1997, the FDIC assigned Tadlock to the Memphis regional office for a six-week period to act as Assistant Regional Director. As soon as he began his temporary assignment, his supervisors met with him and alleged that in his permanent position he had mistreated staff, misinterpreted promotion policies, failed to follow instructions, and played solitaire on his computer. However, he was not disciplined. Late in 1997, when he was fifty-six, he was informed that he no longer had a position in the Little Rock office, but was being demoted and assigned permanently to the Memphis office. Tadlock resigned—and sued in federal court. The court held that he had been constructively discharged because of the demotion and reassignment, and it awarded him a judgment of back pay and reinstatement to his position in the Little Rock office. The judgment was affirmed by the U.S. Court of Appeals for the Eighth Circuit on May 30, 2002.

Remember always, protect yourself. If you feel that your employer has made your professional life miserable and has "constructively discharged" you, start building your court case before you resign.

Resigning with Respect

If you have had enough, and you can't take any more, call it quits. Tell your supervisor or human resources department of your resignation, and do it in person. Would you like to be told by voice mail or e-mail that you have been fired or laid off? Neither will your employer appreciate a voice mail or e-mail that you have left—for good. When telling your boss or employer that you are leaving, be honest but tactful. You will be asked why you are resigning, just as surely as you would ask why you were being fired. Prepare and rehearse your answer to that question.

Do not most, if not all, employees resign to advance their careers? Why not simply say you are leaving to pursue another position or to change your career direction, rather than say, "Take this job and shove it, you ****!"

Speaking your mind may satisfy a desire to get back at someone you feel mistreated you, but resist the temptation. Remember, "What you say can and will be used against you in a court of law." What you say probably will be reported to management and recorded in your personnel file. Inappropriate comments will come back to haunt you. You may well need your former supervisor or manager to provide you a reference. Do not lose the option of asking for a reference by unduly criticizing anyone in the organization. Your former supervisors and coworkers also can be a valuable resource. They may be valuable members of the personal network you will use to find another job.

In the meeting at which you announce your resignation, emphasize the positives associated with your decision and relating to your soon-to-be former employer. For example, after describing how your plans will benefit you and your family, mention the successes of your employer and coworkers and how much you learned from the experience. Just as surely your future is bright, so is that of your former employer. End your employment on a high note, and never burn your bridges. Who knows? You may be reapplying for a position with your former employer sometime in the future. Burning the bridge eliminates that option.

After you personally advise your supervisor or manager of your decision, follow up with a letter of resignation. Expect the letter to be placed into your personnel file. Write it accordingly. As is reflected in Table 2.2, be brief and to the point.

Table 2.2
Letter of Resignation

Dear _____ :
This will confirm that I have decided to resign to pursue other career interests. I felt it was appropriate to give ___ weeks' notice to help arrange for an orderly transition of my work. I appreciate the opportunity to work for the Company and wish all my friends here the best.

Table 2.3
Letter of Resignation—Required Notice

> Dear _____:
>
> This will confirm that I have decided to resign to pursue other career interests. My [employment agreement] [Employee Handbook] requires that I give you two weeks' notice of my resignation. My last day, therefore will be (month), (day), (year). Of course, I will work with you to ensure an orderly transition of all of my work and projects. I appreciate the opportunity to work for the Company and wish all of my friends here the best.

Short, to the Point, and Upbeat

How many weeks' notice to give is not always set. Many employment agreements and employee handbooks require a certain notice period, but when none is set (such as for most at-will employees), a reasonable amount of notice should be given. Ten days to two weeks is reasonable. Providing reasonable notice will promote good will with your former employer and ease your transition.

If your employment agreement or employee handbook requires or suggests two weeks' notice, you use the letter in Table 2.3.

Again, It's Short and Direct

Note that we do not suggest discussing reasons for your resignation or identifying your new employer, if you have arranged employment already. There is no reason for you to bring up that topic, or to admit that you were looking and found a job while you were working for your current employer.

If you must give a period of notice, but need to shorten it so you can start with a new employer, you may use the letter in Table 2.4.

After tendering your letter of resignation and before finalizing the arrangements for your departure, review your employment contract or employee handbook to determine your final compensation. Make sure you receive all compensation due, including salary, accrued vacation or

Table 2.4
Letter of Resignation—Shortened Notice

Dear _____:

This will confirm that I have decided to resign to pursue other career interests. My [employment agreement] [Employee Handbook] requires that I give you two weeks' notice of my resignation. My last day, therefore will be (month), (day), (year). I would appreciate being able to move up the date of my last day to (month) (day), (year), for personal reasons. Of course, I will work with you to ensure an orderly transition of all of my work and projects before I leave. I would appreciate your cooperation and understanding in that regard. I appreciate the opportunity to work for the Company and wish all of my friends here the best.

sick time, commissions, or expense reimbursements. Every penny will count when you are out of a job.

Occasionally, employers offer severance benefits to employees, even those who resign voluntarily. This is the case where the decision to resign is mutual, proposed by the employer, or where the employer wants to buy its peace with an employee who may sue it for issues arising out of the employment. In return for severance benefits, the employer will require a release and resignation agreement similar to the following example.

RESIGNATION AGREEMENT AND RELEASE

EMPLOYEE AND EMPLOYER enter into this Resignation Agreement and Release ("Agreement") on (month) (day), (year).

1. EMPLOYEE's employment will end, by agreement, effective (date).
2. In consideration of the promises in this Agreement, EMPLOYER agrees to pay EMPLOYEE the sum of $_____, less applicable state and federal payroll taxes and other legally required deductions. In addition, EMPLOYER will pay EMPLOYEE any wages due for services rendered up to the date of resignation, as well as all accrued, unpaid vacation pay.

3. EMPLOYER agrees not to contest EMPLOYEE's claim for unemployment compensation.
4. In consideration of the promises in this Agreement, EMPLOYER releases Employer from all claims and damages that may have arisen out of the employment, whether known or unknown. EMPLOYEE specifically recognizes and agrees that this release includes, but is not limited to, any claim arising under any federal law, including Title VII of the Civil Rights Act of 1964, the Age Discrimination in Employment Act of 1967, as amended, the Older Workers Benefit Protection Act, the Employee Retirement Income Security Act of 1974, as amended, the Americans with Disabilities Act, the Rehabilitation Act, the Fair Labor Standards Act, the Equal Pay Act, and the Family and Medical Leave Act of 1993; and any cause of action or claim arising under any state laws or local ordinances
5. EMPLOYEE agrees to maintain the confidentiality of this Agreement, and of all confidential information provided to him/her, during the employment. EMPLOYEE agrees to return all confidential and nonconfidential property of EMPLOYER, and not to use such information at any time for any purpose. In the event EMPLOYEE breaches this provision, he/she shall return to EMPLOYER all amounts paid under this Agreement, but the release in paragraph 4 shall remain in effect.
6. EMPLOYEE agrees that for a period of _____months, he/she will not compete with EMPLOYER in any geographical area where EMPLOYER does business. EMPLOYEE further agrees not to solicit any customers of EMPLOYER to engage in any business with EMPLOYEE that competes with any business of EMPLOYER or solicit any of EMPLOYER's employees to end their employment relationship with EMPLOYER.
7. In the event that EMPLOYEE breaches this Agreement, EMPLOYEE agrees to the entry of a temporary restraining order, preliminary injunction, permanent injunction, and judgment in damages caused by the breach. EMPLOYEE also shall pay EMPLOYER's costs and expenses, including reasonable attorneys' fees.
8. EMPLOYEE represents that he/she was advised by EMPLOYER to consult an attorney before signing this Agreement; he/she has been offered at least twenty-one (21) days to consider whether to sign this Agreement; he/she has read and understands the Agreement; he/she understands the release of claims, and has signed this Agreement voluntarily. EMPLOYEE may revoke this Agreement within seven (7) days.

[Signatures]

Entering into an agreement for your resignation, in which you receive severance in return for giving your employer a release has many benefits, not the least of which is extra compensation to you. It also puts a period at the end of the sentence. Your employment is officially over, and you did it on your terms.

Even if you do not receive severance benefits, you are entitled to compensation due you, such as accrued vacation, commissions and prorated bonuses. Your employment agreement, employee handbook, or benefits policy will provide these forms of compensation. In addition to monetary compensation, did you have a pension or 401(k) plan? Find out what your rights are with respect to these benefits before you leave. Getting answers after you leave may be more difficult.

Now what? Move on to greener pastures? Not so fast.

Remember, protect yourself and your family. Did you have an employer-provided health insurance plan for yourself and your family? Do not delay. Make alternate arrangements for family health insurance coverage during the period in which you are unemployed. One of your options is under the Consolidated Omnibus Budget Reconciliation Act (COBRA). Under COBRA, if your employer has more than twenty employees, it must continue your health insurance under the company's health plan even if you quit. Your employer must notify you of your right to continue coverage within fifteen days of benefits termination. You then have sixty days to notify your employer that you have elected to continue coverage. Continuation coverage will last eighteen months, but it is costly. You must pay the entire cost of the coverage. Your former employer no longer has to make an employer contribution to the total cost of the premium. In addition, your employer may add an administrative charge of 2 percent to the cost, to cover its expenses in administrating your COBRA benefits.

If you find that COBRA benefits are too costly or do not provide the benefits you need, you must shop around for coverage. If you belong to any professional or trade associations, investigate whether they offer group health insurance.

As soon as you find a new position, immediately arrange for health insurance coverage. Ensure that you have the health insurance you need. Many of us have suffered an injury or have a condition that makes obtaining individual health insurance difficult. Many insurance companies, for example, exclude "pre-existing conditions." The Health Insurance Portability, and Accountability Act of 1996 (HIPAA) may help those of us with pre-existing medical conditions. HIPPA applies generally to all employer-provided health insurance plans. In short, HIPAA prevents group health plans from denying coverage or charging you extra for benefits based on your or your family's health history. You should contact your new employer's benefits administrator for a full explanation of the group health coverage.

When you apply for a new position, be prepared. Revise and update your résumé. We provide specific advice about résumé writing in chapter 7. However, a word to the wise is in order here. After the tragic events of September 11, more and more employers are conducting background investigations of job applicants. Prospective employers probably will conduct a background investigation of you during the job application process. Knowing that your background most likely will be investigated, be scrupulously honest in describing your educational and employment background in your résumé.

You have significant rights in any background investigation. For details, see our explanation of the Fair Credit Reporting Act later in this chapter, in the section "How to Fire Your Employee." Understanding your employer's obligations under that statute will help you understand your rights under it. This is a good example why we deal with your resignation in the same chapter as your being fired. Both you and your employer have to know and understand each other's rights—to protect your own.

Be prepared for prospective employers to contact your references and conduct an investigation of your background. Background checks can include:

- Verification of your Social Security number and citizenship;
- Verification of your educational degrees and professional certifications;
- Verification of your state licensing;
- A check of your driving record;
- A check of criminal records (convictions only—many states have laws protecting the confidentiality of arrest records);
- A check of court records and filings, such as bankruptcies;
- A check of your military record;
- Interviews of your neighbors;
- Interviews of your references;
- Interviews of your former employers.

  A special note: When a prospective employer contacts your former employer, your former employer may disclose any truthful information about your employment. This is why we strongly recommend taking the high road of honesty with your former employer. When a prospective employer contacts a previous employer, most employers, fearing a claim of defamation or breach of confidentiality, will only provide the dates of your employment, final salary, and job title.

- A review of your credit report from credit reporting agencies.

Employers are more inclined than ever to conduct background checks of job applicants, to avoid liability for claims of negligent hiring. Liability for hiring an employee with a criminally violent past can be substantial if the employee harms another employee or customer. For example, these are real cases from public court records:

Robert Bennett (not his real name) was hired by Brooks Transport, Inc., (not its real name) as a truck driver. Bennett was involved in an accident with a motorist. He was intoxicated at the time of the accident. The motorist, who was severely injured, sued Brooks Transport for negligent hiring.

(The need to conduct a background investigation is made obvious in the Bennett case: An employer owes a duty to its other employees and to the public to ascertain the qualifications and competence of the employees it hires, especially when the employees are engaged in occupations that may be hazardous to the safety of others. An employer may be liable for negligent hiring if it hires an incompetent or unfit employee whom it knows, or by the exercise of reasonable care should have known, was incompetent or unfit.)

Brooks had conducted a background check of Bennett. It obtained a state motor vehicle drivers report that indicated no violations in the past three years. Unfortunately, Brooks Transport went no further. It did not obtain a report from the State Police, which would have shown Bennett's conviction for possession of illegal drugs and two convictions for driving under the influence.

You can probably guess what happened. The judgment was for the injured motorist on his negligent hiring claim.

Here is another case:

James Foster (pseudonym) was hired as a bartender by The Warehouse (not its real name), a popular singles bar. Late one evening, Stuart Flynn (pseudonym) went to The Warehouse with a friend for a night of dancing and libation. Flynn's friend, unhappy with how a drink was mixed, tossed it at Foster. Foster jumped across the bar and punched both Flynn's friend and Flynn, breaking his cheekbone and injuring his eye. The Warehouse knew when it hired Foster that he had a record of violent criminal conduct. The jury, holding that The Warehouse was liable for negligent hiring, awarded Flynn substantial damages.

The lesson The Warehouse learned the hard way is that not only are background checks necessary, but they also may (and sometimes should) be used to screen job candidates.

In addition to a background check, many employers require job applicants to submit to a drug test, a job skills test, or a personality or psychological exam. Drug testing may be regulated or prohibited at the application stage by state law. Job skills tests, such as typing drills, mathematics tests, writing ability tests or physical agility tests, also may be administered if they are job related.

Missing from the litany of issues employers will examine in a background check is a medical inquiry. Many states have laws protecting the confidentiality of medical records. The federal Americans with Disabilities Act (ADA) also limits medical examinations and inquiries. Employers may require a medical examination, but only at certain stages of employment.

The Americans with Disabilities Act prohibits medical tests and disability-related inquiries at the job application stage. Making disability-related inquiries may be a pretext for screening out disabled, but qualified, applicants. The ADA does not define "medical-related inquiry." At the job interview, or in the job application, the employer may not ask:

- "Have you had or have you been treated for any of the following conditions or diseases?" (listing them)
- "Describe any physical or medical conditions for which you have been treated in the last five years."
- "Do you suffer from any conditions or diseases that would make it difficult for you to perform the duties of the job?"
- "Do you take any prescription medications?"
- "Do you have any physical limitations that would make it difficult for you to perform this job?"

However, the employer may ask at a job interview:

- "How are you?"
- "How did you break your . . . ?" (if you have a cast)
- "Can you perform all of the job functions?"
- "How would you perform the job functions?"

Once the employer has made a job offer to the applicant, it may conduct a medical inquiry and require a medical exam, but only if it does so for all job applicants. During employment, an employer may require a medical examination only if it is "job related and consistent with business necessity."

We included this discussion of background investigations and permissible and prohibited medical inquiries to help prepare you for what you will face when you re-enter the job market. In addition, now that you know how a resignation and transition to a new employer may work from your perspective, let us try to learn a lesson from how it looks from an employer's perspective:

HOW TO FIRE YOUR EMPLOYEE

We are human beings, not human assets. We are born with certain inalienable rights, as our Declaration of Independence states. Employees do not leave those rights outside the door of the office or plant each workday. Human rights of freedom, dignity, and respect we have so cherished historically must be the principles guiding employers during the entire employment relationship, from the application process through ending the relationship.

How should an employer establish and reinforce these principles so they are consistently applied? The same way our forebears did in 1787—adopt a constitution—and follow it. Just as any free nation, large or small, must have a constitution to establish the government's relationship with its citizens, all employers, large and small, must have laws (employment policies) governing the employer-employee relationship. Just as citizens are entitled to have their actions measured against an established legal standard set forth in a system of laws, employees are entitled to have their performance measured against an established system of employment policies and productivity standards.

We are a society founded on law. We agree to conform our conduct to the rules and regulations enacted by our elected officials. In the workplace, employers and employees each agree to conform their conduct to the legitimate expectations of the other. This can be achieved only by having an agreed system of laws—employment policies governing the employer-employee relationship.

Having established personnel policies also benefits employers in another significant respect. The employer-employee relationship is governed by two sets of "laws." The most apparent on a day-to-day basis, of course, is the employer's personnel policies. Let us not forget, however, the pervasive state and federal regulation of the employment relationship. From the Americans with Disabilities Act prohibiting disability-related inquiries in the job application process (see the discussion above), through wages and hours rules of the Fair Labor Standards Act, through federal and state antidiscrimination laws, and through state and federal laws governing wrongful discharge, governmental regulation of the entire employment relationship (from hiring to firing) is pervasive. Having and adhering to employment policies will help employers stay out of legal trouble and will help them achieve their goal of having a workforce that knows, understands, and follows its rules. It will also help employees understand what is expected of them and better enable them to meet the employer's expectations.

For all of these reasons, all employers should have employment or personnel policies. We suggest that employers adopt an employee handbook or personnel policies manual that will apply to all employees, from the CEO to the intern. Equality under the law is not a principle confined to criminal law—it applies to the workplace, too. If personnel policies and work rules are applied selectively or in a discriminatory manner, the employer would be better off having no rules or policies at all. Courts, juries, and arbitrators resent and will punish discriminatory or selective application of rules or policies.

To help ensure the enforceability of employment policies, we suggest that during the job application or initial employment process, employees be given a copy of the employee handbook or policy manual and be required to sign the written acknowledgement. This procedure will enable the employer to enforce its policies as an agreed system of laws governing the employer-employee relationship.

A sample written acknowledgment is presented in Table 2.5.

Table 2.5
Written Acknowledgment

I, [Insert employee's name], acknowledge that I received a copy of [insert

employer's name] Employee Handbook, on [insert date]. I have read it, have

been given an opportunity to ask questions about it, fully understand all of its

contents, and agree to abide by it.

[Signed by employee]

We learned in civics class that ex post facto laws are unconstitutional. For those of us whose memories of high school civics has faded, this means that our government may not enact a law making criminal some conduct that was legal when it was committed, subjecting us to criminal prosecution under a law enacted after the fact.

Why should this not apply to the employer-employee relationship? An employer should not impose a policy after an employee has started working and then accuse the employee of not following it. The appropriate method of imposing a new policy or amending an existing one is to "publish" it to employees. Give them a copy to insert in their employee handbook or policy manual, and have them agree to it. This is accomplished by having them sign a new acknowledgment each time a policy is revised or added. Doing so will help ensure that all personnel policies will be enforceable. This also will ensure that all employees know what rules they are expected to follow. While "ignorance of the law is no excuse," an employer's failure to notify employees and obtain their agreement to rules and regulations they are expected to follow may prevent the employer from being able to enforce them.

Perhaps the most important policy employers must have to enforce their rights, and to avoid being accused of wrongful, selective, or discriminatory enforcement of their policies, is a discipline policy. A common discipline policy provides for gradually increasing penalties for rules infractions of different severity. This is commonly called a progressive discipline policy.

Here is a sample Progressive Discipline Policy:

General Principles. The Company has established these Personnel Policies to help ensure that all employees work together cooperatively and according to agreed standards of conduct. These Policies will help us collectively to serve the needs of our customers and clients. The Company and all employees agree that reasonable rules of personal and professional conduct established in these Policies are necessary if we are to work together safely and productively.

Furthermore, it is Company policy that all employees be informed of all policies and rules governing their conduct and abide by those policies and rules. Together with these Policies, your supervisor will help you understand what is expected of you in performing your job. When a performance issue arises, it is Company policy to advise you of the issue and to give you an opportunity to improve your job performance to meet the Company's expectations.

Policy. Degrees of discipline generally are progressive. Certain conduct, however, may be serious enough to justify immediate action including, but not limited to, immediate suspension or discharge. These serious offenses include intentionally endangering others, fighting or other violent behavior, the use or sale of alcohol or illegal drugs on Company property, theft or intentional destruction of Company property, etc. Progressive discipline will follow these stages:

First Stage

The first stage of progressive discipline is an oral warning. An oral warning will be given to address less serious offenses such as excessive tardiness, excessive unexcused absences, leaving the premises without authorization, interfering with the work of others, or minor violations of these Personnel Policies.

There is no set rule as to how many oral warnings may be given before a written warning is given. All oral warnings, however, will be recorded in the personnel file of the employee.

Second Stage

The second stage of progressive discipline is a written warning. A written warning will be given following one or more oral warnings or for more serious offenses. Such more serious offenses include possession of drugs or alcohol on Company property, reporting to work under the influence of alcohol or illegal drugs, destruction of Company property, insubordination, dishonest or unethical business practices, or repeated violations of these Policies. An employee may also be suspended with or without pay in lieu of a written warning or after repeated written warnings.

Written warnings will be provided to the employee, who will be expected to sign it, acknowledging its receipt. The Company encourages employees to work with their supervisors to address the issues that caused the written warning, and to avoid similar problems in the future.

Third Stage

The third stage of progressive discipline is a suspension without pay or discharge. Serious or repeated instances of policy violations will result in suspension or discharge for cause.

As this sample Progressive Discipline Policy reflects, when employees violate policies or work rules, they should be informed of the violation and be given an opportunity to improve. This common sense principle should be fundamental to the employer-employee relationship. This common sense principle is similar to due process. As we discussed before, constitutional due process means notice and an opportunity to be heard. This due process concept is so ingrained in our society that it should be followed in the workplace just as it is in our criminal justice system. Employees have a right to expect that any deficiencies in their performance will be brought to their attention (the "notice"), and they will be given a chance to improve (the "opportunity to be heard").

By no means is this employment principle borrowed from the Constitution an inconvenience or detriment to employers. Quite the contrary, employers will benefit by following employment due process. Wrongful discharge and discrimination litigation has exploded in recent years. Whether an employee claim is resolved in a court or in arbitration, an employer is far more likely to prevail if it follows rules and procedures that are fundamentally fair and afford due process pursuant to a progressive discipline policy.

Another means employers should use to help ensure a successful defense of any claim of wrongful discharge or discriminatory discipline procedures is to document absolutely everything. When a company issues an oral warning, a written record should be placed in the employee's personnel file. In addition, a complete record of a written warning, in addition to the written warning itself, should be placed in the personnel file.

The record of a written warning placed in the employee's personnel file should include:

- Date of the warning;
- Description of the infraction that gave rise to the warning;
- Description of the evidence that the infraction occurred;
- Names of any witnesses and their knowledge;
- Accurate and complete description of what the employee was told;
- The employee's response;
- Corrective actions or measures discussed with the employee; and
- The employee's signature.

This detailed account of the circumstances of a written warning is not useless paperwork. On the contrary, documenting employee discipline is essential. Employers frequently are called upon by the EEOC, a court, or an arbitrator to explain disciplinary actions and to defend themselves against a claim of wrongful discharge or discrimination. Having this detailed account of the infraction and the discipline will dispel any notion that the employer's disciplinary action was a pretext for wrongful discrimination.

The issue of "pretext" arises most frequently in employment discrimination cases. A short legal description of how one proves employment discrimination will demonstrate the importance of completely documenting disciplinary measures and procedures.

Employment discrimination may be proved by either the direct or indirect method. An employee can use the direct method to prove discrimination if the employer made a discriminatory comment or specifically told the employee or others that the adverse employment action (such as a suspension, demotion, layoff, or discharge) was because of the employee's race, sex, ethnic background, age, or other federally protected classification. It is rare for such blatant, direct proof of discrimination to exist. The more common means of proving discrimination is the indirect method. This is used when, for example, the employee's performance was satisfactory and the adverse employment action was not a result of progressive discipline. The employee's natural inclination is to conclude: "I didn't lose my job because of something I did. No one ever complained about my work. It must have been discrimination."

The indirect method of proving discrimination was approved by the U.S. Supreme Court in 1973 in the landmark case *McDonnell Douglas Corp.* v. *Green,* 411 U.S. 792. In that lawsuit, a mechanic and laboratory technician had been laid off. When his former position reopened, he applied for the position but was rejected. He alleged that he was rejected because of his civil rights activities and because of his race. He had no direct evidence of discrimination. The Supreme Court then outlined the alternative indirect method of proving discrimination and allowed his case to proceed.

To show discrimination under the McDonnell Douglas indirect method, an employee must show that: (1) he or she is a member of a federally protected class; (2) he or she met the employer's legitimate expectations; (3) he or she suffered an adverse employment action; and (4) other similarly situated employees who were not members of the protected class were treated more favorably. If the employee proves these factors, the employer must show a legitimate, nondiscriminatory reason for the employment action. The employee then must show that the employer's stated reason for the employment action was not the true reason, but merely a pretext for discrimination.

This single example demonstrates the necessity of proper documentation of employee discipline. First, an often-disciplined employee may be able to prove that he or she met the employer's legitimate expectations, unless the employer makes and maintains records to the contrary. Second, to prove that similarly situated employees were treated similarly, the employer must have records that show it enforces its policies evenhandedly as to all employees, regardless of race, sex, ethnic group, age, and so forth. Finally, an employer can readily show that its stated reason for the discipline or adverse employment action was not a pretext for discrimination by showing a well-documented investigation leading to the conclusion that the employee violated a policy or work rule and that discipline was warranted.

Not only is proper documentation of the discipline process a necessity, but also proper investigation procedures are critical. To defeat any claim that the employer was not justified in imposing discipline, the employer must engage in a proper investigation.

Legal Warning to Employers I

Before launching into an investigation of employees, or job applicants for that matter, employers must comply with the federal Fair Credit Reporting Act (FCRA). As unlikely as it sounds given the name of the statute, the FCRA governs certain employer investigations and may give rise to liability to job applicants or employees if the employer does not follow the provisions of the statute. Many employers do not have the staff or capability to conduct a full investigation of serious allegations of employee misconduct. In those situations, the employer may request that an outside agency or firm conduct the investigation and submit a report. This situation triggers the application of the FCRA. The FCRA will apply to employee investigations if the employer retains an outside firm other than its law firm to conduct the investigation instead of performing the investigation itself.

The FCRA was enacted primarily to protect the privacy of consumer report information and to guarantee that the information supplied to consumer reporting agencies is accurate. The FCRA also protects individuals from having their personal affairs investigated without their knowledge or consent. In 1996, Congress amended the FCRA to apply to background investigations of job applicants and investigations of employee misconduct.

Increasingly, after the tragedy of September 11, employers conduct background investigations of job applicants. In addition, following U.S. Supreme Court decisions in employment discrimination and harassment cases, employers must investigate allegations of discrimination or harassment to defend against large damages claims.

The FCRA requires that no more than three days after requesting an outside firm to conduct an investigation and report its results, the employer must notify the applicant or employee in writing that a report concerning his or her character, reputation, personal characteristics, and mode of living has been requested and may be used. The employer must obtain a signed authorization from the employee before conducting the investigation.

This notice requirement may sound more onerous than it will be in practice. All employers should include with every job application a separate consent form, signed by the job applicant, disclosing that the employer may request an investigation by a credit reporting agency and may obtain a report, in connection with the job application. Of course, the employer should have the job applicant sign the separate consent form as well as the application form. As to investigations of employee misconduct, the employer should have the accused employee sign a consent form for the investigation.

Whether the employer relies on an outside investigator or conducts its own investigation, any investigation that might lead to employee discipline must include a full examination of the facts. First, the employer should examine the employee's personnel file. This will reflect, for example, whether the employee was given an oral or written warning in the past for similar or other policy infractions. This could be relevant to whether an oral or written warning, or the more serious disciplinary actions of suspension or discharge, is appropriate. Next, any investigation should review any other documents, such as incident reports, customer complaints, performance records, or productivity reports.

After reviewing the written record, the employer should interview witnesses, including the affected employee.

Legal Warning to Employers II

Interviewing an employee in the context of an investigation that may result in that employee's discipline raises another issue under the rules of the National Labor Relations Board (NLRB). The NLRB has ruled that even in a nonunion workplace, an employee is entitled to have a coworker present during any interview when the investigation could result in discipline. The employer must allow the employee to designate a coworker to be present, if the employee asks. The employer need not offer to allow the employee to have a coworker present and need not advise the employee of that right. The accused employee may assert this right where the employee reasonably believes, under the circumstances of the interview, that the employer is conducting a disciplinary interview that may result in an adverse employment action.

The coworker present at the interview should be allowed to provide assistance and counsel to the employee, but may not disrupt the interview. If an employee asks to have a coworker present, the employer has two choices. It can proceed with the interview or refuse to go forward with it unless the employee waives his or her right to have the coworker present.

A comprehensive and well-documented investigation will serve several useful purposes. First, of course, the investigation will reveal whether the accused employee has violated a rule or policy and should be disciplined. Second, other employees will see that the employer takes allegations of discrimination, harassment, or policy violations seriously. Third, other employees will feel more secure and be more likely to avoid the type of behavior that prompted the investigation. Fourth, if the employer's decision to discipline the accused employee is challenged, the employer will have a developed record of evidence to support its decision.

Finally, apart from the disciplinary process, a full investigation of a possible policy violation may be illuminating for internal purposes. The investigation may cause the employer to question or amend its policy. Perhaps it was too broad or narrow and did not encompass what the employer had intended. Perhaps it was not clear enough for employees. Perhaps it was not emphasized to employees, in which case an education program may be instituted. Perhaps it should not be a policy at all.

Legal Warning to Employers III

Polygraph examinations have been the subject of significant publicity recently with politicians and celebrities taking them voluntarily to "prove" their innocence of some alleged offense. Especially since September 11, many employers, too, may be inclined to use them to ensure the veracity of their job applicants or of their employees during an investigation of possible misconduct. Before proposing or imposing a polygraph examination, employers must comply with the Employee Polygraph Protection Act of 1988.

As a general rule, an employer may not require or even suggest an employee take a polygraph test. Consistent with this rule, no employee or prospective employee may be disciplined, discharged, or discriminated against in any manner for failing or refusing to submit to a polygraph test. The statute does not apply to local, state, or federal governmental agencies, such as law enforcement agencies, employees in certain businesses such as armored car personnel, or security personnel in facilities having a significant impact on the health and safety of any state (nuclear power plant, public water works, toxic waste facilities, etc.). Employers desiring to administer a polygraph test should consult the statute for specifics as to any applicable exemptions.

The only exception to the general rule prohibiting polygraph tests concerns investigations involving economic loss or injury to the employer's business, such as theft, embezzlement, misappropriation, or an act of unlawful industrial espionage or sabotage. In such an investigation, the employer must have a reasonable suspicion that the employee was involved in the incident or activity under investigation. In addition, the employee must have had access to the property that is the subject of the investigation.

If an employer asks an employee to submit to a polygraph test, the employer must provide a notice to the employee, signed by a person (other than the polygraph examiner) who has authority to bind the employer legally. The notice must describe the specific incident or activity being investigated and the basis for testing particular employees. The notice must state, at a minimum:

- An identification of the specific economic loss or injury to the business of the employer;
- A statement indicating that the employee had access to the property that is the subject of the investigation;
- A statement describing the basis of the employer's reasonable suspicion that the employee was involved in the incident or activity under investigation; and
- The date, time, and location of the test, and of the employee's right to obtain and consult with legal counsel or an employee representative before each phase of the test.

With these requirements met, the polygraph examination may proceed, but there are restrictions:

- Throughout the test, the employee may terminate the test at any time;
- The examiner may not ask questions in a manner designed to degrade, or needlessly intrude on, the employee;
- The examiner may not ask questions concerning:
  - Religious beliefs or affiliations;
  - Beliefs or opinions regarding racial matters;
  - Political beliefs or affiliations;
  - Any matter relating to sexual behavior; and
  - Beliefs, affiliations, opinions, or lawful activities regarding unions or labor organizations.

Any employer violating the Employee Polygraph Protection Act may be prosecuted by the secretary of labor for a civil penalty of not more than $10,000, may be enjoined from future violations (this would make any future violation punishable as a contempt of court with a possible jail sentence), and may be liable to the employee or prospective employee for damages.

Significantly, employees may not waive their rights under this federal statute. Because of the general prohibition of polygraph examinations, and the very specific exceptions, employers should consult with an attorney before suggesting or administering a polygraph examination in any investigation.

As you can see from the dramatic penalties in the Employee Polygraph Protection Act, polygraph examinations are very serious investigative tools that must be used with utmost caution. The statute was enacted to address abuses and abusive use of lie detector tests in employee investigations. Most courts do not allow the results of lie detector tests to be entered into evidence at trial, because their reliability is not generally accepted in the scientific community. What must be generally accepted, however, are the very strict requirements for their use in the workplace. Employers should beware of running afoul of the strict requirements of the statute, lest they lose in a proceeding for violating the statute much more than they lost in the underlying incident they were investigating.

A thorough investigation also will be a self-evaluation for the employer. Examining the written record and interviewing supervisory (and other) employees will reveal the nature of their relationships and how they view each other, the employer, and their jobs. In short, a full investigation will benefit both the employer and employees. A knee-jerk, intemperate, rash decision to discipline an employee benefits no one. It may land the employer in court, unable to explain or defend its actions. The accuser then becomes the accused.

Adverse employment decisions do not have to be the result of disciplinary action associated with policy violations. Frequently, the adverse employment decision to lay off or fire an employee may be unrelated to performance. The principle of treating all employees with dignity and respect arises in the exit interview, where an employee is advised of the adverse employment decision.

Finally, a word about allowing the employee to make a graceful exit. In addition to due process rights, employers should afford employees privacy rights. Employees should not be disciplined, or advised of a layoff or discharge, in front of other employees. Holding an employee up to public ridicule or embarrassment in front of friends and coworkers will earn an employer an express pass to court—do not pass go; do not collect $200. Avoid the vindictive or punitive inclination to make an example of an errant employee. Instead, make an example of yourself. Take the high road, while vigorously enforcing policies and rules that apply equally to everyone. Employees will not admire a punitive employer, but they will respect one that enforces its policies evenhandedly and firmly.

The exit interview should take place in a room apart from other employees. The telephone should be turned off. No one should interrupt the exit interview. Privacy is paramount. This is a time for complete privacy between the employee and the employer's representatives. Complete privacy not only protects the interests of the employee, but also those of the employer. Other employees may not be in the exit interview room, but they are "watching." They will find out eventually about the adverse employment action against their former coworker (and perhaps friend) and will identify with him or her. The next time it may be them! Treating departing employees with dignity and respect will enhance the employer's standing in the eyes of remaining employees.

Affording dignity and respect to employees also means conducting exit interviews professionally. The employer should have two representatives present, usually the employee's supervisor and a management representative. We discussed above the NLRB rule that an employee may request a coworker to be present at any investigative interview as a result of which discipline may be imposed. This should not apply to exit interviews, because the investigation has been conducted and the deliberation and decision have already been made. All that remains is disclosing the decision to the employee.

Treating the affected employee with dignity and respect in an exit interview is largely a matter of attitude. Obviously, an exit interview will be emotionally charged. Firing or laying off an employee has been likened to a divorce. The employer must set the tone by being both understanding and direct:

"We called you here to let you know that we have to let you go. Your last day in the office will be June 15. You will receive your last paycheck on June 30. We appreciate all of your efforts on behalf of the Company and wish you well in the future."

Do not turn the exit interview into a discussion of the reasons for the decision. While it is appropriate and advisable to tell the affected employee in general terms why the decision was made, whether it was performance related or not, do not engage in a detailed discussion of the reasons for the decision. A debate of the pros and cons of the decision serves no useful purpose and will only exacerbate an already emotionally charged situation. It is human nature to blame others for a bad situation. Do not be surprised if the employee, out of anger, self-doubt, shame, or feelings of rejection, blames others for his or her plight. In response to such emotions, the employer's representatives must be sympathetic but firm. If the employee is likely to challenge the decision in court or arbitration, the employer should have counsel prepare an agenda and script—and stick to it.

CONCLUSION

We have discussed in this chapter how to resign and how to discharge an employee. Both employers and employees should also be aware of the hot buttons concerning disciplinary actions. Employee disciplinary actions are rarely reviewed or subject to an appeal. Adverse employment decisions, however, are the basis of a large percentage of EEOC, court, and arbitration claims.

Both employers and employees should consider whether a disciplinary action is actually work-related or instead is based on a prohibited factor such as race, sex, age, national origin, or disability. An adverse employment action based on a discriminatory motive is prohibited by federal, state, and local discrimination laws.

Employers and employees also should consider whether the adverse employment action is actually in retaliation for the employee's actions protected by state or federal law. Retaliatory discharge actions frequently are the subject of large damages awards in favor of employees. Retaliatory discharge may arise in very unexpected situations.

For example, if an employee alleges harassment or discrimination, the employer must fully investigate the allegation. If the employer finds the allegation to have been made without basis, or worse, in bad faith, the natural reaction of the employer may be to discipline the employee for making serious allegations with no factual basis. Do not succumb to that natural reaction.

Any employer that disciplines or discharges an employee for asserting a right protected by law or public policy may be liable for retaliating against the employee. The irony in such a situation is that even though the employer may not be liable for the alleged harassment or discrimination, it is liable to the accuser for retaliatory discipline or discharge.

The best way to avoid litigation arising out of firing an employee is not to fire him or her at all, but let the worker resign with severance benefits— and give you a release of claims. A sample Resignation Agreement and Release is set out above.

With that, we have come full circle. Whether you, the employee, decides to resign or you, the employer, decides to discipline or discharge an employee, both of you are governed by the same basic principle, for which we take no copyright credit. Do unto the other as you would have the other do unto you.

CHAPTER 3

Bulletproofing Your Career

PACK YOUR OWN PARACHUTE

You are responsible for your own career. Your overall success depends on your willingness first to decide your life's mission and then to establish personal goals and objectives. Ensuring personal career success and enhancing job security are not passive activities. You must be proactive. You must take deliberate steps to influence your destiny—you simply cannot wait for good luck to come your way. You must decide what you desire and what you are willing to settle for, in terms of the nature of your work, your finances, and your relationships with family, friends, and associates. You must choose an occupation or profession that is compatible with your interests and personality, as well as your knowledge base and unique set of skills.

As incongruous as it may sound, safeguarding your career begins prior to its inception. To enter the position you desire and then to be secure within that position, you must approach your career in a planned and purposeful manner. You must consider your career to be a journey, rather than a series of events or work sites. Entering the right position does not depend on the actions of others—it depends primarily on you.

Finding the right position for you largely depends on the level of your self-awareness. Self-knowledge involves your recognizing preferences, strengths, and weaknesses relating to your attitude, values, and interests; skills and achievements; knowledge and personal beliefs. Such self-awareness frequently requires a personal audit. Have you ever reviewed your preferences, strengths, and weaknesses? Have you conducted such a personal audit? If so, what did it say about you:

- Did the analysis of your previous experiences and accomplishments reveal the type of work you are likely to enjoy or dislike?
- Did it reveal the type of work you are likely to succeed in or struggle with?
- Did it reveal preferences and strengths you are applying to your current position?

A personal audit should help you answer certain questions. For example:

- Regarding your personal values . . .
  - Do you prefer to help others, work with others, or influence others?
  - Do you prefer to enhance your personal, financial, or social standing?
  - Are you more interested in pursuing knowledge, being artistic, or applying your physical capabilities?
  - Do you prefer to work alone, to work independently but have contact with others, or to work with others?
- In terms of your personal skills . . .
  - Do you possess certain specialized skills that you can apply to a particular role or position?
  - Do you possess certain general skills that you can apply to a variety of roles or positions?
  - Do you possess certain problem-solving skills that allow you to analyze and solve complex problems?
  - Do you possess certain interpersonal skills that allow you to communicate with and influence others?
- Regarding your personal interests . . .
  - Do you enjoy gathering, analyzing, and interpreting information?
  - Do you enjoy expressing yourself artistically (in word and/or in action)?
  - Do you enjoy working with and helping people, or being alone?
  - Do you enjoy leading or managing projects, organizations, teams, and individuals or following through under the direction of others?
- In terms of your personal attitude . . .
  - Are you assertive and aggressive?
  - Are you cheerful and easygoing?
  - Are you self-confident and poised?
  - Are you friendly and empathetic?
  - Are you helpful and kind?
  - Are you persevering and tough?
- Regarding your personality . . .
  - Does being around people or spending time alone energize you?
  - Do you base decisions on what is right for the situation or on one standard that never changes?
  - Do you live spontaneously, or are you more comfortable following a set plan?

Did answers to such questions lead you to your current position? Is your current position or role a suitable one, one that capitalizes on your preferences and strengths and mitigates your weaknesses and limitations? This analysis will also help employers assess their employees and applicants' readiness to enter into a new or open position. Employers also must be proactive in assessing the desires and abilities of their employees to ensure that the applicant or employee is the right fit for the position.

Safeguarding your career does not end with its inception. Change is constant in today's work world. Your career success largely depends on your ability to understand and respond to the changing nature of work—the kinds of work people do and the way in which they are asked to do that work. You must monitor local, regional, and global trends. You must remain aware of changes occurring within particular industries and professions. You must monitor changes taking place within leading companies—trends relating to downsizing, reengineering, and outsourcing. You must monitor steps companies are taking to maintain their competitive advantage, steps such as entering into joint ventures or establishing strategic alliances with organizations in their supply chain. You must remain aware of how changing technology affects business processes and how those process changes in turn impact capabilities needed throughout the workforce. A key to business success in turbulent times is adapting to changing economic conditions. So, too, with your career, you must be conscious of changes affecting the workplace and be willing to adapt to change or evolving employment trends.

Knowledge of current practices and emerging trends is useful only if it leads to informed decisions and responsible action. Although careers traditionally were vertical (you climbed the corporate ladder), they are now horizontal (you accept a lateral position elsewhere) or more closely follow a lattice (you accept a demotion to enter a new organization or industry ultimately to advance your career). These current trends are the hallmark of a mobile workforce. The workforce is mobile by necessity, having to undergo frequent change in response to a turbulent business climate. Such a business reality suggests a career consisting of varying speed, pauses, and changing directions. Such a reality requires you to: initially set the course for your career, monitor the progress you are making, recognize and respond to changing business requirements, and continually take action to capitalize on your strengths and mitigate your limitations. You must also reconsider the way you define "success" as it relates to your career. If you consider climbing the corporate ladder the cornerstone of a successful career, unfortunately you have already established an expectation you are not likely to realize in today's world.

As we discuss in later chapters, researchers project significant shifts in the marketplace and in the nature of work; such shifts will directly and indirectly impact everyone's employability. While individuals with certain skill sets will have greater employment opportunities, others with different skills will encounter fewer. For some, lifelong learning in the form of cross training and "retooling" will become an economic necessity rather than a passive desire.

Regardless of marketplace pressures and the changing nature of work, employers constantly seek individuals with certain characteristics. We have found throughout our careers that employers consistently seek employees:

- Willing to make sound decisions;
- Willing to take reasonable risks;
- Able to contribute without being closely managed or supervised;
- Considered to have a positive, can-do attitude;
- Who are able to communicate with others;
- Who are comfortable working with individuals of other cultures;
- Who are comfortable working with individuals from other geographic regions;
- Who are efficient as a result of possessing organization and time management skills; and
- Who are well rounded, in terms of orientation, viewpoint, and perspective.

Such characteristics reflect a fundamental tenet: employers are more likely to employ and retain individuals who have successfully applied their limited skills over individuals who possess a broader set of untested and unapplied skills. It is understandable that employers value someone who does his or her best with limited skills over one who does not make use of better skills. Effort usually is recognized and preferred over pure, but unrealized, ability.

To thrive in any business environment, it is imperative that workers, through formal education and training, attain marketable skills. Such skills enable you to help an organization deliver on its value proposition, whether that proposition involves the creation and distribution of a product or the development and delivery of a service. Personal capabilities, even during relatively stable times and in relatively favorable environments, are simply not enough. To be a valued employee, you must be competent (skilled) as well as self-motivated and self-confident.

Awareness of your skills and assets enhances your job security only if it helps you minimize personal limitations and weaknesses. Awareness is beneficial only if it helps you address the multitude of challenges created by prevailing business practices and emerging business trends. In essence, actions you take, rather than mere awareness or understanding, will help "bulletproof" your career.

We believe the following actions will help you navigate your career, regardless of where you are in your career cycle and regardless of whether the business environment is turbulent or stable:

- Establish, enhance, and then maintain (easier said than done, given today's business environment) relationships with individuals throughout your organization, industry, and business world. Such relationships will prove invaluable as you attempt to learn about prevailing office politics, emerging business trends, and potential development and employment opportunities. More opportunities will open to you through networking with professional colleagues and coworkers who move to different firms than through poring over want ads. Plan for your future by marketing yourself within your profession.

- Identify, and then work with, someone willing to serve as your mentor. This individual will help you both understand the current business environment and emerging trends and assess your knowledge, skills, and abilities within that context. Perhaps the most important role the mentor plays is helping you refine your career plan and then helping you identify the development events (such as workshops or seminars) and practices (such as leading start-up projects or product development teams) that will help you execute that plan.

- Conduct an annual review of your career plan. Just as employers conduct annual performance reviews, you should conduct an annual self-evaluation. Identify accomplishments, challenges, and opportunities. Determine how your plan may need to be revised to meet current and emerging business trends and to reflect your personal growth and changing interests. Evaluate your plan within the context of current and future positions, current and potential career sites. The changes you make to your plan become the foundation for your next year's career plan.

- Become active in trade organizations or professional associations. Even if you are uncomfortable doing so, volunteer to lead or participate in discussion groups, task forces, and special interest associations or committees. Getting over the initial anxiety of joining and taking the plunge will show you that you are not alone. Many of your colleagues feel the same—you may as well feel that way together. Capitalize on opportunities to serve as a guest editor or to help review the organization's journal, magazine, or newsletter. Such experiences will get your name out and enhance your professional standing as well as your awareness of industry practices and business trends, and they will be an invaluable tool in your professional and personal development.

- Through personal and professional relationships, solicit information about current business practices and emerging trends. It is not necessary that you solicit such information from individuals directly associated with your particular occupation or profession. For example: ask a real estate agent about housing trends and forecasts; ask a community leader about local demographic trends; ask a government official about planned development; ask a commercial lender about lending forecasts, expanding businesses and nonperforming loan trends. Such discussions will give you insight into changes occurring within the workplace and the workforce capabilities those changes will require. Such intelligence will not only be useful as general knowledge, but will also become an invaluable part of your annual career plan.

Such actions enhance your self-awareness and business acumen, and help you to be more responsive to prevailing business practices and emerging business trends. Whether business conditions are uncertain or relatively stable, such actions help you bulletproof your career.

Unfortunately, as we learned in the previous chapter, we do not work in a world whose driving principles are loyalty, trust, and prosperity. Rather, standards of fairness and respect often are sacrificed. In such a business world, we are all at risk. While much of this book provides practical information for those who have been laid off, this chapter focuses on what you can do now to reduce your risk of being laid off.

In many ways, typical ground rules apply in a turbulent business environment. For example, you must still be willing and able to contribute to your organization's success. However, displaying the following characteristics, which typically do not warrant special acknowledgment or recognition, may become noteworthy in such an environment:

- Exhibit flexibility by accepting temporary assignments elsewhere, by working unusual schedules or overtime, or by applying newly learned tools and techniques. These behaviors reflect your cooperativeness and adaptability—characteristics employers value.

- Remain enthusiastic by not spreading rumors or openly criticizing the organization or its management team.

- Accept responsibility when things go badly and credit others when things go well.

- Continue to handle stressful events with dignity and poise.

- When feeling overwhelmed or out of control, calm down and relax. Defusing volatile situations will enhance your value to any organization in turbulent times.

- Become acutely familiar with office politics, about how decisions are made and who typically makes them. Try to fit into the framework of office politics instead of bucking it, unless doing so would cause you to compromise your principles.

- Project a positive first impression. First impressions count, regardless of who tells you otherwise.

- Anticipate and be responsive to problems, taking the time to not only point out problems but to also share potential solutions.

- Take responsibility for your personal development, seeking out opportunities to cross-train.

- Make decisions and behave in a manner that reflects an understanding of—and support for—the organization's mission, vision, and values.

- Understand and work to exceed performance objectives, striving to outperform quality, time, and cost standards.

- Maintain a healthy outlook, interpreting (and describing) problems as challenges and opportunities.

- Continue to be as good as your word, refusing to waver on your honesty and integrity. Especially for those in a professional services profession, your reputation and integrity are as important as your ability. A mentor of mine (M. D. M.) taught me that we attorneys have nothing if not our reputation and integrity—never sacrifice them for some transitory benefit. We discuss these principles further in Chapter 10, "Loading and Using Your Toolkit."

- Continue striving to deliver on your organization's value proposition when working with colleagues and customers.

- Remain even keeled when it comes to your emotions and attitude.

- Do nothing to embarrass a colleague, your supervisor or manager, or your organization.

- Counter a potential lack of focus by employing planning, organization, and time management tools and techniques. You may find many of the tools introduced in this book to be helpful.

- Continue to be aware of your appearance and how you appear to others. Remember, too, first impressions are lasting. Trial attorneys know that many jurors decide cases based on opening statements, before they hear any evidence—despite judges advising them not to do so.

- Watch what you say and do; your comments and actions may be misinterpreted. What you say and do may be used against you later.

- Counter the turbulence by focusing on daily (rather than weekly) or weekly (rather than monthly) objectives. Take each day at a time. When faced with adversity, do the next right thing. Thus:

- When in doubt, strive to do what is right, just, and fair.

- When in doubt, be compassionate, strive for excellence, and be innovative.

In addition, seek out opportunities to establish and maintain a good reputation among your colleagues and supervisors. While others attempt to hide among the masses, you should take steps to gain visibility; enhance credibility; and project self-confidence, passion, and commitment toward the organization's vision and mission. Your objective is not to win a promotion or receive a salary increase. Rather, your intent is—to the extent possible—to influence the decision-making process. More specifically, you might influence decision makers by:

- Volunteering for special assignments, such as participating or leading start-up or product/service line development teams;

- Taking undesirable projects others eschew, distinguishing yourself as a person who will pitch in when needed;

- Assuming responsibility for mission-critical activities, especially highly visible ones;

- Volunteering for assignments directly or indirectly linked to revenue-producing activities;

- Showcasing your knowledge, skills, and abilities in a manner that is visible and acceptable to key decision makers;

- Willingly going above and beyond what is typically expected of an individual occupying your position within the organization;
- Becoming recognized as being a key player in the knowledge network;
- Contributing information, suggestions, and opinions to the organization's knowledge database or to its knowledge manager;
- Contributing expertise and thought leadership to trade organizations or professional associations—when such contributions are known to be coming from you as a representative of your organization;
- Updating your skills so they match industry trends or skills critical to your organization's success;
- Being courageous, when those around you fail to be so;
- Exhibiting a strong work ethic—workforce honesty and reliability oftentimes falter when times get tough; and
- Being mature, when those around you are not.

To help you assess your current focus, consider completing a Personal Engagement Checklist (see Table 3.1). Answering "no" to any of the questions on the checklist should propel you to immediate action. For example, if you have not previously or are not currently:

- Volunteering for special assignments . . .
  - Which assignments have surfaced during the past thirty days?
  - Which special assignments have others in your role or position recently accepted?
  - With whom can you meet to voice an interest in a current or future assignment?
- Assuming responsibility for mission-critical activities . . .
  - Which activities are currently available?
  - What potential gains and losses are associated with your assuming responsibility for those particular activities?
  - With whom can you meet to voice an interest in assuming responsibility for these—or other similar future—assignments?
- Volunteering for undesirable but necessary projects . . .
  - What types of projects do most colleagues avoid?
  - What risks and benefits are associated with your taking on such a project?
  - How would management view your volunteering for such a project?
- Volunteering for revenue-producing activities . . .
  - Which revenue-producing activities have surfaced during the past thirty days?
  - Which revenue-producing activities have others in your role or position recently accepted?
  - With whom can you meet to voice an interest in such a current or future activity?
- Showcasing your assets in a visible and acceptable way . . .
  - Which assets are most relevant to your organization's success?
  - How might you showcase those assets?
  - What are your colleagues doing to showcase their assets?

Table 3.1
Personal Engagement Checklist

Am I Currently or Have I Been . . .	Yes or No
Volunteering for special assignments?	
Volunteering for undesirable but necessary projects?	
Assuming responsibility for "mission critical" activities?	
Volunteering for revenue-producing activities?	
Showcasing my assets in a visible and acceptable way?	
Going above and beyond what is expected of someone in my position?	
Recognized as a key member of my organization's thought network?	
Contributing to my organization's Knowledge Database or Manager?	
Recognized as representing my organization at external meetings?	
Updating my skills to ensure industry/organization relevancy?	
Acting in a courageous manner?	
Maintaining a strong work ethic?	
Acting like the mature professional that I am?	

- Going above and beyond what is expected of someone in your position . . .
  - What opportunities have surfaced during the past thirty days?
  - What prevented you from capitalizing on these opportunities?
  - What have others done reflective of someone's going above and beyond expectations?
  - What can you do to mirror what others have done?
- Recognized as a key member of your organization's thought network . . .
  - Are you a member of your organization's thought network?
  - What might you do to become part of that network?
  - What can you do to publicize your being a key member of that network?
- Contributing information to your organization's Knowledge Database or Manager . . .
  - What can you offer your organization's Knowledge Database or Knowledge Manager?
  - What must you do to contribute to the Database or Manager?

- • Have mentoring opportunities surfaced within the past thirty days?
- • What can you do to let others know you have contributed to the Database or Manager?
- • Recognized as representing your organization at external meetings . . .
  - • Do you belong to trade organizations or professional associations?
  - • Do you actively contribute to such organizations or associations?
  - • If you contribute to such entities, what can you do to gain recognition for having represented your organization?
  - • What can you do to raise internal awareness about your representing your organization at trade organization or professional association meetings?
- • Updating your skills to ensure industry and organization relevancy . . .
  - • Are there continuing education opportunities in your profession?
  - • What can you do to ensure the relevancy of your personal skills?
  - • What discussion groups, professional associations, or trade groups should you join?
  - • Should you consider attaining a nondegree, professional certificate?
- • Acting in a courageous manner . . .
  - • Who are recognized as heroes in your organization?
  - • What did they do to be considered a hero?
  - • What opportunities are there for you to think and act in a similar manner?
- • Maintaining a strong work ethic . . .
  - • How can you send the message "I am still with the program"?
  - • What are others doing or not doing when you think, "That person is still with the program"?
- • Acting like the mature professional you truly are . . .
  - • How can you send the message "I am thinking and behaving at a mature level"?
  - • What are others doing or not doing when you think, "That person is acting professionally"?

Such behaviors and actions not only reduce the likelihood of your being discharged, but also show that you have reflected on and understand the role you play within such a changing organization and tumultuous business environment. You may find, nonetheless, that your organization is laying off entire departments or that it is asking departments throughout the organization to reduce staff allocations by a certain percentage. Under such circumstances, you—regardless of your performance or level of contribution—may not survive.

CREATING AN EXIT STRATEGY

A close colleague recently met with an entrepreneur to learn about how to manage risks associated with forming a partnership. An interesting point surfaced during this discussion: regardless of how optimistic you are about the potential success of the venture, you must begin at the end. You must enter the partnership with a clear understanding of how you will exit the partnership, should the need arise. Our colleague learned that one must not wait until the enterprise is at risk or the business relationship is in peril to decide on such issues. In today's turbulent business environment, prudence dictates the subject of "exit strategy" being raised—and decided upon—even before the venture is established.

We employees function within an equally turbulent and risky environment. It therefore makes sense for such logic be applied to everyone's career, not just someone wishing to establish a partnership. To begin at the end requires some forethought. To frame your thinking around this, we recommend you think about two critical points: (1) the moment you decide you no longer wish to work within an organization, and (2) the questions typically included in a job interview. In terms of the typical (although perhaps currently not as typical as in past years) career cycle, these two points normally occur at the end. So let's begin there.

Upon accepting a job offer, you are usually very excited. You think about the success you will realize. The accomplishments you will garner. The rewards you will gain. Such a time is typically happy and exciting. Now, shift forward several years. You look at yourself in the mirror and suddenly realize you no longer wish to work for your employer. Yesterday's optimism has vanished. Accomplishments perhaps remain unfulfilled. Rewards perhaps remain unattained. You suddenly realize you no longer eagerly anticipate spending another day at the office, but rather dread the thoughts of simply having to "show up on time."

To turn this rather negative exercise into something positive, you must shift your focus and think about conditions likely to contribute to your developing such a mind-set. Using such thoughts (your no longer wishing to work for your employer) as a basis of a hypothetical situation, what:

- Factors would most likely contribute to your having such a mind-set?
- Events would most likely need to occur to create such a mind-set?
- Concerns would most likely surface before you drew such a conclusion?

By identifying these factors, events, and concerns, you will be able to counter them proactively throughout your career so they do not occur, and you will recognize them (and take appropriate action) if they do. Both of these courses of action help bulletproof your career.

What factors might contribute to your decision to leave the company, firm, or institution? For example, what if you discover your management is guilty of illegal activity? What if you discover your organization is contributing to the pollution or depletion of our natural resources? What if you discover that discrimination prevails throughout your worksite or corporate headquarters?

What events might contribute to your coming to such a realization? For example, what if you are passed over for a much-deserved promotion? What if you are not recognized for contributions you make to an important project? What if do you do not receive a much-deserved bonus or commission?

What concerns might make you come to such a conclusion? For example, might you initially feel you are not being given an opportunity to contribute or to achieve? Might you feel you are not being recognized for your contributions? Might you feel you no longer receive satisfaction through the work itself?

This exercise sensitizes you to conditions that may never surface; however, they are conditions you must recognize and act upon if they do. This exercise allows you to be proactive, to assess conditions contributing to your desire to remain with the organization and to be alert and responsive (for example, updating your career transition Action Plan) when such conditions begin to change. This exercise also raises your awareness of factors and events most likely to propel you toward a career or job change. Such awareness is absolutely critical, in that it helps you realize how tenuous your affiliation with your organization might be and how career management is an ongoing process rather than a one-time event.

We also recommend that you shift the scenario forward. Hypothetically, you have decided you no longer wish to remain affiliated with your organization and have submitted your letter of resignation. You are about to end your final day of employment and are being asked to complete a brief exit interview. How might you respond to questions typically asked during an exit interview?

For example, if you decided to leave an organization, how likely is it that you based that decision on one or more of the following reasons?

- There were certain aspects of your current job you did not like.
- Your new position provides certain, unique challenges and opportunities.
- Your new organization is recognized for its—
  - Commitment to its customers or clients.
  - Concern for its employees.
  - Willingness to invest in the development of its employees.
  - Cutting-edge thinking, products, or services.
  - Efficient systems and processes.
- There were aspects of your previous job you did not enjoy doing.
- You did not like the manner in which your supervisor—
  - Provided guidance and direction.
  - Provided feedback.
  - Recognized your effort and performance.
  - Developed or trained you.
  - Assigned you to particular tasks or projects.
- Certain aspects of the new organization "draw" you to it.
- Certain aspects of your current organization "push" you away.

- You were not allowed to contribute ideas about how to improve your organization's services or products.
- You were not allowed to contribute ideas about how to improve the manner in which your organization functions or operates.
- Your next organization is more likely to display a more desirable corporate style when—
  - Dealing with its customers or clients.
  - Dealing with its employees.
  - Investing in the development of its employees.
- Your next supervisor is more likely to demonstrate a more desirable management style when—
  - Giving you guidance and direction.
  - Providing feedback.
  - Recognizing your effort and performance.
  - Developing or training you.
  - Assigning you to particular tasks or projects.

This scenario, like the previous one, sensitizes you to conditions that may never surface. These are conditions, however, that you must recognize and act upon (i.e., activate your personal network) if they arise. This exercise allows you to be proactive and assess conditions contributing to your desire to remain with an organization, and to be alert and responsive when such conditions begin to change. This exercise raises your awareness of conditions most likely to cause you to begin considering a new career or job. This insight is critical, in that it helps you realize how little job security you really have. Such insight helps you recognize an important tenet: career management is an ongoing process rather than a one-time event.

CONCLUSION

Actions we outline in this chapter may help you bulletproof your career. However, as we stressed in Chapter 1, layoffs frequently occur and they simply are beyond your control. If you are laid off, these suggestions will contribute to your ability to respond productively and will increase the likelihood of your becoming employed elsewhere. While the remainder of this book provides information likely to increase your employability, it is in your best interest to keep in mind that previous performance does count, that your track record does make a difference, and that your being offered your next position does depend on your consistently doing the right things for the right reasons, even under unfavorable circumstances. Remember, a forced career change is not a boot out the door, but a boost to a higher level, and you can assist the boost by bulletproofing your career.

CHAPTER 4

It Still Happens to People Like Us

THERE IS NO SILVER BULLET

It happened to Jack—for the third time in as many years—on July 24, 2001.

It was a Tuesday.

Jack was laid off at a meeting with his supervisor (who had commuted from London to New York to meet with members of his global IT team) to discuss, among other things, his year-end review.

Jack was not then—nor is he now—alone in being laid off.

During that same week, tens of thousands of other employees throughout the United States were also laid off. That week, the media announced job cuts including those at Lucent Technology (involving more than 10,000) and Hewlett Packard (involving another 5,000).

The workplace is facing very turbulent times. No profession or industry is immune. For example, within a recent year:

- Ford, the nation's second largest automaker, announced layoffs.

- Motorola, the telecommunications equipment giant, announced layoffs.

- Steelcase, the nation's second largest office furniture manufacturer, announced layoffs.

- Even before the Enron scandal, Arthur Andersen, the premier accounting and consulting firm, announced layoffs.

The nation's unemployment rate in April 2003 was 6 percent, an eight-year high. The number of unemployed workers stood at 8.8 million; approximately 2 million had been without jobs for twenty-seven weeks or more. The average duration of unemployment was 19.6 weeks, a twenty-year high. From November 2001 through April 2003, the unemployment rate ranged from 5.6 percent to 6 percent (The Employment Situation: April 2003: On-line). Almost every region had been significantly impacted—as of April 2003, states with the highest unemployment rates were Alaska, Oregon, Washington, Pennsylvania, Michigan, California, Wisconsin, Vermont, Idaho, and Massachusetts (Unemployment Weekly Claims Report 2003: On-line). This was not a short-term issue; the unemployment rate also reached 6 percent in December 2002 (The Employment Situation: December 2002: On-line). An exceptionally brutal year for America's workforce was 2001. In late 2001, more than 3.1 million unemployed workers drew unemployment benefits (Strope 2001: B3). More than 250,000 layoffs were announced in a single month and more than 1.3 million were laid off during the first nine months of 2001 (Eisenberg 2001: On-line).

Financial analysts suggest that current trends reflect not only a large— but also a rising—number of layoffs.

What happened to Jack that Tuesday morning might already have happened to you. If not, you—by virtue of working in today's business environment—may soon also be subject to a job cut (layoff or discharge).

Today's turbulent times are here to stay. Ongoing business decisions and actions constantly contribute to this tumultuous environment; we witness large firms, corporations, and institutions eliminating higher paying jobs, while smaller organizations continue to create those same kinds of jobs. The continuously changing landscape of the business world also contributes to this tumult; we witness part-time and contract employees now making up a significant, rather than a marginal, portion of the workforce.

Bridges (1994: 29–63), after analyzing social and industrial trends, concludes that today's business world does not demand (nor does it expect) employee loyalty. Rather, it seeks the knowledge, skills, and abilities the employees possess. He concludes that all jobs, in essence, are now temporary and that job security resides "in the person, not the job." Bridges stresses that companies, firms, and institutions no longer provide job security. In today's environment, employee capabilities and assets (rather than their employer) provide job security.

Many in the workforce assume that job cuts result only from declining sales or slumps in revenue. Bridges (1997: 12–26) reports this is not the case; that even an upturn in the economy may not significantly reduce the number of layoffs! The bottom line is this: the need for organizational flexibility and adaptiveness, rather than declining sales or slumps in revenue, is driving the changes in today's work world.

Tischler (2001: On-line) argues that being laid off is not the worst thing that can happen to you—that remaining in a bad job for security reasons is worse. In fact, she suggests that losing your job may be the best thing that will ever happen to your career! To turn this challenge into an opportunity, she recommends that you use this time to re-create your future. She stresses that being laid off provides an excellent opportunity for you to decide which company you would like to work for and who will have "the privilege" of having you work for them. As we see it, your point of view is critical to your future success. Do you view being laid off as a "boot out the door" or a "boost to the next level," namely your next career move?

Perhaps Tischler is right. We all know people (perhaps ourselves!) who remain in a job for all the wrong reasons. Inertia has kept many of us in a position we found unfulfilling. While such dissatisfied employees may "hold on to their job," we find they often:

- Sacrifice their self-confidence and self-respect;
- Lower their standards to match those of the organization;
- Become bitter and display passive-aggressive behavior;
- Settle for having a good (rather than perhaps ever having a great) day;
- Look forward to Fridays and dread each Monday;
- Allow their mediocre attitude to influence the way they interact with their colleagues and the manner in which they serve their customers;
- Allow that mediocre attitude to hurt their performance, contributing to the downward spiral of job (dis)satisfaction;
- At best, they have nothing good to say about the company when around family and friends;
- Even worse, refuse to defend the company when it is criticized or defamed; and
- Fall into the routine of withholding suggestions and otherwise performing at a suboptimal level.

Careful analysis of these mind-sets and behaviors of disaffected employees reveals the high personal cost of holding on to job security under such circumstances. We should recognize that holding on to an unfulfilling and dissatisfying job is not worth the personal cost.

As Tischler points out, being laid off is as much an opportunity as it is a problem. As we discussed in chapter 3, "Bulletproofing Your Career," we must each approach our career in a planned and purposeful manner. Because the factors that impact our career constantly change, we must periodically review and modify our plan. This review and the resulting actions allow us to:

- Assess the prevailing business environment (hot products and services, hot skills). Can we reform ourselves to take advantage of those changes?
- Assess our personal assets (knowledge, skills, abilities). Do we need to seek out training or additional education to adapt to changing conditions?

- Assess our personal limitations (personality, attitude, knowledge, skills, abilities). Do we need an "attitude adjustment" through career or psychological counseling as much as we need a career boost?
- Capitalize on emerging opportunities by appropriately applying our assets. Do not be shy—take the plunge into the emerging market.
- Minimize the most significant risks by taking steps to reduce the impact of our limitations on the services we provide or the products we create. This is another attitude-awakening issue. Accentuate the positive—do not dwell on the past or on your self-perceived limitations.

Although perhaps extremely upsetting and unquestionably inconvenient, being laid off does provide an excellent opportunity for you to review your career plan and make necessary adjustments. That is where the "boost to the next level" comes in. You must motivate yourself to recognize job market conditions, assess where you may fit in to those conditions, improve yourself to steer your career in the right direction. For example, if the real estate market grinds to a halt and no clients seek you out for real estate law advice, learn another area of practice. If newer automobiles no longer have carburetors and distributors, take courses in emerging technologies to retool your automotive service career.

Slightly adjusting your career plan may not be enough. We must, from time to time, leave an occupation or profession and enter another one. The compelling reason for such a career change varies; for example, it might involve a significant shift in technology. To illustrate this point using an example from times past, consider the case of professional buggy whip manufacturers. Whip manufacturers once created an important and valued product. Because of market demand, individuals capable of creating such devices were valued; many individuals therefore considered this to be a desirable trade and entered it as their chosen career.

The introduction of automobiles into mainstream America drastically (albeit not very quickly) reduced the need for buggy whips and subsequently decreased their value. At that specific point in our not too distant past, both employers and employees had to decide whether they would continue manufacturing buggy whips or whether they would apply their knowledge and skills elsewhere. This shift in technology eventually forced many workers to enter another career.

It is important to note that this career change proved necessary not because employers demanded it, but rather because customers (or rather the lack of customers) demanded it. The same situation occurs today—but rather than manufacturing leather buggy whips, we manufacture gravity pumps and fuel injectors. While being laid off may not be the most desirable course of action, it does give you an opportunity to review your career plan and—to the extent necessary—make significant adjustments.

While being laid off may be theoretically beneficial, naturally, it is difficult to see the benefit immediately, because the immediate effect of a layoff is the complete disruption of your life. It impacts your relationships, your financial security, and your means of:

- Expressing yourself professionally;
- Contributing to a worthwhile business venture;
- Achieving personal satisfaction at a professional level; and
- Receiving recognition from colleagues and associates.

We have used the following "tool" (one of many presented in this book) throughout our careers. We find it to be extremely useful, whether tackling a personal obstacle or working with a team to address a business issue.

We encourage you to take some time right now to use the Barrier/Solution Table. It will help minimize your fears and propel you into action (see Table 4.1).

Instructions for Using the Barrier/Solution Table

Take a moment to consider how being laid off might impact your life. Using the Barrier/Solution Table, list "Barriers" (challenges, problems,

Table 4.1
Barrier/Solution Table

Barrier	Potential Solutions

limitations, obstacles) would have to be addressed as a result of your being laid off.

For each Barrier, identify at least three potential "Solutions" (counter-measures, fixes, answers). Be creative—do not limit yourself when identi-fying potential solutions. Do not sell yourself short. Your career and life experiences are valuable tools you can draw upon in meeting and over-coming barriers that block your way to a new position or a career change.

Once you have listed three potential solutions, numerically rate all three in terms of:

- Feasibility;
- Likelihood of Success;
- Required Cost (time, financial, emotional); and
- Overall Benefit (certain solutions will address multiple barriers).

For Feasibility, Likelihood of Success, and Overall Benefit, the range of potential ratings is –5 to +5 (–5 if, for example, it is not very feasible, or +5, if it is extremely feasible).

For Required Cost, the range of potential ratings is also –5 to +5, though you assign a –5 if the cost is extremely high and a +5 if the cost is extremely low.

A completed table may look something like Table 4.2.

Using the above as an example, give the potential solutions to the fol-lowing ratings:

- Join or continue attending professional association meetings and seminars has a total score of +5 (doability = –1, likelihood of success +2, cost = +2, benefit = +2).
- Distributing work samples and writing samples to potential employers has a total score of –1 (doability = –3, likelihood of success = +3, cost = –4, benefit = +3).
- Writing a book, having potential employers be part of the target readership earns a total score of +2 (doability = +2, likelihood of success = +2, cost = –5, benefit = +3).
- Writing a series of magazine articles likely to be read by potential employers acquires an end score of +3 (doability = +3, likelihood of success = +2, cost = –5, benefit = +3).
- Writing a series of articles for trade journals, industry publications, or newsletters and sending them to potential employers earns a total score of +3 also.

In these examples—after taking all factors into account—the most promising solutions are for you to join or continue attending professional

Table 4.2
Completed Barrier/Solution Table

Barrier	Potential Solutions
Being laid off takes me out of the mix. It keeps me away from meetings where I can interact with other people in my field. It drastically reduces my ability to gain exposure (to "get my name out there" and to have my name recognized by potential employers).	Join or continue attending professional association meetings and seminars.
	Distribute work samples and writing samples to potential employers.
	Write a book and have potential employers be part of the target readership.
	Write a series of magazine articles that potential employers are likely to read.
	Write a series of articles for trade journals, industry publications, or newsletters and send them to potential employers. Include them with your résumé or request for an interview to distinguish you from other job candidates.

association meetings and seminars and to write a series of articles (for publication in magazines, trade journals, and/or industry publications or newsletters) that potential employers are likely to read. The other two potential solutions are not as likely to yield the desired outcomes.

Using this or a similar tool, consider your personal situation, identify barriers and potential solutions, assign the ratings, add up the results, select the best solution, and act!

In summary, this section introduced information for you to take into consideration and one of several tools. Faced with the adversity of a changing job market, you should be proactive; act, do not simply passively react. "Act, don't react." Take control of your future by assessing your skills and your goals, and determine where you can best fit into potential employers' plans. The next section provides information useful in preparing for, or responding to, being laid off.

THE SEVERANCE SEESAW

Shortly after his out-counseling session, Jack attempted to capture emotions associated with the event. He, along with other friends and colleagues, shared their personal notes, journals, and diaries (in confidence) with us for use in this book. Their thoughts serve as the basis for this section.

We have attempted to capture thoughts and emotions typically experienced by someone being laid off. Our intent is to give this aspect of the severance process the coverage it needs and deserves, one of us by virtue of having been trained to serve as an out-counselor, having out-counseled others, and having been severed by two organizations and the other of us having been trained as an attorney and counselor and having moved from one firm to another unexpectedly.

Our desire is not to raise your level of discomfort if you have been laid off, nor is it to raise your anxiety level if you are at risk of being laid off. Rather, it is to:

• Depict what you may feel if you encounter such an event.
• Help you cope with some of the emotions you are likely to experience.
• Share with others the emotions you may be experiencing if you have just been laid off.

Total shock.

Out of town on a business trip to enter a meeting expecting to discuss your wins and accomplishments. But rather to be told "the reason you think you are here is not the reason you are here. We have decided it is not gong to work out and we need to sever our relationship."

Total loss of focus. You have entered the "Twilight Zone." This is not happening. You sit there, stunned, just barely able to hear, much less comprehend, what they are saying. You listen as they tell you that after August 2 you no longer have a position with the firm.

Your first thought: "Why me?"

You ask: "Was there a misunderstanding?" "No, there was no problem with your performance" is the answer they give you. You think, but cannot speak: "Then why?"

They very formally—almost robotically—go through the motions . . . your last day in the office is today; your last day with the firm is August 2;

we will not contest your receiving unemployment; we will pay you for your accrued but unused vacation time.

Of course they will not contest my receiving unemployment, of course they will pay me for my vacation time. I'm entitled to it.

Thoughts are racing through your mind at 100 miles per hour.

You again ask, "Why?" Again, you are told it is not your performance. You must trust what they say, but how can you trust them when they are doing this to you?

Uncertainty, fear, then anger.

You are caught up in a series of events over which you have no control. You realize your destiny has already been decided.

You want to ask questions.

So much to think about in so brief a period of time—decisions to be made, actions to be taken.

You feel helpless, betrayed, abandoned.

"We need to go down the hall so you can speak to someone from the outplacement firm. He will answer questions you may have." You feel like you are being rushed.

You need more time—to think through all of this, to ask the right questions, to say the right things.

You realize they want to end the conversation.

They stand.

You stand, not knowing what to say, how to act.

Numerous, conflicting emotions run through your mind at the same time.

You shake their hands and are then escorted down the hallway to meet with the outplacement firm's representative.

All of this seems so very unbelievable.

You are taken into a small office. The outplacement specialist is waiting. He stands and shakes your hand. His first question is, "So, how are you?" Is he insincere or just patronizing? He comes across as being friendly. He acts as though he understands what you are going through. How can he understand?

You realize he seems sincerely interested in your well-being and gives you some solid advice.

He tells you not to do anything for the next seventy-two hours. You think to yourself, "But that is three days of an already short transition period."

You ramble, still unable to focus. Still not believing what just occurred. You try to summarize your feelings by saying, "I feel like I am standing on the edge of an abyss."

The specialist indicates that everything will work out. After all, something similar to this had previously happened to him, and he came out fine.

He points out that you were not laid off due to poor performance—you have strong credentials and will land on your feet. He assures you this is happening because of the numbers—that you should not take it personally.

He begins asking questions about your separation agreement. You suddenly realize you did not comprehend what was said during your out-counseling session.

They said six weeks of severance pay, you heard two.

They said your voice mail would be operational until the end of the month, you heard immediate disconnection.

You feel the need to get out of the office building. To get away, to go to the hotel room. To call your wife and give her the bad news. To prepare her for your arrival home. To set the stage for your deciding how the family will survive this. And to assure her that this was not your fault.

You say you must pick up your bags for the trip to the airport.

Before you depart, he wants to make sure that you will be all right. He asks if there is anyone you can talk to. He voices concern about your being alone on an airplane.

You say you need to call your wife; he suggests you give her the news in person. You now feel you must immediately telephone your wife—but what will you tell her?

You feel isolated, as if a shell of numbness has enveloped you. You feel like you did when you were young, sick with a fever. Things and people around you appear to be distant.

You see one of your colleagues exit his office. He sees you, turns and walks quickly in the opposite direction. You think, "Not even enough courage to look me in the eye."

You leave the building and walk to the hotel. You call your wife—you tell her you have bad news. You want her to know that it is not as bad as it seems. That you will discuss things when you get home. Her only response is, "I am scared."

You refocus. You now stand in your driveway. You can't remember much about your commute home—the flight, the route you took from the airport, the volume or flow of traffic.

Looking at your home, you think about your family. About how disappointed they will be when you give them the news.

You see your wife for the first time—only hours after you received the news. You can tell that she has been crying—but that she does not want you to know. You look into her eyes. You don't know what to say. You want to apologize. You want to make everything right.

Words are spoken. . . .

Silence is marked. . . .

That night, you are exhausted. You fall asleep at around 1:00 A.M.; wake up at precisely 4:21 A.M. You can't sleep, you can't think—you still can't believe what happened less than twenty-four hours ago. You realize you do not have to get up and go to work. There is no work to go to.

You sit around in a fog for the remainder of the day. Sitting next to the local pond, you reflect. You look at your watch—it is 9:30 A.M. Moments later, you look at your watch again—it is 2:30 P.M.

You reflect on the past. You think about the future.

Several days pass. You can now discuss this without becoming emotional.

Now is the time to tell your children, "Dad has to look for another job."

But what do you tell them? What do you say?

That we will get through this . . . that everything will work out.

There are emotional and psychological costs associated with any significant, personal transition. The preceding narrative, based on our personal experiences, reveals such costs in graphic detail.

Here are several points to remember:

- Individuals responsible for "severing" others may assume they can relate to those being severed.

  Discussions with individuals who have served as out-counselors and who have also been severed revealed the following conclusion: you do not know what being laid off is like unless it happens to you.

- Individuals previously responsible for severing others may assume they know how they would react if the roles were reversed.

  Discussions with individuals who have been laid off revealed the following conclusion: You do not know how you will actually react until it happens to you.

- Individuals at risk of being laid off may feel that they could not handle such an event.

  Discussion with individuals who have been laid off revealed the following conclusion: Initially, you may feel incapable of surviving this crisis. You eventually realize you will get through this, that everything will work out. This, too, will pass. You survive—your support network of family and friends catches you.

THE VEILED OPPORTUNITY

Much of the information presented in this chapter, by its very nature, places a negative connotation on the severance process. As perhaps it should, in that a layoff is typically unplanned and the manner in which it occurs frequently causes undue stress and financial hardship. Layoffs therefore unsettle us. They somehow unbalance us.

Although we may take prudent steps to bulletproof our career, layoffs still happen to people like us. While the act of being laid off will unsettle and unbalance us, it in essence does create an opportunity. We discuss in greater detail how you should capitalize on this opportunity in chapter 8. The effects of layoffs are both negative (on which we typically focus) and positive (which we typically do not recognize, or worse, which we ignore). Layoffs ultimately become our nemesis or our salvation.

To capitalize on this life-changing event, you must unveil the opportunity it presents. To regain your balance following a layoff, we recommend that you:

- Shift your viewpoint.

  When it happens to you, you take it personally. How can you not, when you are the one being personally impacted by this business decision? Not only have you been a compliant employee, but you also have probably sacrificed time with your family "to get some work done."

  Shift your viewpoint so that you do not focus only on what has occurred to you. Look around you, at the countless others also involved. You were not targeted; this may be one of those times it helps to think you were simply a number.

- Rely on your personal values.

  You were not in your previous position by accident. You were there because you possessed needed knowledge, skills, and abilities. You were also there for a much more fundamental reason: you felt your personal contribution to the company, firm, or institution was the right thing for you to do. For days, weeks, months, or years you used your organization as a vehicle or mechanism for your contributing to your profession, occupation, and/or community.

  Just as you have done in the past, rely on your personal values. Think about how you wish to contribute to your profession, occupation, and community, and then seek out other vehicles and mechanisms for doing so. There are other opportunities out there, in the form of companies, firms, and institutions that will allow you to benefit others.

- Reframe your thinking.

  You consider your job to be a means of your doing good work. It also provides you and your family financial security. Being laid off may naturally cause you to focus on these two aspects of employment.

  However, there is more to life (and to employment) than being allowed to do good work and earn an income. The mission statement in a local school includes the following phrase "We will nurture students so they become lifelong learners." Reframe your thinking so you approach this event as a lifelong learner. Rather than focusing on only two aspects of employment, think about it in the following terms: What might I learn from this? How might this challenge help me refine my current skills? Or develop new ones?

- Focus on the big picture.

  Being placed in an "at-risk" situation causes certain things to occur. For example, our senses are heightened, time appears to stand still (or slow down), and we are able to focus on the situation that threatens us. Unfortunately, such a focus may lead to tunnel vision.

When it comes to layoffs, as we stress throughout this book, it is important that "we sweat the small stuff." However, our attention to detail must not prevent us from stepping back and "seeing the big picture." While you are being laid off, pay particular attention to what is happening around you, and to those around you. While you create your transition action plan, do not be constrained by your previous jobs and responsibilities. When chasing a particular job opportunity, do not be blind to other opportunities surfacing elsewhere.

- Reinterpret the situation.

Being laid off forces you to look for another job. It also sensitizes you to other career opportunities.

Being laid off is an act with numerous consequences. It typically requires one to search for other career or job opportunities. Reinterpret the event by thinking about (and then acting upon) the other consequences. For example, being out of work gives you the gift of time. Individuals previously devoting sixty or more hours a week to their job may find themselves in a position to devote time and energy to: shaping up physically, through diet and exercise; shaping up mentally, through reading or writing; and reconnecting with family and friends.

- Rely on the support of family and friends.

If your son or daughter happens to be a baseball or softball pitcher, you are undoubtedly familiar with the saying, "He (or she) has dug himself (or herself) into a hole. The coach must now let him (or her) climb out of the hole." Individuals typically apply the same logic to a layoff. They take personal responsibility for the problem, and they therefore assume personal responsibility for solving the problem.

If your son or daughter happens to be a baseball or softball infielder or outfielder, you are undoubtedly familiar with the saying, "Team, great job backing up the pitcher! You really helped him (or her) get out of the hole." While the pitcher may be a key asset when it comes to the games of baseball and softball, pitchers do not win—nor do they lose—games on their own. Pitchers rely on the defensive play of their infielders and outfielders. Individuals must apply the same logic during a layoff. Do not even attempt to win this game single-handedly. Rely on your family and friends.

- Exercise your imagination.

As previously stated, being laid off does give you the gift of time. Unfortunately, the need to do good work and to earn income frequently magnifies the need for us to spend all, or a majority, of that time seeking a new career or job.

Being laid off also gives you the gift of discovery. Exercise your imagination. How might your capabilities and assets be applied to other disciplines, such as the field of medicine? For example, how might you apply the totality of your life experiences to the solution of breast cancer? Or to something else that afflicts society, depriving children of their parents and communities of their vital contributions? Do not simply "look for" another job. Explore. Discover. Imagine.

- Rely on your inner self.

Being laid off causes uncertainty and ambiguity. It causes one to question oneself, to doubt. It frequently causes individuals to doubt both the value they brought to their previous organization and the value they are capable of bringing to their future employer. Such a traumatic event shakes us psychologically and emotionally to the core. Under such circumstances, it is not a surprise that individuals lose their self-confidence.

Rather than focusing on the uncertainty, think about the constants that make up a significant portion of your life. Rather than giving in to self-doubt, think about your previous position(s) and responsibilities. The values, capabilities, and assets that qualified you to enter your previous position are still there. You still possess those values, capabilities, and assets that contributed to your success while in that position. Your core values, capabilities, and assets will serve as your bridge to the future. Just as you can take comfort by relying on your family and friends, be confident in relying on your inner self.

Layoffs do happen to people like us. They are not to be taken lightly—being laid off is a life-changing event. However, to appreciate and capitalize on this event, you must unveil the opportunity it presents. The information provided in this section pertains to mind-sets likely to help you more fully appreciate (and thus capitalize on) a layoff. While this section contains information of a conceptual nature, chapter 8 provides practical tools and techniques.

CONCLUSION

As we discussed in chapter 1, job cuts (by chance and by design) are becoming a way of business life. In such an environment, we are all at risk of being—or may have already been—laid off. This chapter introduced information for you to consider and one of several tools. Faced with the adversity of a changing job market, you must act rather than simply passively react. "Act, don't react."

This chapter also highlighted typical thoughts and emotions anyone feels after being laid off. While everyone is different, you must recognize that you probably will have such thoughts and feel such emotions if you are laid off. Being aware of them allows you to realize that such reactions are normal, and that while the thoughts and emotions are spontaneous and normal, your response must be planned and purposeful. Such calculated action/response reduces the likelihood of your making a mistake by which you may surrender your rights that cannot be returned or burn bridges that cannot be rebuilt.

The next chapter outlines the process, the results, and the outcomes of the out-counseling process. This information will allow you to assess your situation and decide potential responses/follow-up actions.

CHAPTER 5

Cutting the Cord

The meeting in which you are laid off . . .
The meeting in which you are out-counseled . . .
The meeting in which you are severed from the organization . . .

THE OUT-COUNSELING PROCESS

From Your Employer's Viewpoint

Regardless of what you call it, your out-counseling session will follow a pre-set sequence of activities. When a significant number of employees are laid off, or when an organization has planned or has undergone a series of layoffs, the protocol may be established by outside consultants or in-house human resources professionals and attorneys. The protocol, by design, provides you with information about your severance and reduces both the likelihood of an altercation occurring during the process and a lawsuit for wrongful discharge, discrimination, or retaliation afterward.

Most organizations follow an established and approved process when "severing" employees. In many cases, individuals conducting the out-counseling sessions have received special training and/or have participated in skills-building sessions. In most sophisticated organizations, two corporate representatives attend the out-counseling session. Reasons for this include the security of having two people attend in the event of an altercation, and the usually silent attendee (in legal terms, the "prover") can report or testify as to what both the employee said and what the corporate representative said during the session, in the event of a lawsuit. The point is that most out-counseling sessions are pre-planned, well planned, and designed to protect the organization, rather than you.

The out-counseling session may or may not come as a complete surprise to the individuals being laid off. If it is not a complete surprise, you should consider it a gift that you have already had an opportunity to begin working through this personal transition. Our goal in bringing you the advice in this book is to raise your awareness of an ever-more frequent occurrence in the workplace and to help you plan your future. Forewarned of a possible career transition is forearmed for the future. Remember, the layoff is not a "boot out the door," but a "boost to a higher level."

The out-counseling session will be very brief. The organization's representative will attempt to:

- Give you the news;
- Hand you the severance agreement;
- Explain key points; and
- End the meeting as quickly as possible.

This is the proverbial "Get in. Get it over with and get out." You may be told, "You will have an opportunity to ask questions, but not now, not to me. You can ask questions to a different person at a later time." Again, the overall objective is for your session to conclude as quickly—and as amicably—as possible.

From Your Viewpoint

Even if you knew about it in advance—just like the death of a terminally ill loved one—the out-counseling session is shocking. As we discussed in chapter 5, the session raises numerous thoughts and emotions. You may attempt to address these thoughts and emotions by soliciting additional information. The organization's representative, however, is trained not to ad-lib. The script is as set as the decision.

Nonetheless, you will want to know why. You will want to ask, "Why me?" You will want to find out what you did, but should not have done. You will want to find out what you could have done, but failed to do. You will feel lost and alone. You may feel violated.

You are likely to detect the out-counselor's discomfort and desire to end the session quickly. Through his or her comments and actions, you are likely to detect a desire to avoid conflict. You may sense the out-counselor's cold-hearted attitude toward your personal tragedy.

The out-counselor may say that you will have an opportunity to ask questions at a different time or to a different person. You will not wish to do so. The out-counselor and the employer will hope you do not. From their perspective, it is over. From yours, you have to begin anew.

Given the nature of out-counseling, all of your questions and concerns cannot be adequately addressed during the session. It is therefore important that you focus on a few key issues that will help you adjust and move on, as well as help you determine whether your layoff was wrongful:

- Ask the out-counselor to verify or confirm the reason for your layoff (at a minimum, whether or not it is due to your performance).
- Ask for the name of the person you should contact for answers to future questions, especially about severance and COBRA benefits.
- Listen closely to what is being said and take notes. If you do not have paper and a pen, ask for them—don't be shy.
  - What effort was made to identify other job opportunities for you within the organization? Volunteer to consider or to be considered for another position or training for one.
  - Who will be asked to assume your role/responsibilities (is the person younger—possible age discrimination)?
  - Who else is being included in this round of layoffs? Does any federally protected group (race, sex, religion, ethnic group, age, etc.) bear the brunt of the layoffs?
- After your session, ask the outplacement specialist (if such services are being offered to you) similar questions:
  - What reason was he or she given for your out-counseling?
  - Whom should you contact for answers to future questions?
  - Did the out-counselor or your file reveal anything that might suggest you will have problems finding a future position?

Do not be surprised if you become emotional during the session. Remember, being laid off is not always a reflection of you or your performance. Try to manage your emotions so you can listen to what is being said and observe what is being done.

Do not become hostile or act aggressively toward the out-counselor or outplacement specialist. Becoming hostile or aggressive does not help you—it (1) hinders future negotiation of severance benefits (if negotiation is possible); (2) could result in your discharge for cause, a blemish on your record, instead of a layoff unrelated to your performance; or, worse (3) could result in criminal prosecution!

The Result of Out-counseling

Your out-counselor will tell you when your last day in the office will be, when your last day with the organization will be, what your final compensation will include (salary, accrued vacation time, etc.), and how you are to proceed during the brief transition period.

Although rarely done, at times the individual being severed is asked to vacate the premises immediately and is escorted while doing so.

Make no mistake about it—at the end of the out-counseling process, you will no longer be a member of the organization. Regardless of what your organization calls it—at the end of the out-counseling process, your employment will have been terminated.

You cannot immediately do anything about your dismissal. The decision has already been made, endorsed, and approved by all necessary parties, and implemented. You can, however, review, question, and (if appropriate) challenge the conditions and stipulations of your severance package—before accepting them.

You may want to consider retaining an employment lawyer and/or an employee benefits specialist to review your severance package. Many packages contain releases, agreements not to compete, and confidentiality agreements that may not be in your best interest. Of course, it is up to you to protect your interests for the future, because your soon-to-be-former employer will not do so.

The Impact of Out-counseling

While these actions result in your employment with the organization being terminated, the impact is much greater. It carries psychological and emotional costs.

Holmes and Rahe (1967: 216), in the article "The Social Readjustment Rating Scale," present a well-known tool used to assess stressful effects of significant life events. They report that stressful events require significant coping behaviors, and that such "expenditures" may precipitate illness or have an additive effect in contributing to illness.

Holmes and Rahe rank being fired as the eighth most significant event that can occur to an individual. Being fired is less significant than only the following events:

• Death of a spouse;
• Divorce;
• Marital separation;
• Jail term;
• Death of a close family member;
• Personal injury or illness; and
• Marriage.

Holmes and Rahe also report there is an approximately 33 percent chance of your becoming ill during the next year if you score 151 or more points on their Life Change Index.

Being fired (47 points), along with the associated business readjustment (39), changes in financial state (38) and work responsibilities (29), causes your score to surpass the 151-point threshold. We cannot avoid the physical effects of losing our employment.

Events generally perceived as being positive are also stressful. These events include marriage, Christmas, vacation, and the arrival of a baby. Such events, when combined with being laid off, also contribute to one surpassing the 151-point threshold.

The Social Readjustment Rating Scale was developed for adults. Coddington (1972: 13–16), using a similar tool developed for children, discovered that:

- For preschoolers, a parent losing his or her job ranks twenty-seventh (followed by a "decrease in the number of arguments with parents," which ranks twenty-eighth).
- For elementary school children, a parent losing his or her job ranks twenty-eighth (similar to one experiencing an "outstanding personal achievement," which ranks twenty-seventh).
- For junior high or middle school student, a parent losing his or her job ranks twenty-fifth (similar to one's "not making a desired extracurricular activity," which ranks twenty-fourth).
- For a high school student, a parent losing his or her job ranks twenty-ninth (followed by one experiencing an "outstanding personal achievement," which ranks thirtieth).

This information should be good news to those of you who fear being laid off will emotionally or psychologically devastate your children. Research proves this is simply not the case, that children are more adaptable at times than adults.

In addition to emotional and psychological costs, being laid off carries financial costs that impact you and every member of your family. In some cases, this impact may even touch your extended family. The next two sections provide detailed information about what you are likely to experience and receive when being laid off, as well as more information about how you can recognize—and address—the psychological, emotional, and economic costs associated with the traumatic event.

AGREEING TO DISAGREE

Perhaps the only thing you will receive during the out-counseling session is the separation letter or agreement. Although its primary purpose is to serve as a formal record of your separation, your out-counselor will rely on it to expedite your out-counseling session.

The typical separation letter provides detailed information relating to your:

- Last day in the office.

- Final day with the organization.
- The amount and timing of your last paycheck.

A word of note: Many states have wage payment and collection statutes that contain provisions as to when your last paycheck must be provided to you and what the final paycheck must include, such as salary, commissions, earned bonus, and accrued but unused vacation time. Check with an attorney to determine what your state's laws provide.

- Expectations during the transition period; and
- Stipulations set forth by your organization.

The following severance letters are examples of what you might receive.

Personal and Confidential
Date: June 24, 2003
To: Mike Southard
From: John Blanch
Subject: Separation Memorandum

   The purpose of this memorandum is to confirm your separation from the firm. The terms and conditions of your separation are as follows:

- Your last day of employment is July 1, 2003.
- Your last day in the office shall be today.
- On June 27, the firm will pay you your regular pay. On July 10, you will be paid for 6/30–7/1, plus six weeks of severance pay, paid as a lump sum, less applicable taxes.
- The firm will also pay you for any unused Personal Time Off (PTO) through June 27, 2003, less applicable taxes. This will be paid to you in your final paycheck.
- Your group insurance will continue through July 31, 2003.
- Upon the termination of your group insurance, you have options under COBRA to continue your medical and dental insurance. Information on COBRA will be sent to your home at a later date.
- The firm will not oppose your applying for or receiving unemployment insurance benefits.
- You will submit no later than July 2, 2003, any property in your possession belonging to the firm.
- Upon request, you agree to state in writing that you have complied with your obligations set forth in the preceding paragraph.
- The firm hereby waives amounts you may owe related to a signing bonus, relocation assistance, and/or educational assistance.

- The firm will pay for outplacement services. You will schedule this assistance by calling the number on the attached form.

Nothing in the agreement entitles you to any salary, benefits, or severance pay beyond that provided in paragraphs 1–9 of this Agreement.

You agree to cooperate with the firm in all matters relating to the completion of work on the firm's behalf and the orderly transfer of work to the firm's partners or other employees.

You must adhere to provisions regarding matters of confidentiality and non-solicitation of clients and/or personnel.

You will direct all reference requests to Human Resources. If contacted for a reference, the caller will be provided with your title and the beginning and ending dates of your employment.

The firm's obligations are contingent upon your adherence to your obligations under this Separation Memorandum.

Confidential
Date: June 24, 2003
To: Mike Southard
From: John Blanch
Subject: Separation Agreement

On behalf of ABC Corporation, I am sorry to inform you that effective July 1, 2003, you will no longer have a position within the company.

This Agreement confirms stipulations concerning your separation from the company. Terms and conditions of this separation:

- Your last day of employment is July 1, 2003. Your last day in the office shall be today.
- On July 15, 2003, you will receive pay for 6/30–7/1.
- On or before July 15, 2003, you will receive 12 weeks (480 hours) of severance pay, paid as a lump sum, less applicable deductions and taxes.
- On or before July 15, 2003, you will receive pay for all unused Vacation Time Off, less taxes and applicable deductions.
- As part of your executive compensation package, you are authorized (as per corporate policy) to exercise your stock options. You will—under separate cover—receive detailed information on how to exercise your stock options.
- As part of your executive compensation package, you will receive (less taxes and applicable deductions) a lump sum payment equal to 17% of your annual salary, as is stipulated in the 2002–2003 Executive Performance Bonus Plan.
- You will—under separate cover—receive detailed information on your benefits package, your insurance coverage, as well as options you will have available under COBRA.
- You will—under separate cover— receive detailed information about options pertaining to the Corporate Pension Program.

- You will return any and all ABC corporate property in your possession to corporate representatives on or before your last day of employment.

- We have arranged for you to receive outplacement services. We will contact you prior to your last day of employment with the date and time of your initial meeting with the outplacement firm's representatives.

We ask that you direct all questions to John Fox, Transition Representative (Human Resources, Extension 1234).

We regret this action, but are confident in your future success.

As is reflected in these two examples, Separation Agreements typically consist of the following key parts:

- Date of separation agreement;
- Name of individual being out-counseled;
- Name of out-counselor;
- Terms and conditions of the separation letter;
- Last day of employment;
- Last day in the office;
- Schedule of final paycheck;
- Length of salary continuance or amount of severance pay;
- Eligibility for accrued and unused personal time off;
- Continuance of group insurance;
- Information about COBRA benefits;
- Information about unemployment insurance claims;
- Return of property belonging to the organization;
- Completion of pending work;
- Forgiveness of sign-on bonus or relocation/educational assistance;
- Provisions of outplacement services;
- Provisions of confidentiality and nonsolicitation; and
- Provisions being made for future reference requests.

Although partially addressed in the second example, such letters typically include detailed information about:

- Eligibility for individual or group performance bonus;
- Eligibility for vested portion of the organization's pension program;
- Provisions for stipulations outlined in the individual's employment contract or job offer letter; and
- Provisions of the organization's or federally sponsored programs relating to protected classes (age, for example).

When reviewing your Separation Memorandum or Agreement, beware of statements suggesting your termination is a result of your behavior or performance. If such statements are included in your letter, you are not being laid off! If the Separation Memorandum or Agreement contains any such objectionable statements, ask that they be deleted.

Also, beware of the following omissions:

- Terms and conditions of the separation letter. Compare the separation letter and the Severance Agreement, just as you must compare the offer letter, employment agreement, employee handbook and policy manual to the Severance Agreement.

  A word of note: If the Severance Agreement does not include provisions in the other documents, ask that it be revised to include them.

- Last day of employment.

  If it is not specified, is your last day today?

- Last day in the office.

  If it is not specified, should you immediately clear out your desk and vacate the premises?

- Schedule of final paycheck.

  If not specified, can you assume your organization is aware of your state's regulatory requirements?

- Salary continuance or severance payment and benefits.

  If not specified, are you ineligible?

- Eligibility for accrued and unused PTO.

  If not specified, can you assume your organization is aware of your state's regulatory requirements?

- Continuance of group insurance.

  If not specified, are you ineligible?

- Information about COBRA benefits.

  If not specified, can you assume your organization is acting in accordance with federal requirements?

- Information about unemployment insurance claims.

  If not specified, will your organization challenge unemployment insurance claims?

- Return of property belonging to the organization.

  If not specified, what steps are in place to ensure a smooth transfer of property currently in your control?

- Completion of pending work.

  If not specified, what steps are in place to ensure a smooth transfer of your projects, documents, and work?

- Forgiveness of sign-on bonus or relocation/educational assistance.

If not specified, are such bonuses and assistance forgiven?

- Provision of outplacement services.

  If not specified, are you to assume such services are not being provided?

- Provisions of confidentiality and nonsolicitation.

  If not specified, do confidentiality and nonsolicitation provisions not apply?

- Provisions being made for reference requests.

  If not specified, to whom should you direct reference requests?

- Eligibility for individual or group performance bonus.

  If not specified, are you ineligible to receive such bonuses?

- Eligibility for vested portion of the organization's pension program.

  If not specified, do you lose your previous accrual(s)?

- Provisions for stipulations outlined in your employment contract or job offer letter.

  If not specified, does the organization intend to honor the agreed-upon stipulations?

- Provisions of federally sponsored programs relating to protected classes.

  If not specified, can you assume the organization is following federal mandates?

REVIEWING/ASSESSING THE SEPARATION AGREEMENT

As we previously stressed, you probably cannot do anything about the termination of your employment; the decision has been made, endorsed, and approved. You must, however, review, question, and (if appropriate) challenge the conditions and stipulations of your separation prior to signing and accepting your Separation Agreement. We encourage you to seek the assistance of an attorney experienced in employment law to assist you in this review.

The Pluses/Minuses Table we suggest you use allows you to identify the strengths (+) and weaknesses (–) associated with the Separation Agreement. Although it is somewhat subjective in nature (you decide whether a stipulation or condition is positive or negative), it does allow you to assess the agreement from your point of view. It will help you feel more in control. Such an organized listing of pluses and minuses also will help you identify your strengths that should be acknowledged and the limitations you need to address.

Using the first separation letter included in this chapter as an example, you might create a Pluses/Minuses Table that looks something like Table 5.1.

The results of your Pluses/Minuses Table may serve as a basis for your follow-up with your organization. The table helps you recognize the pos-

Table 5.1
Pluses/Minuses Table

+	-
Will receive all accrued, unused personal time off (PTO).	Does not address payment of bonuses (performance and retention).
Firm will not seek repayment of sign-on bonus.	Does not address amount accrued in pension plan.
	Group insurance ends on the last day of August—cost under COBRA is about $600 per month.
	Severance pay is only six weeks—in this market, job search will probably take six months.

itive aspects of your severance agreement while helping you formulate questions about the negative ones.

The results of your Pluses/Minuses Table serve as the basis for your Discussion Points Matrix. This document helps you focus on important points to be made and issues to be raised during follow-up conversations with or in follow-up letters to your organization. A completed Discussion Points Matrix might look something like Table 5.2.

If your Separation Agreement suggests your layoff was due to job performance, review it closely and think about future implications. You may be able to convince your employer to characterize the layoff neutrally. If your Separation Agreement fails to provide detailed information on the stipulations listed above, review it closely and seek additional and more detailed information.

Table 5.2
Discussion Points Matrix

On the positive side . . .	On the other hand . . .
I will receive all accrued, unused PTO time.	The Separation Agreement does not address payment of bonuses. Am I entitled to a bonus or a partial bonus? Was this issue ever considered? Can this issue be revisited?
The firm will not seek repayment of my sign-on bonus.	The Separation Agreement does not address the pension plan. Was this issue ever considered? Can this issue be revisited? Is this negotiable?
	The Separation Agreement stipulates that group insurance ends on the last day of August—cost under COBRA is about $600 per month. Was continuation ever considered? Can this issue be revisited?

A WORD OF CAUTION

Proceed cautiously and cooperatively. Your employer is not required to provide severance benefits, unless the benefits (1) are required by law (such as civil service benefits); (2) are required in your employment offer, contract, employee handbook, policy manual; or (3) have been agreed upon by your employer and labor union.

You must proceed with caution when attempting to negotiate severance benefits. If you reject the initial severance package, your employer may withdraw the offer. You may not be allowed to go back and accept it later. If you make a formal counterproposal, your organization might reject it and not allow you to go back and accept the original offer!

Proceed with caution when signing a release of claims in order to receive a severance package. If you sign such a release, you might give up all claims you have against your employer, even wrongful discharge, discrimination, or breach of contract claims you do not yet know about. Such claims, if pursued, could result in a substantial court verdict in your favor. A leading consultant in human resource management reports that as much as 71 percent of employee claims that go to trial result in a verdict for the employee. You do not want to give up something that could be much more valuable than the benefits your employer is offering.

Seek the advice of an attorney if your assessment reveals the need for you to negotiate severance benefits or if you feel you may have a claim against your employer.

In summary, this section stressed the importance of your reviewing the Separation Agreement and asking questions about its stipulations and conditions. Such a review must be conducted within the context of the terms and agreements set forth in your job offer letter or employment contract.

The next section presents information you should take into consideration when incorporating your job offer letter or contract into this review.

SEVERED, BUT SMART

At the meeting where the company broke the news to you, the out-counselor told you what benefits you would receive. The company gave you a Severance Agreement describing those terms and asked you to sign it. You thought, "Well, I guess this is all I get. I had better take it before they take it away."

Stop! Do not let your shock or emotions overtake your rational thinking.

The Severance Agreement may not include all of the benefits to which you are entitled. The employer intends the Severance Agreement to confirm your agreement to its severance package. By signing it without analyzing your rights, you may lose more than your employment—you lose compensation, bonus, commissions, vacation pay, or other benefits due to you separate from the Severance Agreement.

The Severance Agreement usually includes a release of claims you may have against the company. You may ask, "Why am I releasing claims?" or "What claims?"

You must explore the answer to those questions before signing any Severance Agreement. Let's start from the beginning. Even if your employer called you an "at-will" employee, telling you that you have no right to the job or to any benefits upon a layoff, do not be so quick to agree or to accept that self-serving position.

When you took the job, did you receive any of these?

- An offer letter;
- An employment agreement;
- An employee manual; or
- A policy manual.

If you received any of these items, you may have rights outside of the severance package your employer proposed. If you prematurely sign the Severance Agreement and it contains a release of claims, guess what you did—you released any rights to receive additional benefits to which you were entitled under the offer letter, the employment agreement, the employee handbook, or the policy manual.

For example, your offer letter or employment agreement may provide that your employment may be terminated only for cause. In that event, you may not be included in a layoff or a RIF (reduction in force). Your employment agreement or policy handbook may provide that you are entitled to one week's severance pay for each five years of service in case of a layoff. Do not assume that Human Resources properly calculated your years of service—or even took the policy into account in drafting your Severance Agreement. Check the policy and the calculations yourself. In fact, it is imperative that you check carefully, perhaps with your attorney, each and every document you signed or received from your employer, including any offer letter, employment agreement, employee handbook, or policy manual, before signing away your rights.

In fact, most states have laws entitling you or someone you designate (your attorney) to review your entire employment file. You should ask to review it. If your employer refuses (which should be unlikely), ask your attorney to make the request. This will serve dual purposes. First, the file may contain a document you do not recall, and perhaps Human Resources did not consider, providing you rights not available to other employees. Second, losing your employment is traumatic. You may not be at fault. To minimize any concern that you did something that caused your loss, check your file to satisfy yourself that nothing in the file indicates any problem with your performance, attitude, commitment or abilities.

In addition, these documents in your employment file, governing the employer-employee relationship, become much more important when you take advantage of out-counseling. This is true for several reasons. First, keep in mind that the decision to out-counsel is a business decision. It may be only part of a far-reaching cost savings campaign. In addition to reducing costs by terminating your employment, decision makers may also attempt to reduce costs by failing to follow through on terms agreed to when you were being recruited and the organization was competing with others for your talent.

Second, the termination process changes the psychological/emotional contract previously in place. That contract is not a legal or formally written one, but rather the contract that exists when mutual trust and respect comprise the relationship. Since out-counseling ends the contract, the organization is more likely to act in its—rather than your—best interest.

Examples may bring these principles to life. The typical job offer letter provides detailed information relating to your:

- First day as an employee with the organization;
- First day in the office;
- Where and when you report for new hire orientation; and
- Stipulations agreed upon by you and the organization.

The following job-offer letters are examples of the one you might have received from your organization.

January 27, 2003
Dear Robert:

On behalf of ABC Consulting, it is my pleasure to extend an offer of employment to you as Director of Information Management, based in our New York office.

We extend this offer, and the opportunity it represents, with great confidence in your abilities. You have made a very favorable impression; we are excited about your joining our firm.

As we discussed, your start date will be March 1, 2003. As agreed, your salary will be at the annual rate of $100,000, with a guaranteed [Note: not based on performance *and* payable even if you are discharged] annual performance bonus of 15%. You will also receive benefits generally accorded to ABC Consulting Directors. As an incentive to join the firm, you will receive a signing bonus of $20,000.

The sign-on bonus is "earned" over two years of employment with us. [This could mean two years of guaranteed employment.] It will be paid to you on the condition that if you voluntarily resign your position with the firm prior to completing two years of service, you will repay the signing bonus (based upon the number of months under 24 not yet worked). [It does not say you have to repay anything if you are laid off. Does this reflect the employer's intent that you will not be laid off?]

The firm's Employee Benefits Program includes group insurance and retirement benefits, payroll deduction plans, and a vacation program. The group insurance program includes multiple medical options, dental, basic and supplemental long-term disability, basic, optional and dependent life insurance options, travel insurance, elective personal accident insurance, and a flex plan. Retirement benefits are provided through a pension plan and a voluntary 401 (k) Plan. The payroll deduction plans offer long-term care insurance and auto/home owners insurance. In addition to paid holidays and sick days, the firm provides a Vacation Program that allows you to accrue 25 vacation days per calendar year.

You will receive periodic performance and compensation reviews. Performance-based compensation adjustments will be made in August of each year.

You will be expected to abide by all ethical standards, including our Code of Professional Conduct. To the extent that you are subject to a non-compete agreement with another party, we expect that you will abide by all provisions of that agreement.

Your employment is conditional upon the satisfactory completion of a background check. In order to comply with the Immigration Reform and Control Act of 1986, you must provide documentation verifying your employment eligibility.

Although your employment will be at-will [or at least we want you to think so], your acceptance of our offer [in legal parlance, offer + acceptance + consideration (services for compensation) = contract] will be just the beginning [Does this not sound like something more permanent than at-will employment?] of a mutually beneficial relationship [mutuality is an indication of a contractual relationship] with our firm.

This letter states the terms of our employment offer to you. [All of the terms of the employer-employee relationship are contained in this we-do-not-want-to-call-it-a-contract.]

To accept our offer, please sign below in the space provided. [Here we go again: offer + acceptance = contract!] For tax purposes, we ask you to include your social security number.

Robert, I congratulate you and extend my warmest regards.

We look forward to your joining our team!

Dear Robert:

On behalf of ABC Systems, it is with great pleasure that I formally offer you the position of Director, Training and Organization Development. As you know, we have developed a national reputation as one of the premier hospitals in the United States.

We have a commitment to excellence and are looking forward to the future with great anticipation as we enter a new era. Your addition to the management team will be an asset that will help us achieve our goals and meet our challenges.

As we discussed, the position is offered at a base salary of $100,000, with a salary review on September 1, 2004. As I mentioned to you, we utilize a pay-for-performance program to evaluate and compensate our management staff. In addition, we agreed to the following:

- Department head benefit package;
- Relocation expenses;
- Temporary housing for up to six months (Not to exceed $1,000 per month); and
- One weekend house-hunting trip

As agreed, your start date will be Monday, August 1, 2003.

Georgia is an at-will state and as such, this letter represents an at-will offer of employment [Here we go again: offer + acceptance = contract! Is it really at-will?]. Also, as with all employees, employment is contingent upon testing negative for drugs and alcohol. In addition to the drug and alcohol policy, you will be expected to abide by each of the policies in the Employment Policy Manual we have provided you. [Does not this sound like the policy manual is part of a contract?]

We will contact you to arrange a convenient drug screening date and time. We have also scheduled you to attend new employee orientation on Monday, August 1, at 7:45 A.M. in Room E-2 of the main building.

Robert, I am pleased you have decided to join us and am looking forward to your arrival. You will make a fine addition to our management team and I am confident you will make a significant contribution.

Please contact me with any questions you may have or if there is anything I can do to further assist in the transition process.

Please sign the two originals of this letter I have enclosed. [Does signing this make it a mutual agreement? A contract?] One copy should be returned in the enclosed prepaid overnight envelope—the other is for your records.

Welcome to the ABC Systems and I look forward to working with you!

Dear Robert:

We are very pleased with your decision to join ABC Consulting as a Senior Manager in our HR Consulting practice. I know that Sarah Jones and the others are looking forward to working with you.

This letter is to confirm the terms of our offer:

- Base salary of $130,000 to be reviewed August 2004 and every August thereafter. [If the base is not reviewed until August 2004, is it guaranteed until then? Even if the employer reduces everyone's compensation?]

- Sign-on bonus of $20,000 payable shortly after you join the Firm. [It sounds like the sign-on bonus is nonrefundable, even if you leave of your own volition.]

- Based on goals set by you and Jane Doe at your first review in August 2004, a variable pay opportunity of $0–$20,000 payable in September 2005.

- Participation in the ABC Consulting Firm's Deferred Compensation Plan.

Your first day of employment will be July 1, 2003. We will provide a New Hire Orientation Session that morning to introduce you to the history, culture, structure, benefits, and policies of the Firm. During the afternoon, you will become familiar with your new work environment and associates within your practice.

You will spend Tuesday in Benefits Orientation and will be introduced to our computer technology.

Within four days of your start date, please verify the location of your Orientation Session by calling (123) 456–7890.

New Hire Orientation begins on Monday mornings at 8:00 A.M. Please inform the Receptionist that you are here for Orientation—a map is enclosed.

Please find the enclosed packet of materials regarding your first days with the Firm, a history of the Firm, and some forms [Is one of the forms a receipt and acknowledgement regarding an employee handbook or employment policy manual?] you will need to complete and submit during your first week with us [Making them a condition of employment?].

Again, Robert, welcome to the Firm!

If I can be of any help now or in the future, please feel free to give me a call.

We often hear the term *legal technicality* used negatively. As you can see from the bracketed comments in these examples, legal technicalities may protect you! Legal technicalities may provide you with additional severance benefits, or even continued employment, if your contract made you immune to being laid off.

Our review of these sample offer letters should show you that you must review very carefully every document concerning your employment before concluding that the Severance Agreement contains all of the benefits to which you are entitled.

As is reflected in these examples, job offer letters typically consist of the following key parts:

- Confirmation that an offer for employment is being extended.
- Confirmation that the offer is contingent upon the successful completion of a background check and/or drug screen.
- Description or title of position being offered.
- Information about annual compensation and performance bonus opportunities.
- Information about the signing bonus, if one is included in the offer.
- Conditions surrounding "forgiveness" or repayment of the signing bonus.
- Description of benefits assigned to the position being offered.
- Information about performance and/or compensation reviews.
- Information about compensation adjustments.
- Information about expectations around your following the organization's Code of Conduct or Values Statement.
- Disclaimer typically stating, "This offer does not create a contract of employment," "This offer does not create a contract of employment for a specified period of time," or "This offer does not constitute a contract." Only a judge can draw such a conclusion!
- What the candidate must do to show that he or she accepts the job offer and the organization's terms of employment.

Offer letters also may include detailed information about:

- Executive compensation package benefits, such as stock options and performance bonuses. [A word of note here: Stock option agreements and performance bonus plans typically are included in separate agreements. Review those agreements carefully before signing any Severance Agreement releasing your rights!]

Table 5.3
Separation Agreement Review Table

Terms Set Forth in Job Offer, Employee Handbook, Policy Manual	How Addressed in Separation Agreement

- Severance stipulations to be followed if—under certain conditions—the organization out-counsels you.
- Outplacement services you will receive if—under certain conditions—the organization out-counsels you.

It bears repeating that we encourage you to review your written job offer, your contract, your employee manual, and your policy handbook. Make a list of terms and agreements outlined in them. Compare that list with the terms and agreements outlined in the severance agreement.

You may find the Separation Agreement Review Table helpful (see Table 5.3). This tool allows you to systematically compare terms set forth in your job offer to the conditions and specifications set forth in your Separation Agreement.

A completed table may look something like Table 5.4.

The above form identifies two issues not addressed in the Separation Agreement:

- Annual retention bonus (you are not voluntarily resigning; your employment is being terminated).
- Annual performance bonus (although it may need to be prorated, you may deserve compensation/recognition for your previous contributions to the organization).

Table 5.4
Completed Separation Agreement Review Table

Terms Set Forth in Job Offer, Employee Handbook Policy Manual	How Addressed in Separation Agreement
Guaranteed annual performance bonus	Not mentioned. It should be!
$20,000 sign-on bonus, forgiven after three years of employment	Firm will not seek repayment
Accrue twenty-five days' vacation each year, as part of executive compensation package	Will receive all accrued, unused vacation time
$5,000 annual retention bonus	Not mentioned

Results of the Separation Agreement Review can become the basis of a Discussion Points Matrix. Using the above data as an example, the completed Discussion Points Matrix may look something like Table 5.5.

A WORD OF CAUTION

As we stressed in the previous section, proceed with caution when attempting to negotiate severance benefits. Seek the advice of an attorney when your assessment reveals the need for negotiation.

CONCLUSION

Being laid off initially will make you feel helpless or without control. Remember, you did not leave your rights outside the room where you were told you were being laid off or discharged. You had them in that room and you still have them. This chapter has provided information and tools you can use to evaluate and follow up on your Separation Agreement. Such action allows you to begin exerting control over your situation and reduces your feeling of helplessness.

Table 5.5
Completed Discussion Points Matrix

On the positive side . . .	On the other hand . . .
The Separation Agreement addresses several stipulations outlined in my Job Offer letter.	It does not address my guaranteed $5,000 annual retention bonus (which was to be paid within two weeks of my termination). Can this issue be revisited? Is this issue negotiable?
	It does not address my performance bonus (which also was to be paid within two weeks of my termination). Can this issue be revisited? Is this issue negotiable?

CHAPTER 6

Getting Back Down to Business

Although we may pretend that being laid off does not cause us stress, it does. We will be healthier and happier adults once we are willing to put it out into the open, recognize it for what it is, and begin addressing it in a planned and purposeful manner.

This toolkit is not meant to provide definitive information on how one should "work through" one's personal transition.

It is, in part, meant to help you realize that dealing with your layoff may be the most challenging—and potentially fulfilling—thing your family will ever have to do. Your layoff presents an excellent opportunity for your family to:

- Better understand each family member's strengths and limitations;
- Better identify each family member's expectations, goals, and aspirations;
- Better understand more of what makes each family member unique;
- Pull together, allowing each member to provide—and receive—mutual support; and
- Work together as one to overcome an event and contribute as one to an individual family member's overall success.

There are certain points to keep in mind as you turn this stressful time into a productive time.

Much of a person's identity is wrapped around his or her career. We went to school, spent years learning a profession, and identify ourselves a part of that profession. Our employers wanted us to feel as though our profession was more important than attending that Little League game or a recital. Work came first. Life had no true meaning outside our professional life. Many of us bought into that philosophy. To many of us, organizational role and responsibility not only added meaning to life, but it was our life. Now, without them, we are rudderless ships, lost in stormy seas.

Information presented in chapter 4, "It Still Happens to People Like Us," suggests that individuals being laid off typically experience feelings of:

- Disbelief

  "Unbelievable." Perhaps the best way to describe your reaction to the news. The feeling that this cannot be happening and that this certainly cannot be happening to me.

- Surprise

  "Utter shock." The sudden realization that this is happening and that this is in fact happening to you.

- Anger

  How can they? How dare they? Who do they think they are? The sudden desire to strike back—or escape—from what is occurring to you.

- Acceptance

  The acknowledgement that this can happen, has happened, and that you will survive (or thrive) psychologically, emotionally, and economically.

These responses are similar to the grieving process, which consists of the following stages:

- Denial and shock

  At first, it may be difficult for you to accept the possibility of your dying or the death of a significant other.

- Anger

  You may become angry at what you consider to be the unfairness of death.

- Bargaining

  You may offer to give up something in exchange for the return of good health or the other person.

- Guilt

  You may feel guilty about things you did—or failed to do—prior to the loss.

- Depression

  You may experience extreme changes in your mood.

- Loneliness

  You may feel lonely and isolated.

- Acceptance

  You ultimately accept and deal with the current reality.

• Hope

  You ultimately look back on the past with fondness and look forward to the future with optimistic anticipation (University of New York 2001: On-line).

REGAINING CONTROL

Try to take charge of your emotions. You cannot, by being emotionally distraught, risk alienating your support group, professional network, or potential employers. It is important that you—alone or with the help of others—reflect on, be in touch with, and in control of your emotions. The following two tools might assist you in this effort.

The Emotional State Assessment (see Table 6.1) allows you to see, and therefore more clearly understand, where you are emotionally.

For example, you (alone or with the help of others) may examine your emotions and conclude that you are at the Acceptance stage (see Table 6.2).

This might suggest that you now accept your severance and perhaps may even consider it to be an opportunity. Such a mind-set is conducive to your speaking to or meeting with your support group, network, or potential employer.

On the other hand, you (alone or with the help of others) might conclude that you are in the anger stage. This would suggest that you view your severance as extremely negative and perhaps may even consider striking back. Such a mind-set is likely to hurt you more than help you. This negative mind-set will influence your words and actions in a negative manner. Negative words and actions will alienate your support group, professional network, and potential employers. They will say or think: "This person is trouble!" In short, such a mind-set might cause damage that will be extremely difficult to repair.

A job search demands prudent action. Every action, from meeting with members of your network to meeting with potential employers, must contribute to the desired outcome of your becoming re-employed.

The Emotional Readiness Assessment may also help you explore your readiness to move forward with your job search. This tool (see Table 6.3) allows you—alone or with the help of others—to assess your emotional state (as being Unacceptable, Marginal, or Prepared) against actions need-

Table 6.1
Emotional State Assessment

Disbelief	Surprise	Anger	Acceptance

Table 6.2
Completed Emotional State Assessment

			X
Disbelief	Surprise	Anger	Acceptance

Table 6.3
Emotional Readiness Assessment

Action to be Taken	Unacceptable	Marginal	Prepared
Speak with members of network			
Meet with members of network			
Speak with potential headhunter			
Meet with potential headhunter			
Meet with potential employer			
Participate in job interviews			

ing to be taken (from "speaking with members of your network" to "participating in job interviews").

This tool, like a majority of the ones introduced in this toolkit, can be modified to better meet your needs (for example, to reflect additional actions needing to be taken).

A completed assessment may look something like Table 6.4.

Using the above results as an example, this Emotional Readiness Assessment suggests that although you are emotionally prepared to speak to or meet with members of your personal network, you are not yet fully prepared to meet with potential employers or to participate in a job interview. Take the process one step at a time. Be prepared for each step.

In his book *Managing Transitions*, William Bridges (1991: 3) stresses that "it isn't the changes that do you in, it's the transitions. Change is not the same as transition. Change is situational: the new site, the new boss, the new team roles, and the new policy. Transition is the psychological process people go through to come to terms with the new situation. Change is external, transition is internal." Buy Bridges's book and read it!

Table 6.4
Completed Emotional Readiness Assessment

Action to Be Taken	Unacceptable	Marginal	Prepared
Speak with members of network			X
Meet with members of network			X
Speak with potential headhunter		X	
Meet with potential headhunter		X	
Meet with potential employer	X		
Participate in job interviews	X		

REBUILDING THE FOUNDATION

Layoffs represent significant change and involve personal transition. Transition associated with being laid off involves three periods:

- Closure

  Allows you to assess previous experiences and accomplishments.
- Reflection

  Allows you to reflect on the past, within the context of new opportunities.
- Launch

  Allows you to become more self-aware and able to capitalize on emerging opportunities.

From being a productive and contributing member of an organization to being out of work represents a significant Closure. Emotionally and psychologically, you realize that one chapter of your life has come to an end. While addressing issues around Closure, focus on the positive and take the following into consideration:

- How did you contribute to the organization's success?
- What did you learn in your previous position that will benefit you in the future?
- What knowledge and skills did you use in your previous position?
- What did you like about the previous position?
- What did you dislike about the previous position?

Consider the Reflection period as a gift. Having taken previous experiences and accomplishments into consideration during the Closure period, you can now think about them in terms of new and exciting opportunities. Think about how your knowledge has increased. Reflect on your strengths. Your knowledge, experience, and abilities cannot be taken away from you.

The Reflection period allows you to move from the past toward the future. While reflecting, it may be helpful for you to take the following into consideration:

- In what ways might you contribute to an organization's success?
- What knowledge, experience, skills, and abilities can you transfer to other positions? Other professions?
- What have you learned from this experience that you can apply to future opportunities?
- What new industries or companies should you consider for your career?
- What assets do you possess that set you apart from—and above—other candidates for positions in which you are interested?
- What characterizes your next, ideal position?
  - Role
  - Responsibilities
  - Job characteristics
  - Work environment

The Reflection period provides an excellent opportunity for you to begin "rebuilding the foundation" by defining your next, "ideal" position and reaffirming your strengths, interests, and preferences. This is yet another opportunity to build yourself up. Being laid off was devastating, but it was "a boost to the next level." Your knowledge, education, and experience differentiate you from the masses, and they will be valuable to your next employer. Begin the process by reviewing your personal strengths, interests, and preferences.

The following Start/Stop/Continue Table will help you review your strengths, interests, and preferences. It then helps you apply this insight to your assessment of emerging options and opportunities. The uncompleted template looks like Table 6.5.

We recommend you review your strengths, interests, and preferences within the following context:

Given your assets and capabilities, what should you—

- Start doing (what you previously did not have an opportunity to do);
- Continue doing (what you previously did and would like to continue doing); and
- Stop doing (what you previously did, but no longer wish to do)?

Table 6.5
Start/Stop/Continue Table

Start	Stop	Continue

Table 6.6 may lead you to realize that, because of your strengths, interests, and preferences, you should take certain actions.

Using Table 6.6's results as an example, your leadership, negotiation, and conflict management skills are personal strengths; your interests and preferences include strategic planning and small group facilitation.

In terms of defining your next, "ideal" position, you should target opportunities that allow you to:

Table 6.6
Completed Start/Stop/Continue Table

Start	Stop	Continue
Applying strategic planning skills	Relying on others— time management	Applying leadership skills
Enhancing project management skills		Using negotiation and conflict management skills
Applying small group facilitation skills		Applying team/people management skills

• Start doing certain things (you previously did not have an opportunity to do);
• Continue doing certain things (you previously did and would like to continue doing); and
• Stop doing certain things (you previously did, but no longer have a desire to do).

To help you envision your next position, you might create a table that looks like Table 6.7. To properly interpret the results, complete the following sentence, "My ideal position will allow me to. . . ." For example, "My ideal position will allow me to start being responsible for cross-functional teams."

Using Table 6.7's results as an example, pursue an opportunity if it requires leadership skills, strategic planning skills, and involves minimal travel. On the other hand, think twice if it lacks senior level support, involves weekly travel, and does not require project management skills.

Identifying and pursuing potential opportunities are reflective of Launch activities. Capitalizing on an opportunity (i.e., accepting the job offer) reflects an actual Launch.

This period exists after you have put the past behind you (the negative "baggage," not what you have learned) and have taken full advantage of the Reflection period.

The Launch period allows you to:

• Prepare to contribute to another organization's success;
• Think about your knowledge, skills, and abilities in terms of new challenges and potential opportunities;

Table 6.7
Sample Start/Stop/Continue Table

Start	Stop	Continue
Being responsible for a cross-functional team	Traveling every week	Working from home office
Being responsible for a revenue-producing department	Working in a position that lacks senior level support	Serving on a leadership team
	Working in a traditionally structured Firm	Reporting to senior level management

- Think about what you have previously learned, in terms of new challenges and potential opportunities;
- Communicate (to potential employers) assets you possess that set you apart from—and above—other candidates;
- Target and pursue desirable industries or companies;
- Target and pursue desirable positions; and
- Accept a job offer and enter into your next role or position.

In summary, as adults, we may pretend that being laid off is not a stressful event. We think stoically, "I can handle it. No problem." Quite the contrary, it is stressful. You must rely on your support network. You must do significant soul searching. You will be healthier and happier once you:

- Put it out into the open;
- Recognize it for what it is;
- Address it in a planned and purposeful manner; and
- Make plans for your future.

Only you can make your future. Assess who you are, where you are, and what you desire to do, and plan a course of action to achieve it. This section has provided information and tools that will help you turn this stressful time into a productive time.

CUTTING TO THE CHASE

Risking obvious understatement, being laid off is very stressful. Again risking obvious understatement, equally profound is the financial loss associated with losing your job.

As with the stress associated with your job loss, you will be in a much better position once you are willing to put the financial issue on the table, recognize it for what it is, and then begin addressing it in a planned and purposeful manner.

This toolkit is not meant to provide definitive financial planning information. It is, however, meant to help you realize that:

- Your layoff presents a financial challenge that you and your family can work together to overcome;
- Your layoff is an event having financial consequences; the event has occurred— you can take planned and purposeful action to mitigate its consequences;
- Your layoff presents financial obstacles and challenges similar to the ones you addressed while employed; and
- Services and benefits are available to you as a result of your out-counseling.

Auditing Your Financial Situation

There are three actions you should immediately take upon being laid off. The first is to audit your financial situation, which should include an assessment of:

- Your liquid assets, including your savings account, checking account, and other savings to which you have easy access. Be sure to include funds that are or will be available as a result of your Severance Agreement.
- Your current liabilities: fixed monthly costs, average monthly expenditures, required monthly expenditures, and optional monthly expenditures.
- "Contingent" assets, such as funds set aside for painting or reroofing your home, that you will access only if the situation requires it.
- Nonliquid assets, such as 401(k) or other retirement funds.

The Current Assets Matrix in Table 6.8 may help you review your current assets.

A completed form may look something like Table 6.9.

Using the data in Table 6.9 as an example, this family has total (not counting real estate and other capital holdings) assets of $37,000. This family has $19,200 immediately available, and an additional $17,800 in emergency funds.

Expenses: Optional or Required?

You should conduct an accurate appraisal of your monthly liabilities. Monthly costs must be accurately categorized as required or optional.

Table 6.8
Review of Current Assets Matrix

Asset	Amount	Liquid	Contingent

Table 6.9
Completed Review of Current Assets Matrix

Asset	Amount ($)	Liquid	Contingent
CD for home improvement	10,000		X
Savings bonds for vacation	3,000		X
80% of savings account	16,000	X	
20% of savings account	4,000		X
80% of checking account	3,200	X	
20% of checking account	800		X

Required costs are associated with your needs, optional costs are associated with your wants.

These are examples of required expenditures: mortgage or rent, insurance (automobile, house, apartment, health, life), taxes, alimony/child support, college loan repayment, retirement planning, and personal savings.

These are examples of optional expenditures: entertainment, personal care, automobile care, gifts, excess groceries, clothing and accessories, excess utilities, and home furnishings.

The Review of Current Liabilities Matrix in Table 6.10 may help you properly assess monthly costs:

When reviewing monthly costs, apply the three questions listed in Table 6.11 to each item.

Such questions may lead you to realize that many of your monthly expenditures are optional, rather than required. Optional expenses are those that can be avoided in the coming months while you and your family overcome this temporary financial challenge. You may wish to follow your previously established spending patterns. If that is the case, remember that the decision to do so results from your not wanting the layoff to impact financial expenditures, rather than your having to make required purchases.

Completed forms may look something like Table 6.12 and Table 6.13.

Using the data in Table 6.12 as an example, this family has monthly expenditures of $5,140. Of this amount, $840 is optional and $4,300 is required.

Table 6.10
Review of Current Liabilities Matrix

Monthly Cost (Description of Item)	Amount ($)	Required	Optional

Although perhaps perceived as being inconsequential, the $840 repre-sents 16.34 percent of the total monthly expenditure (differently stated, it equals more than one mortgage payment every three months).

Table 6.13 depicts the three questions applied to the Entertainment item (cost of the family's weekly trip to a movie theater) used in the above example.

These results suggest that Entertainment is an optional expense (rather obvious to you, perhaps not so obvious to a teenage son or daughter).

Of course, you can consider the house mortgage to be an optional, rather than required, expenditure (you can sell your home and move into a less expensive house).

For purposes of this discussion, such steps are considered to be exigent. The mortgage is therefore considered to be a required expenditure. This

Table 6.11
Required versus Optional Expense Matrix

Question	If "Yes," Likely a Required Expense	If "No," Likely an Optional Expense
If this purchase is not made, will my/this family's safety be in jeopardy?		
If this purchase is not made, will my/this family's health be in jeopardy?		
If this purchase is not made, will my/this family's welfare be in jeopardy?		

Table 6.12
Completed Review of Current Liabilities Matrix

Monthly Cost (Description of Item)	Amount ($)	Required	Optional
Entertainment cost	240		X
Mortgage payment	2,300	X	
Automobile payment (primary vehicle)	600	X	
Boat payment	300		X
Food (total of weekly grocery trip)	800	X	
Food (total of trips to convenience store)	300		X
Utilities	600	X	

Table 6.13
Completed Required versus Optional Expense Matrix

Question	If "Yes," Likely a Required Expense	If "No," Likely an Optional Expense
If this purchase is not made, will my/this family's safety be in jeopardy?		X
If this purchase is not made, will my/this family's health be in jeopardy?		X
If this purchase is not made, will my/this family's welfare be in jeopardy?		X

point raises an important issue: your habits and preferences influence optional expenditures. These expenditures are highly personal; no two individuals or families will have exactly the same items listed as optional expenditures. One question you and your family must answer is, "To what extent do we want this event to impact our lives?" As parents, a typical question is, "To what extent do we want this event to impact our children's lives?"

The tools provided above will enable you to capitalize on current assets and minimize current liabilities—to the extent you deem necessary. Using the above data as an example:

• This family has total assets of $37,000, with $19,200 immediately available and an additional $17,800 available if the situation warrants it.
• This family has monthly expenditures of $5,140—$840 is optional, while $4,300 is required.
• If this individual's family does not change its expenditures, he or she has about three months and three weeks to become re-employed.
• If this individual's family spends only what is required, he or she has about four months and two weeks to become re-employed.

- The individual will have about twelve months and three weeks to become re-employed if the family spends only what is required and liquidates all assets.

- The individual will have about ten months and two weeks to become re-employed if the family does not change its expenditures and liquidates all assets.

Reducing the Monthly Draw

You should take steps to minimize your expenditures and capitalize on your assets. For example, to reduce the monthly draw on your family's assets:

- Take advantage of credit cards offering "debt consolidation" at an annual interest rate less than what you already have available. Be sure to read the terms and conditions to ensure against hidden fees or eventual increases in the interest rate.

- Tell your credit card company that you plan to pay off and close the account unless it lowers your rate. Many will.

- Obtain a credit card with a lower rate (refer to http://www.bankrate.com).

- Decrease the pace of reduction by increasing monthly contributions to the family's assets. For example, the spouse's income does not need to equal that of the individual's being laid off—it simply needs to replace a portion of the monthly draw to be of benefit.

- Eliminate expenses you can easily reinstate later—your membership to the local health or golf club, your satellite or cable television subscription.

- Visit your dentist and doctor while you are still covered by your employee's benefit plan.

- Seek reimbursement for all qualified business expenses. If appropriate, include gym and club memberships, as well as the cost of recently attended workshops.

- As a last resort (some financial planners suggest "never"), access money available in your retirement fund. Many 401(k) plans allow you to take a loan for certain purposes on the condition that you sign an agreement to repay the funds later on certain payment terms.

- Use the library as a resource for books and audiotapes.

- Use your financial institution's ATM to avoid paying additional service charges.

- Buy the grade of gasoline that your vehicle's manufacturer recommends. (Regardless of the grade, use "high detergent.")

- During the cold months, turn the heat down when you are away from the house.

- During the hot months, turn the air conditioning down when you are away from the house.

- Visit credit unions you are eligible to join. Review their services; credit unions often have better rates on checking accounts and lower interest rates on car loans than banks do.

- Projecting three months into the future, identify all previously scheduled events requiring significant expenditures. Identify potential opportunities for decreasing the monthly draw on your assets.

- Develop and follow a monthly spending plan. Follow the plan to decrease the monthly draw on your assets (Pohl 2001: On-line).

With such options in mind, the Action Review Chart (see Table 6.14) may help you identify actions you need to start, modify, or discontinue.

The completed Action Review Chart depicted in Table 6.15 suggests definitive actions you can take to reduce the monthly draw on your family's assets, such as: stop buying premium gasoline, modify your furnace thermostat to sixty-eight degrees, and begin clipping coupons.

The Role Unemployment Insurance Plays

Government officials (U.S. Department of Labor 2001: On-line) stress you can decrease the monthly draw on personal assets by obtaining unemployment insurance. Unemployment insurance:

- Is state operated. Check with your state or local unemployment office for information about your state's program.

- Is designed to partially compensate you for lost wages when you are out of a job or if you work less than full time because of lack of work.

- Attempts to ensure that you will have income while you look for a job up to a maximum of twenty-six weeks.

Table 6.14
Action Review Chart

Stop/End	Continue/Modify	Initiate/Begin

Table 6.15
Completed Action Review Chart

Stop/End	Continue/Modify	Initiate/Begin
Dog obedience training	From satellite television to cable	Clipping coupons
Health club membership	Videos instead of pay-per-view	Monthly spending plan
Buying premium gasoline	Set thermostat to sixty-eight degrees	Use our bank's ATM
Autograph collecting	Use of credit cards	Using public library

- Differs from Social Security because in all but a few states the funds used to pay benefits are collected from employers.

One program (Illinois Department of Employment Security 2001: 4–32) serves as the basis for the following information. If you are thinking about applying for unemployment insurance, keep the following information in mind:

- You must meet eligibility conditions. These ensure you have been recently employed and are now unemployed because of lack of work, not for any other reason.
- You are eligible for benefits for any week you meet these conditions:
  - You were unemployed during that week.
  - During the week you were able to work, available for work, and were actively looking for work (keep a record of all potential employers you contacted or to whom you sent a résumé).
  - You filed your claim for the week as directed by the local Employment Security office.
- You are not eligible for benefits for any of the following reasons:
  - You resigned your job without good cause.
  - You were discharged for misconduct.
  - You failed to apply for or accept a suitable job offered to you.
  - You were terminated because you committed a felony or theft in connection with your work.
  - You are unemployed because a labor dispute has caused work to stop at your place of employment.

- For the same week for which you claim benefits, you are receiving unemployment benefits from another state or under a federal program.
- When filing a claim:
  - You must present the following items: your Social Security card; unemployment insurance forms your employer gave you; and employer names, addresses, and dates of employment for the past eighteen months.
  - You must present evidence of earnings, such as withholding statements or check stubs.
  - If you are a former federal employee, you must present your Standard Form 8 and Personnel Action Form 50.
  - If you were formerly with the armed forces, you must present your DD Form 214 and your Social Security card.
  - You may have to explain why are you unemployed.
  - Report all wages received, including severance pay, vacation pay, or any other earnings.
  - Provide names and birthdates of children under eighteen you support and the names of any older children you support who cannot work because of illness or other disability.
  - Provide the Social Security number of your wife (or husband) you support and information about his or her employment.
  - Be prepared to share information about your efforts to find another job.
  - You receive an identification card, which serves as an ID card and assigns a call day to "certify" for weeks of benefits).
  - You register for work with the state's Employment Service.
- Once you have filed a claim:
  - The Department of Employment Security prepares and sends you a statement called a "finding."
  - The finding shows the ending date of your benefit year, weekly benefit amount, and maximum amount of benefits.
  - Benefits are paid for calendar weeks of unemployment. The calendar week begins on Sunday and ends on Saturday.
  - You cannot receive benefits for a week until you have "certified" for that week. Most states allow you to certify by telephone, mail, or in person.
- You must be available for work during the week for which you claim benefits. You are not considered available for work if:
  - You move into a community where chances of your finding a job are not as good as those in the community you left.
  - The wages, hours, or work conditions you insist on unreasonably limit your chances of getting a job.
- You must actively look for work on your own initiative:
  - Your local employment office assists with your career search.
  - You must maintain an informational log detailing (1) what you are doing to find work, (2) the kind of work you are seeking, and (3) your prospects of being hired.
  - You must keep a record of the dates and places you apply for work. The employment office provides a "work search document" you must use to record your efforts to find work.
- Benefits are paid if you are out of work and meet all eligibility requirements:
  - Your benefit depends on the amount of your previous wages, plus whether or not you have a nonworking spouse, child, or children.

- Regardless of the amount of your previous wages, the total weekly benefit cannot exceed a set maximum amount.
- In 2001, the maximum amount you received for any week of employment could not exceed:
- $315 if you do not have an eligible dependent.
- $372 if you have a nonworking dependent spouse.
- $417 if you have a dependent child or children
- Weekly amounts are subject to change.

Unemployment insurance is a useful mechanism for decreasing the monthly draw on personal assets. Do not let your ego rule here—take advantage of benefits paid for (on your behalf) by your previous employer.

If considering this option, keep the following in mind:

- When writing to your local Department of Employment Security, be sure to include your Social Security number.
- When visiting your local Department of Employment Security, be sure to have your Social Security card with you.
- Contact your local office in advance. You may be assigned a time to meet with a designated representative.
- When waiting to meet with a representative, do not become concerned if it appears that some people are "going out of turn." Representatives handle different matters, and the representative familiar with situations similar to yours will service you at the proper time.
- You are not immediately eligible for unemployment benefits—a "qualifying" week, in which benefits are not paid, is required by law.

CONCLUSION

Being laid off is stressful. Equally unsettling is the financial loss associated with one's losing one's job. The information provided and tools presented in this chapter may:

- Help you and your family work together to overcome challenges associated with your being laid off.
- Help you minimize financial consequences associated with your being laid off.
- Raise your awareness of services and benefits available to you by virtue of being laid off.

Regardless of whether you apply the tools presented in this chapter, we encourage you to put this issue out in the open, recognize it for what it is, and then address it in a planned and purposeful manner.

CHAPTER 7

The Four Cornerstones

A successful career does not occur by happenstance. Nor does a job that is likely to resist the challenges of today's turbulent work environment. Entering the "right" job requires careful planning (see chapter 8), due diligence, and decisive action on your part. Even in today's time of economic uncertainty, entering into a successful career and bulletproofing your job are still possible. They are likely, however, only if you apply what we call "the four cornerstones" of a successful job search:

- Organizing and managing your job search;
- Developing an effective résumé;
- Preparing for, participating in, and following up on interviews; and
- Managing the job offer process.

Just as the four cornerstones add strength and stability to any building, these actions will add strength and stability to any job search. They will help you, regardless of whether you seek a public or private sector position, a position in a professional services firm or a position within a certain industry.

Regardless of your career goals, you must proceed with your job search with a clear objective. You must direct your energy to make your effort effective and efficient. Every action must contribute to attaining your next position, and—as we will stress time and time again—you must make every effort to ensure that these actions yield a position that is right for you!

ORGANIZING AND MANAGING YOUR JOB SEARCH

We cannot overemphasize the importance of preparing for your job search. We encourage you to conduct a personal assessment (as we describe in chapter 8), maintain a positive attitude, and establish an Action Plan (see chapter 8). Once you are prepared to move forward, you must approach your job search as you do any other job or project. You must apply the same organization and management skills.

You must recognize that you lead a very complex life and that multiple priorities are constantly pulling you in different directions. Your job search is not an event unto itself; it will compete with your other family and personal responsibilities. You will therefore have to apply time management skills, or your attention may be drawn away from your job search.

In organizing and managing your job search, there are techniques and tools you may not consider applying. There are techniques and tools you might consider using, if you were operating under different (and less stressful) circumstances. We therefore offer the following tools and techniques for your consideration. They have helped us successfully navigate previous job searches, and have helped our friends and associates successfully navigate theirs.

Creating a Positive Environment

Your typical workday, in all likelihood, is hectic. Your worksite, in all likelihood, may be equally tumultuous. Before beginning your job search, we encourage you to take steps to reduce the clutter. Doing so up front requires a minimal investment of your time, and doing so after your search is underway may be very costly (consider the price you might place on having to forfeit a prospective job opportunity simply because you misplaced notes of a brief telephone call).

To the extent possible, create a workspace you will use whenever conducting your job search. It is important that this room (or area in a room) allows you the freedom and privacy you need when writing letters, speaking on the telephone, and completing and filing forms. Ideally, your workspace will include a desk (its most important feature being plenty of desktop space), a comfortable chair, and a door. The door is important for two reasons: physically, it will help reduce distracting background noise; psychologically, closing it can help you shift into the mind-set that "I am now at work on my current full-time job, my job search."

In addition to your workspace, you will need supplies. We recommend that you purchase enough supplies to last throughout your job search. The reason for this suggestion: once you begin your job search, nothing trivial should distract you from your objective. While the following scenario may not seem like a big deal now, it may later. Once deciding on the stationery you will use for your cover letter and résumé, you discover halfway through your mailings that the local stationery store no longer carries the item or that this item is "temporarily" unavailable. This occurred to a close colleague who happened to reside in a rural area—the nearest stationery store was twenty-seven miles away!

Over the course of your job search, you will save a lot of time if you have supplies readily available. Prior to initiating your job search, take a few moments to think about supplies you will need when: developing (and mailing) your résumé; answering the telephone; retaining magazine and newspaper articles and advertisements; speaking with potential employers; participating in telephone interviews; and developing (and sending) e-mail messages. Table 7.1 lists supplies you are likely to need when involved in such activities.

Table 7.1
Supplies for Conducting a Job Search

Item	Possess (P) or Acquire (A)
Pens and pencils	
Notepads of 8 1/2 by 11-inch paper	
Notepads of 4 by 5-inch paper	
Scissors	
Paper clips	
Ink cartridges or typewriter ribbons	
Envelopes	
Tape	
Typing or printing paper	
Stationery	
Stamps	

This table is rather simple to complete. If you possess the item, indicate so with a "P" and make sure it is available in your workspace. If you need to acquire the item, indicate so with an "A." Take this form with you when you visit the store; it is your shopping list.

Once you have obtained your supplies, make sure they are close at hand. If you will be using the supplies in your workspace, make sure they are within easy reach. If you have multiple telephones in your home, and if they will be used at any time during your job search, place a pen and notepad next to each telephone. (A lesson learned: the pen and notepad should be unusual in shape and color, or they may be moved inadvertently and not be available when needed.)

In addition to your workspace and supplies, certain equipment will help you conduct your job search. In addition to your telephone, you need to have access to a computer with Internet capability, if you plan to access databases and send messages to potential employers; a typewriter or word processor, if you plan to send typed letters to potential employers; a printer for your computer, if you plan to make copies of messages you electronically send to potential employers; a telephone service or answering machine; and a scanner, if you plan to electronically submit work samples, such as reports, documents, or photographs. Be sure to obtain supplies for the equipment you use. For example, we recommend you purchase ink cartridges for your fax machine in advance. You may need to establish a second phone line for your home.

As you will see later in this chapter, you will generate, review, and manage a lot of information during the course of your job search. In order for this information to be useful, it must be organized in a manner that allows you quick and easy access. We therefore recommend that you obtain a cabinet, drawers, or container to hold files during your job search.

Establishing a Routine

You lead a very hectic life. Regardless of your employment status, conflicting priorities impact your daily life. The only difference is this: when you are unemployed and searching for a job, conflicting priorities compete with your effort to attain your next position. You must therefore direct your energy so you are able to spend your time effectively and efficiently. You must establish a daily routine to ensure that every action contributes to your attaining your next position.

Unfortunately, we do not operate within a vacuum. Our job status impacts our family members as well as ourselves. As you change your daily routine, to a certain degree, so must every member of your family. For example, you in all likelihood are not the only person in your family who answers the telephone. If your spouse, parents, or children answer the telephone during your job search, you must make sure they do it in a professional manner and, if you are unavailable, take down information using the supplies you have made available at each telephone. To sensitize your family members to potential callers and the messages they need to give them, we recommend you use a family "action board." This bulletin board should be placed in a location that is central to your family members' lives. For it to be effective, you must update it daily with information about your expected calls, your schedule, and when you are likely to receive (and be able to follow up on) the caller's message.

Conducting a job search in many ways is like writing a high school or college term paper. You have been given an assignment, quality expectations have been set, and you are now free to proceed at your own discretion. No one will be monitoring your progress (except, perhaps, your spouse or significant other); no one will be pressing you to be productive; no one will be monitoring the time and energy you put forth each day on this "priority item." The effort you put forth and the progress you make is entirely up to you. There are steps you can take to help ensure that, at the end of each week, you can look back and say, "This week has been a productive one!" For example, approach your job search as you do any other job. Focus on your objective. Keep quality standards in mind. Draw upon all available resources. Capitalize on your equipment and supplies. Execute your Action Plan. Establish and maintain a regular schedule.

Perhaps the most important thing you can do is to establish and maintain a regular schedule. Does this mean spending forty hours a week on a job search? The answer to this questions is, "It depends." It depends on the business environment, the job market, your career aspirations, your previous schedule, as well as your personal preferences. For example, if you (due to financial reasons) need to attain a job within three months and you find the business environment in turmoil and the job market tight, you might consider spending more than forty hours a week on your job search. If your career aspirations are such that you want to move from the public to the private sector (from industry to a professional services firm or from one industry to another), you again might consider spending more than forty hours a week on your job search. If you previously worked sixty-hour weeks and are physically and mentally adjusted to such a routine, you might consider spending an equal amount of time each week on your job search. Of course, you may simply prefer to invest twenty hours a week in your job search. If this is your preference, do so, but in a planned and purposeful manner (rather than by default, by spending each day watching soap operas or sports).

The amount of time you spend on your job search is not the only issue. Be sure the time you invest is time well spent. Focus on achievement, rather than on activity. You may discover ways to minimize the time you spend on an activity and to maximize your accomplishment. For example, if you access company Web sites and use electronic databases as part of your job search, you may find that it is easier to do so (due to the volume of people using the Internet) during "off" hours. Personal experience suggests that conducting research electronically for two hours at night (from 11:00 P.M. to 1:00 A.M.) yields the same results as conducting the same research for four hours during the day. If you find this to be the case with you, consider adjusting your schedule so that you spend two (rather than four) hours on this activity each day. Apply the time you save on your research to other aspects of your job search.

Managing Your Job Search

Apply the organization skills you have used throughout your career to your job search. If you normally use a pocket calendar, a desk calendar, a portable day planner, or an electronic planner, continue to do so. To help you focus your actions, you might wish to modify your planner so it contains information relating to your job search.

For example, modify your weekly calendar so it also contains information reflected in Table 7.2. (An important note: Table 7.2 reflects only information relating to your job search, not the information you typically track.)

Table 7.3 provides insight into how you are spending your time. To further crystallize your understanding of how you spend your time, we rec-

Table 7.2
Weekly Calendar

Day	Meet	Telephone	E-mail	Mail
Monday				
Tuesday				
Wednesday				
Thursday				
Friday				
Weekend				

Table 7.3
Sample Weekly Calendar

Day	Meet	Telephone	E-mail	Mail
Monday	2	3	8	1
Tuesday	0	1	4	2
Wednesday	2	1	3	1
Thursday	1	4	1	0
Friday	1	3	0	7
Weekend	0	0	12	10

ommend you maintain detailed information on your activities using forms presented later in this section. To determine your progress, you must compare your weekly activities against the goals you established for that week. For example (using data from Table 7.3), six meetings and twelve telephone calls may look quite impressive. However, your interpretation of the progress being made may change if your goal for the week was thirteen meetings and twenty-five telephone calls (not that unusual for an aggressive job seeker)!

It is important that you maintain detailed information on your search activities. The following six logs may help you organize this information. We, and some of our colleagues, have used these logs during previous job searches. Their value therefore has been tested and proven. Use these forms to capture and track information you consider useful and important, and modify the forms to match your needs and preferences.

The form illustrated in Table 7.4 allows you to record information taken from Internet job databases. The form illustrated in Table 7.5 allows you to record information on organizations you contact. The form illustrated in Table 7.6 allows you to record information on search firms you contact.

Networking and research may yield one or more job leads. It is important that you retain detailed information on each job lead. The form illustrated in Table 7.7 allows you to record such information.

Table 7.4
Job Database Log Sheet

Database	Internet Address	User name and Password	Notes

Table 7.5
Organization Contact Log Sheet

Company, Firm, or Institution	Date of Contact	Contact Info (Address, E-mail, Telephone)	Notes	Follow-up Actions

In addition to the information recorded in the previous logs, you should retain detailed information on each of your contacts. This information can be kept in two separate logs: The Personal Contact Log and the Transaction Log. The Personal Contact Log lists your personal contacts, helping you get in touch with your personal contacts efficiently. The Personal Contact Log is illustrated in Table 7.8.

The Transaction Log contains information relating to conversations you have with each personal contact, and the results of those conversations. At any given time, you may be working with dozens of personal contacts. The information this form contains will help you recall previous conver-

Table 7.6
Search Firm Contact Log Sheet

Firm	Date of Contact	Contact Info (Address, E-mail, Telephone)	Notes	Follow-up Actions

sations and prepare for future ones. The Transaction Log is illustrated in Table 7.9.

Whether you use one, some, or all of these forms (and whether you use them as designed or customize them), it is important that you organize them in a manner that addresses your needs and reflects your personal style. As previously stated in this section, you may wish to use a file cabinet or container to organize and manage these forms. If you do not have the space or simply do not wish to use a case cabinet or a container, consider using a notebook binder to create a job search folder. When hole punched and inserted into a binder, these forms allow you to manage your search in an effective and efficient manner. If you have the capability, consider creating electronic files or spreadsheets. Electronic files allow you to sort through data more quickly and to analyze more thoroughly the information you have collected.

Continuous improvement begins after planning ends and execution begins. We encourage you to continuously improve upon the manner in which you conduct your job search. Throughout your search, seek out opportunities to:

- Begin, maximize, or magnify the amount of time you spend on activities that contribute the most to your attaining your next position;
- Stop, minimize, or limit the amount of time you spend on activities that marginally contribute to your attaining your next position;
- Stop, minimize, or limit the number of distractions and disruptions that occur during your search;

Table 7.7
Job Lead Log

Information	Notes
Lead (Company, Firm, Institution)	
Lead address	
Contact	
Title	
Telephone/E-mail	
I received lead from	
Useful information about lead	
My response	___ Telephone Date: _____ ___ E-mail Date: _____ ___ Meeting Date: _____
Results	

- Shorten the duration of distractions and disruptions, if you cannot control the frequency of their occurrence;
- Increase the amount of time you spend on your job search while also increasing the amount of time you spend with your significant other; and
- Enhance the quality of your job search while also enhancing the quality of the time you spend with your significant other.

Table 7.8
Personal Contact Log

NAME	
Title	
Company	
Telephone	
E-mail	
Fax	
Miscellaneous	
NAME	
Title	
Company	
Telephone	
E-mail	
Fax	
Miscellaneous	

This section has presented information and tools you can use to more effectively organize and manage your job search. This information and the tools will allow you to concentrate your effort, minimize obstacles, and maximize results.

DEVELOPING AN EFFECTIVE RÉSUMÉ

There is good news and there is bad news.

The good news is that, as we reported in chapter 2, your job search can be viewed as an opportunity. It allows you to target a new profession, occupation, company, firm, or institution. Once you have decided on a potential employer, you contact it and attempt to interest it in (1) meeting with you to learn more about your personal assets and capabilities and (2) about what you can contribute as a new member of the organization.

Table 7.9
Transaction Log

NAME	
Transaction 1. Date: _____ ___ Telephone ___ E-mail ___ Personal meeting	Summary/Result/Follow-up
Transaction 2. Date: _____ ___ Telephone ___ E-mail ___ Personal meeting	Summary/Result/Follow-up
Transaction 3. Date: _____ ___ Telephone ___ E-mail ___ Personal meeting	Summary/Result/Follow-up

The bad news is that, as we report in chapter 4, millions of people are currently unemployed. Employers who previously received hundreds of résumés for open positions may now receive thousands. So, not only must you now compete with thousands of other job applicants, you must compete with them just to get the potential employer's attention. Under such conditions, you must differentiate yourself (read as "your résumé") from all the others. You must "hook" potential employers so they will want to learn more about you and what you can contribute to their organization.

Job seekers used to create exceptionally long résumés. Detailed information about their professional and personal experiences frequently spanned eight, nine, ten, or more pages. Employers having only one or two résumés to review frequently were able to invest the time to review such detail, make preliminary decisions based on that review, and then act on a potential candidate. Now, facing stacks of hundreds or thousands of résumés, employers no longer have the time to review résumés containing such detailed information. They must screen (or even pre-screen) résumés, following up on those showing most promise. The bottom line is this: your résumé must be concise and, in a minimum number of words and pages, convince the potential employer that you possess the required capabilities and are the best candidate for the position.

Designing the Effective Résumé

It is not our intent to provide full coverage to the subject of résumé writing. Numerous specialty books and resources (including your local librarian and state employment office personnel) can help you with this task. Our experiences are broad-based and multifaceted, however, and we cover key points you might consider as you move forward with this aspect of your job search.

The current business environment and job market dictate that you create a résumé that, in a matter of seconds, will convince a prospective employer to set it aside for further review or follow-up action. Such a résumé must be powerful, in content as well as in presentation. Designing such a résumé requires forethought on your part. To shift into the proper mind-set for creating your résumé, answer the following questions:

- If I were the prospective employer, what would I be looking for in the ideal candidate?
- If I were asked to review hundreds or thousands of résumés, how would I screen them?
- If I were the potential employer, how would I differentiate "exemplary" from "average" employees, and how might such differences be described in a résumé?
- If I were to review hundreds or thousands of résumés and were required to select the top 1 percent, what criteria would I apply?
- If I were the potential employer, with résumés of hundreds or thousands of potential interviewees, how would I decide which five to interview?

Answering these questions will shift you into the proper mind-set for creating your résumé. Such a mind-set allows you to approach this task from the right perspective and ultimately to develop a résumé that differentiates you from all the other candidates. Designing your résumé "with the reader in mind" allows you (1) to create a document containing needed factual information, and (2) to present that information in a manner most likely to address the expectations of the reader.

You must decide what information to include in your résumé. Your goal is a résumé that will make the employer aware of your capabilities and excite him or her to the point of inviting you to participate in a conversation, meeting, or interview. When deciding what to include in your résumé, answer these questions:

- What skills and abilities are employers looking for?
- What results have you produced that reflect these capabilities?
- What are your three to five greatest accomplishments?
- Which of those accomplishments can be communicated in measurable terms?
- Without knowing anything about other candidates, what capabilities do you possess that differentiate you from all of them?
- Without knowing anything about the experiences of the other candidates, what have you experienced that differentiates you from all of them?
- What strengths in these skills differentiate you from all the other candidates: leadership, problem solving, decision making, conflict resolution, negotiation, and interpersonal communication?

You have thus far given a lot of forethought to the needs and expectations of your prospective employer and to the information you must include in your résumé. You must now decide on the format your résumé will take. Keep in mind your objective is to create a résumé that not only raises the potential employer's level of awareness, but one that highlights (or "showcases") your information in a manner likely to propel him or her into action. Again, your underlying goal is to excite the prospective employer to the point of inviting you to participate in a conversation, meeting, or interview.

We have reviewed thousands of résumés. We have had countless conversations with our colleagues about the way résumés are formatted and the information they contain. We have experienced successes (when those hired lived up to the expectations their résumés set) and challenges (when they failed to live up to those expectations). Based on our experiences, we believe effective résumés contain—at a minimum—the following five sections:

- Summary or Profile
- Professional Experience and Accomplishments
- Certifications, Licensures, and Specialty Training
- Education
- Awards and Special Recognition

In today's business environment, employers reviewing hundreds or thousands of résumés may spend only thirty to forty-five seconds on each résumé. Your résumé must immediately convey a single message: out of all the candidates—I am the "the one" for this position or role. You must introduce this important message at the very beginning of your résumé. You do so in a section titled "Profile" or "Summary."

If effectively written, this section immediately captures the reader's interest. You set the stage for such a response by including information most likely to personally interest the reader. When developing this section, review your answers to the set of "If I were . . . " questions. Keep the following principles in mind:

- Keep it brief. It must be concise and to the point;
- In four or fives phrases, highlight your most significant capabilities, experiences, and accomplishments;
- Provide adequate coverage, showcasing the depth and breadth of your capabilities; and
- Provide adequate representation, highlighting the full range of your experiences and accomplishments.

These guidelines will help you create a brief profile or summary that leads the reader to conclude that of all the candidates, you clearly possess the most compelling capabilities, experiences, and accomplishments.

The section titled "Professional Experiences and Accomplishments" reinforces that conclusion. Keeping in mind the key messages you wish to share, and building on the previous information, you provide additional detail. An important reminder: you do not include every detail. The detail you include must be important from the prospective employer's perspective, must support the expectations raised in the Profile or Summary section, and must be likely to lead to the prospective employer's concluding that you clearly possess the most compelling capabilities and are most likely to succeed in the open position or role.

This section allows you to share information about your previous positions, employers, dates of employment, and responsibilities and accomplishments. Include only the information likely to interest and excite the reader. Highlight your strengths, focus on the environments in which you have worked, and showcase the most significant results and outcomes of your effort. Although you strive to provide detail, you must not provide too much detail (remember, you must hook the employer in forty-five seconds or less). To help shorten your résumé, provide the most detail in your most recent experiences and provide less detail in your earlier positions. If you are well into your career, consider summarizing each of your earlier positions and roles in one or two lines or in a brief paragraph.

You strengthen your case by providing information in a section titled "Certifications, Licensures, and Specialty Training." This information reinforces the prospective employer's belief that you are the one most qualified for the job. Keep your underlying goal in mind: cite only the most relevant specialty training, but include all certifications and licensures that may differentiate you from the other candidates. When creating this section, keep the following principles in mind:

- List information about your specialized training in reverse chronological order;
- If you do not possess certifications or are not licensed, omit those words from the heading;
- Generally, list information about your certifications and licensures in order of importance (from the reader's point of view); and
- If relevant, cite dates and identify the granting body (institution, board, or association).

We have said it before, and we will say it again: you must keep the reader in mind when developing this section. Know your audience. We have reviewed numerous résumés listing certain specialty certifications (such as one's being a certified masseuse) and licensures (such as one's being licensed to function as an astrologer in the United Kingdom) that, although of interest and importance to the job seeker, clearly were not relevant to the position or role under consideration. Such information may have been taken into consideration in times when market conditions were different, but given today's business environment, such extraneous and irrelevant information likely will result in your résumé being discarded.

You expand your case by including information in a section titled "Education." Like the information presented elsewhere in your résumé, this information reinforces the potential employer's belief that you are qualified for the job. When creating this section, keep the following principles in mind:

- List in reverse chronological order;
- Include the degree awarded, name of the institution, and date (unless you prefer not to draw attention to your age);
- Include your grade point average, if you feel it will interest or excite the reader;
- Include information about academic awards (if you graduated with honors, be sure to include that information);
- If you have not yet graduated, provide information but provide a tentative graduation date; and
- If you are pursuing a terminal degree (for example, a Ph.D.) and are a candidate for that degree, be sure to include that information.

If you are working toward a degree but have not yet graduated, provide information about your program and give a tentative graduation date. To offset concerns regarding the likelihood of your completing the program, be sure to give your grade point average and include information about the number of courses previously taken and the number of remaining courses. If you are attending college courses but do not plan to complete a degree, include information about the courses you have taken and your grade point average.

You strengthen your résumé with an "Awards and Special Recognition" section. This section is very important, in that it confirms the prospective employer's belief that you are the "right person for the right job." We previously stressed the importance of relevancy, pointing out that you should not list certifications and licenses unless they are directly related to the open role or position. The same guideline applies to this section. However, we encourage you (at least initially) to consider including every award and special recognition you have ever received. For instance, although not directly related to a particular position or role, Scouting awards and recognition for community service reflect qualities most employers are looking for: leadership, stewardship, the willingness to serve, and to make personal sacrifices. The length of your résumé and the overall balance of information provided in each of its sections will ultimately influence the number of awards and special recognitions you are able to list.

Developing an Effective Résumé

Thus far, you have decided on the overall framework of your résumé. You must now produce a document that, through substance and "look and feel," states your case in the most powerful way. As you develop your résumé, take the following guidelines into consideration:

- The document must be focused. It must introduce and then reinforce your key message. It must state your case, from the prospective employer's viewpoint.

- The résumé must be visually appealing. It must be balanced, in terms of the number of words and the amount of white space. It must be symmetrical.

- The résumé must be error-free. All words must be properly spelled. Phrases must contain proper grammar and syntax.

- The information must be accurate. There must be no omissions (in terms of dates of employment) or misstated facts.

- The information must be placed in correct order. If information is listed in chronological order, all data must consistently be placed in that order. The same is true for information listed in reverse chronological order.

- Phrases and sentences must be written concisely. Use active voice, rather than passive voice, for all verbs. Do not repeat verbs in the same section.

- Use verbs that reflect performance and achievement. Consider using verbs such as achieved, created, developed, eliminated, increased, launched, redesigned, reduced, reorganized, restructured, simplified, and streamlined.

- Use proper verb tense. If the activity is still underway, use present tense. If the activity no longer occurs, use past tense.

- Do not use personal pronouns (such as "I") or articles (such as "a"). They do not add any value and simply take up space.

- The heading must contain your name, address, telephone number, e-mail address, and Web site, if you have one.

- Do not use the word "Résumé" as the title of the document. The title is your name, which is included in the heading.

- Do not include the names of references or provide salary information.

- Do not include the names of your previous supervisors or your reasons for leaving your previous positions.

- Place your name at the top of the second and subsequent pages, in case the pages become separated.

- Use bullets, italics, and different typefaces to emphasize key points and to make the information easy to read.

Once you have developed and refined your résumé, use a laser printer or high quality ink jet printer to produce a high quality document. Do not use a dot matrix printer. Print it on an off-white, cream, or bright white standard-size (8 1/2 × 11 inch) paper. Mail the résumé and accompanying cover letter in an envelope that matches the weight, color, and texture of the paper you are using.

Preparing an Effective Cover Letter

While your résumé provides detailed information, your cover letter presents your overall intention and availability to the prospective employer. Although your résumé can stand on its own, the cover letter allows you an initial opportunity to introduce yourself and to begin stating your case. Your cover letter, in essence, establishes the purpose of your contacting the prospective employer, attracts his or her attention, and generates initial interest. Your cover letter should:

- Be formatted and written in a manner likely to hook the prospective employer;

- Be brief, no more than two pages;

- Include information that reflects your knowledge and understanding of the reader's industry, profession, and organization;

- Communicate to the prospective employer that you are conducting a job search and that you are interested in joining his or her organization;

- Introduce your capabilities, experiences, and accomplishments to demonstrate to the reader that you are suited for the open position;

- Highlight three or four experiences and three or four accomplishments that differentiate you from other potential candidates;

- Verify to the prospective employer that your résumé is included and that references are available upon request;
- Communicate to the prospective employer that you are eager to take the next steps; that you will gladly connect by telephone or meet in person; and
- Confirm that the prospective employer can contact you at your address, telephone number, or e-mail address if he or she needs additional or clarifying information.

We both have mixed feelings regarding whether you should include salary and relocation information in your cover letter. We strongly feel that you should not include either in your résumé. If the prospective employer has requested information on your salary requirements and relocation preference, we recommend you include it in your cover letter. If you do include this information in your cover letter, we recommend you give a salary range, indicate that your total compensation package is negotiable, and be as liberal as possible (but as candid as necessary) when dealing with the relocation issue.

When structuring your cover letter, take these guidelines into consideration:

- Begin by stating that you are considering options or pursuing opportunities (and briefly, why) and that you are interested in the potential employer's organization;
- Then, summarize your key experiences and accomplishments, taking into account the information previously provided;
- Next, insert information about your references, compensation requirements, and relocation preference; and
- Conclude by stating that you are eager to follow up by telephone or in person.

Once you have developed and refined your cover letter, use a laser printer or a high quality ink jet printer to produce a high quality document. Do not use a dot matrix printer. Print it on an off-white, cream, or bright white standard-size (8 1/2 × 11 inch) paper. Mail the cover letter and the accompanying résumé in an envelope that matches the weight, color, and texture of the paper you are using. Follow up in a week or ten days if you do not receive a call or a letter.

Managing Your Pool of Professional References

As part of the selection process, prospective employers solicit information about your capabilities, experiences, and accomplishments. Most of this information is obtained through conversations, meetings, and interviews with you. Some of this information is obtained through conversations with individuals who previously worked with you. Information from these "professional references" may be obtained through happenstance or in a planned and purposeful manner. As the job seeker, you can influence much of what the prospective employer learns about you by managing the referral process.

A clear majority of prospective employers ask for the names of three or more professional references. When asked to provide professional references, how do you respond? Do you simply provide the names of three or four individuals whom know you and trust? If so, you are not capitalizing on the potential the referral process offers.

Manage the reference process in a systematic way. When deciding on your professional references, follow these guidelines:

- Decide on the six key messages you would like to send the prospective employer. These key messages may relate to your ability to lead, make decisions, solve problems, negotiate deals, resolve conflict, and communicate to diverse groups.
- Identify three people you trust who can comment on your capabilities, experiences, and accomplishments.
- Answer this question: Are these three individuals able and willing to share these six key messages with prospective employers?
- If the answer to this question is "no," identify three other people. If the answer is "yes," contact each person.
- Ask each prospective reference if he or she is able and willing to share information with prospective employers. If the answer to this question is "no," identify someone else. If the answer is "yes," inquire further.
- Ask each prospective reference if he or she is able and willing to share one, several or all six of your key messages with prospective employers. If the answer to this question is "no," identify someone else. If the answer is "yes," prepare the individual to serve as a professional reference.

Job seekers typically fail to prepare individuals properly to serve as their professional references. Once you have identified the most appropriate individuals, you must help them prepare to serve as your reference. We are not suggesting that you "put words in their mouths" or otherwise manipulate them. We are suggesting, however, that you take steps to ensure that in ten minutes or less your references share the most salient points with the prospective employer. The steps you take help your references organize their thinking, rather than your manipulating their thinking. Once you have selected your three (or more) references, help prepare them to serve as your professional reference by:

- Asking each reference which capabilities, experiences, and accomplishments about which they are most comfortable commenting. Each reference may cite five or six capabilities, two or three experiences, and three or four accomplishments.

- Compare the information the references are planning to share. Are there gaps needing to be addressed? Are there redundancies (some repetition is good, in that it verifies what is being said) needing to be addressed? If each reference is sharing the exact same information, alert them to this fact and determine if there is other information he or she is willing to share with the prospective employer.
- Compare the information the references are planning to share against the key messages you would like to communicate to prospective employers. Are some or all of them being communicated? If so, you are in great shape. If not, alert each reference to this fact and determine if he or she has other information to share more closely associated with the key messages you need to send.

You are well on your way to managing the reference process when you have closed the gaps, minimized the redundancies, and ensured that information to be provided will reflect the key messages you are wanting to send to the prospective employers. Further prepare your references by alerting them to the questions they are likely to be asked. Your objective here is to sensitize them to the questions, so they can begin thinking about how they will share key information about you when answering such questions. Here are some of the questions we as prospective employers have typically asked references:

- How long have you known this individual?
- In what capacity do you two know each other?
- How much authority or responsibility did this individual have?
- Did you view this individual as a leader?
- Did this individual work well with others—in other words, is this a team player?
- From your viewpoint, what were this individual's most significant personal and professional accomplishments?
- What do you consider to be this individual's most valuable contributions to the organization?
- From your perspective, must this individual be closely supervised?
- Is there anything I have not asked that I should ask?
- Is there anything you have not yet told me that you would like to tell me before we end this conversation?

You may learn that your reference will be unable to speak with prospective employers (for example, he or she may be working on a demanding project in another part of the world). If this is the case, ask him or her to write a letter of recommendation. We have reviewed hundreds of letters of recommendation. Some were effective, but a clear majority provided limited value. If an individual invests the time to develop a letter of recommendation for you, following these guidelines will help maximize the impact of their effort:

- Begin by providing background information—how long and in what capacity he or she has known you. Include general information about your overall authority and responsibilities.
- Next, provide more detailed information about you. Keeping the factors previously covered in mind, provide information on your capabilities, key experiences, and accomplishments.
- Conclude with a vote of confidence. Such a vote of confidence may take the form of a statement similar to the following, "As my previous comments indicate, I am impressed with this individual's skills and abilities and therefore, without reservation, recommend him (or her) for the position he (or she) is seeking."

Following these recommendations requires an investment of your time, an investment you may not have taken during previous job searches. You may feel you should not have to spend this much time preparing your professional references. The business environment (with increased litigation over negligent hiring and retention) now demands that prospective employers be much more thorough in their selection process. This in turn demands you place much more emphasis on (and invest the needed time in) this aspect of your job search.

Sample Cover Letter

We offer the following cover letter as an example. The information it contains is fictitious. This cover letter accompanies the sample résumé.

Dear Mr. Langston:

Your company is an industry leader and is recognized for its high standards of customer service. You are searching for a Senior Vice President of Human Resources. Dracks Customized Solutions, Inc. recently redeployed its Global HR leadership team—I am currently seeking new opportunities for which to apply my leadership skills.

My credentials are broad-based:

- Global experience while with Dracks Customized Solutions.
- Leadership experience while with the Acoma and Dracks corporations.
- Management experience while with the Fortcum Corporation.
- An earned Doctorate in Management from Netlock University.

My previous leadership responsibilities are similar to those of your Senior Vice President of Human Resources:

- Worked with the corporate leadership team to develop annual goals for the North American HR function, define and prioritize regional HR initiatives, and sponsor strategic HR programs.
- Supervised teams of Relationship and Account Managers.
- Created an organization-wide, internal Change Management function and led global change management initiatives.
- Led education (degree-granting) and training (including CEU) programs.

I have been recognized for the following accomplishments:

- Developed and co-sponsored a Continuous Quality Improvement (CQI) effort that yielded double-digit savings in costs associated with supply chain management.
- Led an education and training program cited by the *Chronicle of Industrial Education* as being "best in class."
- Working with management within a union environment, over a six-year period decreased employee grievances by 28 percent.
- Helped facilitate the consolidation of two industry giants; described as being "the most successful merger in U.S. history."

The attached résumé highlights my previous accomplishments. References are available upon request. Contact me at 111/222–3333 or at KCALL@street.com if you need additional information or if you would like to schedule a meeting.

Cordially,
Kent Callihan

Sample Résumé

We offer the following résumé as an example. The information it contains is fictitious. This document does not represent a particular individual's career, nor does it include the names of actual organizations. This résumé accompanies the sample cover letter.

KENT CALLIHAN

12345 Treetop Lane	KCALL@street.com
St. Lipton, IL 11223	(111) 222–3333

Profile

HR leader with a proven track record in union and nonunion environments. Budget responsibility of up to $9.9 million and direct management responsibility of up to sixteen functional leaders. Previously responsible for double-digit gains in efficiencies and productivity and recognized as a leading HR strategist. Seeking an organization wishing to enhance its internal capability by strengthening its HR function.

Professional Background

Position: Senior VP of Human Resources

Organization: Dracks Customized Solutions, Inc.

Dates of Employment: March 1989—June 2003

Responsibilities and Accomplishments

- Worked with the corporate leadership team to develop annual goals and objectives for the North American HR function, define and prioritize regional HR initiatives, and lead multifaceted HR projects.
- Established and led continuous improvement project teams responsible for double-digit reduction in administrative costs associated with the employee benefits program.
- Helped create a Global Employee Commitment Program, consisting of a series of assessments and follow-up actions. The program yielded double-digit gains in employee satisfaction, as measured on a 100-point scale.
- Led a team that developed an electronic "HR Manager's Desk Reference." It contained methodologies and tools used by managers throughout the entire organization.

Position: Global Vice President of Human Resources

Organization: Acoma Corporation

Dates of Employment: 1984–1989

Responsibilities and Accomplishments

- Served on the Global HR Leadership Council.
- Helped plan and facilitate Shared Services HR Management Team meetings.
- Supervised a team of Relationship and Account Managers—over a five-year period, the team experienced a double-digit decrease in turnover while realizing a double-digit increase in productivity.
- As "thought leader," helped create an organization-wide Change Management function. The team facilitated the consolidation of two industry leaders, a merger *Enterprise Digest* describes as "the most successful merger in U.S. history."

Position: Director Organization Development—Americas

Organization: Fortcum Corporation

Dates of Employment: 1978–1984

Responsibilities and Accomplishments

- Created matrices and templates used to guide the global rollout of the corporation's three-year strategic plan.
- Helped represent management at monthly meetings with union representatives. Over a six-year period, employee grievances decreased by 28 percent.
- Provided leadership for education (degree-granting programs) and training (including CEU programs). The *Chronicle of Industrial Education* cited Fortcum's model as being "best in class."
- Worked with Steedly University School of Business faculty leaders to develop and implement a co-sponsored Continuous Quality Improvement (CQI) effort. This program, reported as being the first of its kind in the nation, yielded double-digit savings in costs associated with supply chain management.

Professional Certifications

Quality Improvement Facilitator Certification—Sturdivant Institute

Quality Improvement Tools Instructor Certification—Sturdivant Institute

Diagnostic Assessment Center Facilitator—Laxicon Learning Institute

Diagnostic Assessment Center Administrator—Les Aminos University

Academic Accomplishments

Ph.D. in Management from Netlock University (1989).

Program Emphasis: Management and Organization Development.

M.B.A. from the Penley State University (1985).

Program Emphasis: Strategic HR Management.

B.S. in Business Administration from Winslet College (1981).

Program Emphasis: HR Management.

Awards

Netlock University Alumnus of the Year (2000)

St. Lipton Commerce Commission Leadership Award (1998)

CAPITALIZING ON THE JOB INTERVIEW

You have reached an important milestone.

Your cover letter, résumé, exploratory discussions, and preliminary conversations have raised the prospective employer's awareness of your capabilities and the value you would bring his or her organization if you were to be placed into the open position or role. In addition, the actions you have previously taken have interested and excited the prospective employer to the point of asking you to participate in a job interview.

The job interview serves two purposes:

- It gives the potential employer an opportunity to interact with you and to learn more about your capabilities, experiences, and accomplishments.
- It gives you an opportunity to interact with your potential employer and to learn more about his or her organization's mission, vision, values, culture, as well as its management and operating style.

Consistent with how we approached the section about developing a résumé, it is not our intent to provide full coverage to the subject of interviewing. Again, numerous specialty books and resources, including your local librarian and employment office personnel, can help you with this task. Our experiences are broad-based and multifaceted, however, so we offer key points for you to consider as you move forward with this particular aspect of your job search.

Preparing for the Job Interview

Our experience suggests there are certain things you must do to prepare for any interview, whether it is by telephone or face to face with an individual or a group. In preparing for the job interview, follow these guidelines:

- Conduct research or review previous research findings.

  Learn as much as you can about the organization and the position you are seeking. Find out about the company's vision, mission, values, and management philosophy. Be able to describe the organization's structure, history, products and services, and key competitors. Be prepared to comment on recent events involving the organization.

- Prepare to answer frequently asked questions.

  Review the information you have on the organization and the position you are applying for. Within the context of that information, be prepared to answer the following fifteen frequently asked questions:

  What are your strengths and weaknesses?

  How do you respond to criticism?

  How do you give feedback to your colleagues and subordinates?

  How would your colleagues and subordinates describe you?

  Why would like to work with us (in this particular industry or profession or in this particular company, firm, or institution)?

  What were your most significant accomplishments in your previous position?

  What were some of your previous responsibilities?

What problem have you had to address and how did you solve it?

What crisis have you experienced and how did you manage it?

How would others describe your management style?

What risks have you recently taken and how did they turn out?

Why are you no longer working for your previous employer?

What was the title of your most recent supervisor and what was his or her level of responsibility?

What would your most recent supervisor say about your management style and your ability to accomplish goals through others?

What has been your most significant project or initiative, what role did you play, and how did you contribute to its success?

- Prepare to ask questions during the interview.

Most interviewers give you an opportunity to ask questions, either throughout or at the end of the interview session. This presents another opportunity for you to learn more about the company (its industry, products, competitors, and customers) or firm (its profession, services, competitors, and clients). Review the information you have on the organization and the open position. Within the context of that information, formulate six or seven questions similar to the following—

Recent newspaper and journal articles suggest your organization is an industry leader. What, in your opinion, has contributed to this success?

I have read that your organization has traditionally resisted downturns in the economy. What, in your opinion, enables it do so?

In comparison with your competitors, you are experiencing phenomenal growth. What, in your opinion, differentiates you from your competitors?

What two or three core values do you expect everyone affiliated with your organization to possess?

Success can be attributed to individual or team effort, or a combination. In terms of individual contributions and teamwork, how does your organization function?

I am very excited about the possibility of my joining your organization. Do you have any concerns that I need to address or any questions I need to answer?

- Begin managing your shyness now.

Think about what you can do in advance of the interview to raise your comfort level. Then do it! Consider the following actions:

Learn as much as you can about the individual(s) you will be meeting. If possible, identify points of commonality (interests, education, positions).

Attain a photograph of the individual you will be meeting. This is much easier now, given the access to information the Internet provides. Study the photograph.

Think about why they are interested in interviewing you. Consider yourself from their point of view. Your shyness may simply not be an issue for them. If it is, they will in all likelihood assume your shyness is temporary. Thinking about each scenario should raise your comfort level.

• Begin managing your nervousness now.

This issue may be addressed using some of the same techniques presented in the previous bulleted item. Begin taking control of your nervousness and using it to your advantage by:

Learning as much as you can about the company, position, and interviewers, through your research.

Raising your comfort level by studying your notes and otherwise preparing for the interview.

Mentally rehearsing every aspect of the upcoming interview.

Literally rehearsing for the upcoming interview, soliciting feedback from family and trusted friends.

Sharing your feelings with family and trusted friends. They may be able to provide valuable insight and suggestions.

As previously stated, you have reached an important milestone. You must put forth the necessary effort to prepare for this important event. By doing so, you can enter the interview with the necessary knowledge and self-confidence.

Participating in the Job Interview

You are now fully prepared to participate in the job interview. You possess the necessary knowledge and self-confidence. You look forward to sharing more information about your capabilities, experiences, and accomplishments. Your objective is to further verify the prospective employer's belief that you are "the right one for the position."

Set the stage for your success by following these general guidelines when participating in the job interview:

• Arrive at the interview site on time;
• Dress in the appropriate manner;
• Display self-confidence and a proper attitude;
• Listen carefully and answer the questions you are asked;
• Be certain with your answers;
• React to surprises in an appropriate manner; and
• Be attentive and responsive to the interviewer(s).

To further ensure a favorable outcome, we recommend you take the following into consideration when participating in the interview:

- Maintain eye contact with the interviewer, but do not stare or glare.
- Answer questions from the interviewer's viewpoint, rather than yours.
- Monitor body language. This will help you realize when you need to expand on a point, change direction, or end a point.
- Focus on personal accomplishment, but also acknowledge the contributions of others.
- Answer in a brief and concise manner. Do not ramble.
- Never criticize your previous employer or supervisor.
- Do not comment on how much you need a job. Do comment on how much you want this particular job.

We have thus far provided some general guidelines you should follow and some rather specific actions you should take to set the stage for a successful interview. This will be without merit if you inadequately or inappropriately respond to the interview questions. Experience tells us that you are likely to be asked certain questions during your interview. We present these questions for your consideration. (An important note: although not stated in the form of a question, you in all likelihood will be asked to describe your response to situations and to react to various scenarios. We include these "questions" as well). We categorize these questions into the following five areas:

- Capabilities

  What skills and abilities do you possess that will most significantly contribute to your success in this position?

  What skills and abilities do you possess that make you stand out from the other candidates?

  Please describe a recent situation requiring you to apply one of your unique skills. How did the situation turn out?

  Based on what you know about this position in our organization, what do you consider the immediate challenges of this position?

  How would one of your colleagues describe your communication skills?

  How would one of your subordinates describe your leadership skills?

  Please describe a recent situation requiring you to solve a significant problem. How did the situation turn out?

  Do you prefer to work alone or work as part of a team?

  Describe a recent project that you were asked to lead. Include the approach you used and the steps you took in planning, preparing for, and managing the project.

- Experiences

  What types of projects and initiatives have you previously led?

How many direct reports have you previously supervised at any one time?

What is the largest budget you have ever been responsible for?

What experiences do you possess that differentiate you from the other candidates?

Of all your previous experiences, which one(s) did you like the least?

Of all your previous experiences, which one(s) prepared you the most for this position?

If you could relive one of your previous experiences, which one would it be and what would you have done differently?

Of all your previous experiences, which one(s) did you learn the most from?

Of all your previous experiences, which one(s) did you enjoy the most?

What has been your most challenging assignment?

- Accomplishments

Describe a defining moment that occurred during the course of your career.

In terms of your contributing to your organization's success, what has been your most memorable experience (in terms of a project, program, or initiative)?

What has been your most personally satisfying and fulfilling project, program, or initiative?

What, in your opinion, has been your most important achievement?

Looking back on your most recent position, describe your most important accomplishment(s).

Are most of your accomplishments due to your leadership skills or to your contributing to a team effort?

In reviewing your résumé, we see that you have received several awards. What accomplishments contributed to your receiving those awards?

Here is the scenario: you joined our organization and have functioned in this position for three years. Looking back over the past three years, what has been your most significant accomplishment?

Some individuals evaluate their level of accomplishment on one or two criteria, such as the impact he or she has on the bottom line. What factors do you use when evaluating your level of accomplishment?

- Knowledge of the Industry (or Profession) and Organization

Summarize your understanding of this industry (or profession).

Why do want to work in this industry (or profession)?

Summarize your understanding of this position.

What do you know about our management philosophy?

What can you tell us about our customers (or clients) and products (or services)?

Who are our competitors and, in your opinion, how do we compare to them?

Summarize your understanding of how our organization is structured and organized.

Have you recently read anything about our organization? If so, what was the article about and what was your reaction to it?

What do you know about our history?

• Professional Development (Education, Training, Certifications, and Licensures)

What specialty certifications do you hold? Do they expire? Do they apply to this state, industry, organization, or position?

How have these specialty certifications contributed to your previous accomplishments?

What licensures do you hold? Do they expire? Do they apply to this state, industry, organization, or position?

How have these licensures contributed to your previous accomplishments?

In reviewing your résumé, we see you majored in (field). Why did you choose this particular field of study?

Why did you attend this particular college (or university)?

What were your most favorite college courses? Why?

What aspect of your college experience most significantly contributed to your previous accomplishments?

What was your overall grade point average?

What was your grade point average for your major field of study?

Do you feel your grade point average is a reflection of your overall ability or a reflection of the amount of effort you were willing to put forth?

Describe your most interesting or fascinating professor. What is the most important thing you learned from this individual?

Describe the professor you enjoyed the most. What is the most important thing you learned from this individual?

What specialty training have you received that has contributed most significantly to your previous accomplishments?

Of the specialty training you have received, describe the trainer or instructor you enjoyed the most. What is the most important thing you learned from this individual?

Of the specialty training you have received, what instructional methodologies and training techniques do you consider to be the most effective?

Of the specialty training you have received, describe the most interesting and fascinating instructor or trainer. What is the most important thing you learned from this individual?

These questions represent the ones you are likely to be asked during your job interview, whether that interview is by telephone or in person and whether it involves one or more interviewers. Also, expect to be asked questions about any and all of the information you present in your résumé. We can recall instances where entire interview sessions were driven by questions relating to information presented in the résumé. Be prepared to provide detailed information on every point included in your résumé.

Expect to be asked questions and be given scenarios to evaluate your level of self-confidence and self-motivation. However, our experience tells us you should expect these characteristics to be evaluated within the context of the questions presented above rather than your being asked separate questions ("Give us an example of your being self-motivated"). A special note regarding technical interviews: do not be surprised if a skills assessment is included in your interview session. The skills assessment may include a role-play (where you are given information, issued limited equipment and supplies, and asked to apply your skills and abilities) or a simulation (different from the role-play in that you are given the equipment and supplies you would have available in "real life").

While answering these questions, there are certain key messages you need to convey to the interviewers. Table 7.10 lists three underlying questions, along with their associated key messages.

We have thus far focused on the questions likely to be asked during your job interview. Prior to the end of your interview, be sure to ask two or three thought-provoking questions from the list you developed while preparing for the interview. If necessary, ask ad hoc questions to round out your knowledge of the company (its industry, products, competitors, and customers) or firm (its profession, services, competitors, and clients).

We recommend you conclude the interview on a positive note and with a rather straightforward question. For example, conclude by saying "I have enjoyed meeting with you, sharing information and ideas with you, and learning more about your organization. I am interested in joining your organization, feel I can contribute to your organization's future success, and am confident I would do well in the position under consideration. What are our next steps?"

Following Up on the Interview

Some time ago, an individual interested in a Vice President of Sales position participated in a series of interviews. In short, his interviews went well and he was one of two final candidates. He left the meetings feeling comfortable with his performance and optimistic about the future. To show his gratitude, he sent each interviewer's executive assistant a dozen roses. At the time, a dozen roses cost about $75 (a total investment of almost $1,000). The other final candidate's interviews went equally well. To express her gratitude, she sent each interviewer's executive assistant a "thank you" note (on a $2.50 card). The company's somewhat frugal Chief Executive Officer undoubtedly took this factor into consideration and extended the job offer to the latter candidate. We consider this to be an

Table 7.10
Interview Questions and Messages

Interview Question	Your Key Message
Why do you want to work here?	I have researched your organization and therefore know your organization. I am very interested in working here and feel that I can contribute to your organization's future success.
Are you right for this job?	I have worked in similar situations, under similar conditions. I have accomplished a lot, contributing to my organization's success. My success has been through my personal contribution, as well as my being a team player. I look forward to applying my assets and learning to this role/position.
Why should I hire you?	I possess the needed capabilities, have a proven track record, am self-confident and self-motivated, and I want the job!

excellent example of how your follow-up actions help or hinder (seldom are the results neutral) your case.

Following the interview, do not expect to receive immediate feedback from the prospective employer. There will be a delay in your being notified of the results. The reason for this delay is that in all likelihood you are one of several candidates, discussions have to occur, and decisions must be made. We find the process typically takes one to two business weeks.

While awaiting word from the potential employer, you can further strengthen your case. Whatever actions you decide on, they must feel right to you and match your personal style. With that said, consider:

- Immediately sending a brief note to the interviewers, thanking them for taking time out of their busy schedules to spend time with you to discuss the position under consideration. In the note, highlight two or three of your strengths.

- Immediately sending a brief note to each support professional who helped orchestrate the interview session(s), thanking them for helping arrange such a positive experience and for making you feel welcome.

- Telephoning the prospective employer if you have not heard anything twelve business days following the interview.

- Telephoning the prospective employer twelve business days following the final interview, if you participated in multiple interviews spanning several days.

While awaiting word from the prospective employer, continue with your job search. If other job options surface, pursue them. If given the opportunity to interview elsewhere, do so. Your goal here is to do all you can to support your candidacy, while keeping your options open by identifying and pursuing other potential job opportunities. Such action will put you in the most favorable position if you are turned down for the position.

If you are not offered the position, it is important that you keep in mind the following edict, "There is always another day!" The employer, although he or she has decided to hire someone else, can still play an invaluable role in your job search. For example, follow up with the employer and thank him or her for initially considering you for the position. Voice a continuing interest in the organization and ask to be considered for opportunities that surface in the future. This happened to me (B. K. S.) early in my career. I responded to the "bad" news in a positive manner and as a result was contacted three months later—the individual initially placed into the position (through an internal transfer) discovered that he did not possess the requisite skills and therefore opted to transfer back into his previous position. Two weeks after the employer re-established contact, I was sitting in the company's New Employee Orientation!

MANAGING THE JOB OFFER

Reviewing the Job Offer

Information provided elsewhere in this book can help you address issues relating to the job offer. For example, apply the results of your self-assessment to help verify that this is "the job" for you. Apply the guidelines for evaluating job offer letters to evaluate the soundness of your job offer (its requirements, specifications, and conditions).

Although you probably considered these issues prior to applying for the job, now is the time for you to ensure that:

- The salary is consistent with industry (or profession) standards and matches your "market value."

- The salary is consistent with what others in comparable positions earn within the organization.
- Salary increases are consistent with cost-of-living increases, if your accepting the position requires you to relocate.
- The salary you will receive falls within a range that allows you ample growth (so you are not surprised to learn that your salary is the top of the range and you therefore will only be eligible for cost-of-living adjustments and future market adjustments).
- Benefits (insurance coverage, vacation and other forms of leave, retirement and pension) are consistent with industry (or profession) standards.
- The benefits you are being offered are consistent with what others in comparable positions receive within the organization.
- The bonus structure (including sign-on, relocation, retention, performance) you are being offered is consistent with industry (or profession) standards.
- The bonus structure you are being offered is consistent with what others in comparable positions receive within the organization.

When reviewing a job offer, it is important that you consider a variety of factors and not be overly influenced by one. For example, you may accept a job offer because it contains an attractive salary. However, losses associated with the benefits and bonus structure may nullify gains made on the salary. It is therefore important that you review your job offer in a comprehensive manner. Completing the Position Review Form (see Table 7.11) will help ensure such a comprehensive review.

To complete this document, transfer information presented in the job offer onto the form. If the job offer does not address a particular item, inquire as to whether this item was inadvertently overlooked (not included in the letter, but is part of the job offer) or whether it is not included in the job offer.

If you receive two job offers, it may be helpful to compare both job offers at the same time. The Position Comparison Form will help you perform such a comparison. This document, illustrated in Table 7.12, can be used in its current form or be modified to match your personal preferences.

To complete this document, transfer information presented in each job offer onto the form. If either job offer does not address a particular item, inquire as to whether this item was inadvertently overlooked (not included in the letter, but part of the job offer) or whether it is not included in the job offer. Placing parallel information together for such a side-by-side comparison likely will help you evaluate the strengths of both job offers.

You may be offered a job that would require you to relocate. When deciding whether or not to accept such a job offer, it is of the utmost importance that you take cost-of-living factors into consideration. For example, you may be inclined to accept a job in another state or city because it offers an attractive salary in comparison with your current

Table 7.11
Position Review Form

Item for Review	Information Relating to Job Offer
Base salary	
Sign-on bonus	
Guaranteed annual bonus	
Annual retention bonus	
Other annual bonus opportunity	
Stock options	
Health insurance	
Long-term care insurance	
Disability insurance	
Life insurance	
Dental insurance	
Eye care insurance	
Relocation expense reimbursement	
Retirement program	
Vacation leave	
Sick leave	

salary. However, if you were to accept the job offer and relocate, you may quickly discover that costs associated with residing in the new location nullify the salary and bonus increases!

Completing the Location Comparison Form will help you conduct a realistic appraisal of the job offer, within the context of the local area's annual cost-of-living. There are several ways you can obtain data to incorporate into this document. First, contact your state employment office. You may find it has "cost-of-living comparison" data available on the

Table 7.12
Position Comparison Form

Item for Review	Job Offer 1	Job Offer 2
Base salary		
Sign-on bonus		
Subsequent bonus opportunity		
Stock options		
Life insurance		
Health insurance		
Disability insurance		
Relocation reimbursement		
Company automobile		
Vacation leave		
Sick leave		
Retirement program		

nation's larger metropolitan areas. Second, conduct an electronic search of the Internet using the keywords "cost-of-living comparison." Your search engine should lead you to several useful Web sites and databases. Finally, contact your local chamber of commerce or real estate association. Each organization typically monitors the local cost-of-living and therefore has access to similar information on the nation's larger metropolitan areas. The Location Comparison Form, illustrated in Table 7.13, can be used in its current form or be modified to match your personal preferences.

To complete this document, insert information on the current (or previous) job and local living expenses and information on the potential job and the surrounding area's living expenses onto the form. Placing parallel information together for such a side-by-side comparison likely will help you evaluate the strengths of each job offer, within the context of what it costs to reside in each location.

The Dual Location Comparison Form allows you to conduct a similar side-by-side comparison of two job opportunities (see Table 7.14).

Table 7.13
Location Comparison Form

Item for Comparison	If I Remain Here	If I Relocate
Base salary		
Sign-on bonus		
Annual bonus opportunity		
State taxes		
Local taxes		
House payment		
Rent payment		
Utilities		
House insurance		
Apartment insurance		
Automobile insurance		
Gasoline for automobile		
Commuting expense (taxi, train)		
Food		
Clothes		
Recreation		
Entertainment		

You may wish to modify this form to include the same items listed in Table 7.13. To complete this form, insert information on each job offer and each area's living expenses. As with the previous form, this document will help you evaluate the strengths of each job offer, within the context of what it costs to reside in its location.

Table 7.14
Dual Location Comparison Form

Item for Comparison	Job Offer 1	Job Offer 2
Base salary		
Sign-on bonus		
Annual bonus opportunity		
State taxes		
Local taxes		
House payment		
Rent payment		
Utilities		
House insurance		
Apartment insurance		
Automobile expense (gas, insurance)		
Food		
Clothes		

Addressing Issues and Resolving Concerns

If concerns regarding salary, benefits, or bonus structure surface, you must address them prior to accepting the job offer. If you feel the salary is unacceptable, share information about your expectations (not in specific terms, but in terms of an acceptable range) with the employer and solicit information about the salary structure (for the organization, in general, and for the position under consideration, in particular). If you consider the benefits to be unacceptable, take a similar approach, but attempt to obtain information (along with supporting evidence) suggesting that the strength of one benefit compensates for the limitation of another. If such information is unavailable, share your specific concerns with the employer and solicit information likely to verify or discount your concerns. If you find the bonus structure to be unacceptable, share your concerns with the employer and ask for more information about the bonus program for positions similar to the one under consideration.

You have invested a lot of time and energy to get to this point, and you do not want to jeopardize a job offer by inappropriately voicing concerns about a certain option. The organization has also invested a lot of time and energy and in all likelihood will not wish to jeopardize a job offer over a trivial point. Now is the time to work out the details and resolve any issues, as long as you and the organization move forward in an appropriate manner. Here, you must approach the employer in a positive, non-threatening, cordial, and professional manner. Your expectations must be reasonable, taking into account the capabilities you bring to the organization and the environment within which the organization operates. In return, the prospective employer must listen to and be responsive to your concerns, be willing to provide additional information, and within reason take steps to address your concerns and resolve any issues.

Because of the time and effort both parties have already invested, it is in everyone's best interest for the job seeker and prospective employer to work together to address concerns and resolve issues. This typically occurs; negotiations over job offer requirements, specifications, and conditions generally end in a mutually acceptable manner. However, if you are unable to negotiate a mutually acceptable agreement, it may be in your best interest to turn down the job offer.

CONCLUSION

This chapter has presented information crucial to a successful job search. This information (and accompanying templates) will help you organize and manage your job search; develop an effective résumé; prepare for, participate in, and follow up on a job interview; and manage the job offer process.

Just as the four cornerstones add strength and stability to any building, these actions will add strength and stability to your job search, regardless of whether you are seeking a public- or private-sector position or a position in a professional services firm or within a certain industry.

CHAPTER 8

For the Survival-Savvy

The primary impressions that employers and out-counselors communicate during the layoff process is that you should be confident; that if you are prudent in your job search something will come along; and that you may ultimately consider this to be one of the best things that has ever happened to you during the course of your career. These comments and advice seem so vague they are meaningless.

Some people think being prudent in your job search means depending solely on your existing personal network. The idea of a job termination ultimately being the "best" thing that has happened in the course of your career may be an optimistic one, but to turn such optimism into reality requires an action plan containing multiple components and an understanding of the role each plays in today's job search. A close colleague frequently paraphrases a rather famous quote, "When conducting a job search, be bold and mighty forces will come to your aid." Boldness, in today's job market, is simply not enough. We provide information in this chapter that enables you to move forward, and offer resources you can call upon if such assistance is needed.

DEVELOPING YOUR ACTION PLAN

Upon coming to a fork in the road, the path you take is unimportant unless you are attempting to reach a particular destination. The same can be said of your job search. It is critical that you not simply begin searching for another job—you must initially define your objective, you must then determine the path to take, and then decide on the steps to take along the way. Finally, success requires two main ingredients: an exceptional action plan and its effective execution.

Using tools provided in chapter 3, "Bulletproofing Your Career," initially you must assess your capabilities, then evaluate the prevailing and emerging business environment, and ultimately identify your target industry, profession, organization, or position. Once you have decided on your target, you create your Action Plan. The Action Plan helps you focus your time and effort—your goal is for your time and effort to yield the greatest possible gains.

As we reported in chapter 3, your personality influences the way you make decisions and interact with the world. When it comes to your job search, your personality may (if you are an introvert) cause you to focus on sending out e-mails and listing your résumé on databases or (if you are an extravert) cause you to rely on your personal network and on leads generated at job fairs. Your Action Plan will help you offset personal preferences, such as the ones influenced by your personality. For example, we recommend that your Action Plan include at least five or six methods for seeking out opportunities and for marketing your availability. These methods typically consist of a combination of the following: using on-line data sources and databases, relying on personal networks, using search firms, contacting investment firms, contacting potential employers, using outplacement firms, working with an alumni association, and participating in job fairs. Your Action Plan should contain:

- Specific actions associated with each method (such as telephoning, mailing, or meeting);
- Critical dates (usually spanning a period of twelve to sixteen weeks); and
- Assessment criteria (so you can measure the progress you are making).

Certain fears or concerns inevitably surface when one becomes laid off. Such fears can be addressed by counter-measures stipulated in the Action Plan. Four common concerns, along with their potential counter-measures, are outlined below:

- You would like to work in a particular industry. The only problem is that you do not have any experience working in that industry.
  - Stress your familiarity with and knowledge of systems, processes, tools, and techniques within the desired industry.
  - Conduct extensive research of the desired industry, so you become familiar with its products and processes, suppliers, and distribution channels.
  - Stress your capabilities and assets that are transferable to the desired industry.
  - Stress your familiarity with and knowledge of the systems, processes, tools, and techniques that can be applied to the desired industry.
- You were recently laid off for the X time in the same number of years. You are concerned that potential employers will feel you are guilty of "job hopping."

- Be candid in sharing information with potential employers. However, be sure not to criticize previous employers. Keep in mind that employers know that layoffs are not within the control of employees.
- Stress the positive aspects of previous positions, focusing on responsibilities and accomplishments.
- Provide personal references from those previous employers.

- You have been with the same company for X years. You would now like to pursue other opportunities, but are concerned that potential employers will feel you have been with one company for too long.
  - Stress your familiarity with and knowledge of systems, processes, tools, and techniques.
  - Stress your capabilities and assets that are transferable to the desired company.
  - Stress your familiarity with and knowledge of systems, processes, tools, and techniques that can be applied within the desired company.
  - Stress experiences, accomplishments, and learnings, rather than the number of years spent in your current company.
  - Stress your familiarity with and knowledge of systems, processes, tools, and techniques within the desired company.

- You know the potential employer will not ask for your age, but you feel there may be a concern about your age.
  - Stress the challenges you have encountered, the solutions you have helped create, the lessons you have learned, the wisdom you have gained, the breadth and depth of your experiences, and your proven track record.
  - Stress your capabilities and assets that are transferable to the desired organization.
  - Stress your familiarity with and knowledge of systems, processes, tools, and techniques that can be applied within the desired company.

Regardless of the job search paths you pursue or the counter-measures you use, your search in all likelihood will require a résumé. Our goal is not to present "Résumé Writing 101" (for more information about creating an effective résumé, refer to chapter 7). However, we do recommend you consider these guidelines when creating your professional résumé:

- Format it so it makes a positive impression;
- Be descriptive yet concise;
- Be concise but do not abbreviate;
- Design for maximum readability;
- Customize for each job opportunity;
- Be relatively brief (generally, only two pages);
- List previous responsibilities and accomplishments; and
- Communicate capabilities and assets.

In summary, your résumé must present a compelling story. Its format and contents must project a professional image; its tone must project commitment and self-confidence. We encourage you to invest the time to create an effective résumé—doing so will facilitate your communicating with your personal network, responding to recruiters and interested employers, contacting investment firms, following up on potential job opportunities, working with alumni associations and outplacement firms, and participating in career fairs.

ESSENTIAL RESOURCES

Using the Internet

If you do not have a computer or if you do not have Internet capabilities, visit your local employment security office. It is in everyone's best interest for you to become employed. Your employment security office will have computers—with Internet capability—available for your use. If your computer skills are minimal, most offices will assign someone to assist in your initial job search efforts. If your office does not provide such assistance, go to your public library and ask for help.

While we, unfortunately, cannot significantly enhance your basic computing skills, we can introduce you to some useful electronic tools. If you are a novice at using the Internet, increase your familiarity as part of your personal transition. For assistance, contact your local community college and ascertain whether it offers computer workshops. Such workshops, typically lasting only one or two days and costing $100–$150, can greatly enhance your skills and expand your awareness of how the Internet might benefit your job search.

Web site addresses accompany each of the following sections. If you would like to expand on this information, we recommend you search the Internet to obtain additional information. To search for additional information, we recommend you initially use the Google (www.google.com) search engine. We recommend you use Google for the following reasons:

- The pages Google lists first are the ones other Web sites link to most often (the number of linkages often reflects quality of information provided); and
- Google stores Web pages, allowing you to access expired pages (expired pages are normally not available).

We recommend you consider using other search engines when you are conducting "specialty" searches. For example, if you are searching for a particular topic (for example, search firms located in your particular area), you might consider using Yahoo! (www.yahoo.com) because it will provide a list of links to search firms in your particular area. On the other hand, if you are searching for articles written about industry performance over the past twenty-four months, you might consider using HotBot (www.hotbot.com) because it will allow you to specify time frames, directing you only to articles written on that particular topic within the past twenty-four months. Finally, if you are cannot find the information using those search engines, we recommend you consider using a metasearch engine such as Dogpile (yes, you read it correctly). Dogpile (www.dogpile.com), which conducts searches over numerous search engines, will in all likelihood uncover the information for which you are searching. We recommend you consider using this search engine as a last resort, primarily due to the number of irrelevant hits you are likely to encounter. Of course, your need to obtain information during your job search may greatly outweigh your having to access and review irrelevant data sources and data.

Regarding the on-line resources listed below: some of the sites may not exist when you conduct your job search. We therefore recommend you search the Internet using these keywords: executive search, résumé, job search, recruitment, investment, outplacement, career, and career counseling.

On-line Data Sources and Databases

These sites are extremely valuable in that they list positions currently available (by industry and by location), allow you to electronically post a résumé, offer career planning advice, and/or sponsor chat rooms and other special services. These include:

- Monster.com at http://www/monster.com
- Chief Monster.com at http://www.chiefmonster.com
- Hot Jobs at http://www.hotjobs.com
- Yahoo! Careers at http://www.yahoocareers.com
- Headhunter at http://www.headhunter.net
- Recruiters-On-Line at http://www.recruitersonline.com
- Future Step at http://www.futurestep.com
- CareerPath at http://www.career-path.com
- Management Jobs at http://www.managementjobs.com
- Careers at http://careers.wsj.com
- JobOptions at http://www.espan.com
- Women.com at http://www.women.com/career

An on-line database can significantly shorten your job-hunting process. To capitalize on this resource, be sure to create a personal account and profile, enter your résumé into the system (using the database's standardized form, by uploading it onto the system, or by cutting and pasting your personalized résumé into the designated file), and make it easy for interested employers to respond by including your e-mail address on your résumé in a hyperlink format. Many newspapers have Web-based job sites that allow for local job searches. When looking for a job in a particular city, check out that city's newspaper Web site.

Personal Networking

As we look back on our careers, many of our transitions into new companies and firms were initiated and then assisted by someone in our personal network. Your personal and professional friends can be your most valuable resource. The bottom line is this: the more people you have in your personal network, the more people there are who know about your personal values, your capabilities and assets, and your unique skills. Your personal network will undoubtedly bring current (and even emerging) job opportunities to your attention and then, in many cases, will help you attract the ones most suitable for you. Never underestimate the power of your network; not only will it help you identify and pursue opportunities, but it also will share ideas with you about how to do so successfully, and then frequently will help bridge the gap between your past and future positions. However, never overestimate the power of your personal network. Personal contacts seldom compensate for the lack of skills and ability, nor do they offset the effects of one's having a faulty track record. You may need to use the other career-building tools we suggest in this book to overcome these possible deficiencies.

For these reasons, personal networking is typically an important component of any career transition Action Plan. Your personal situation will dictate the extent to which you should follow this path. For example, a scenario that best illustrates the need for aggressive personal networking is the individual who, after moving into a major metropolitan area, learns that she is being laid off. An individual in such a situation would not be able to call upon her local connections and relationships for support, simply because they have not yet been established. Rather than remain isolated, this individual would need to aggressively develop her personal network. But how exactly might she accomplish that?

There are several avenues available for individuals wishing to establish a new or expand upon an existing personal network:

- Attend and actively participate in general business seminars and workshops. Attendees invariably discuss their industry, position, and responsibilities. This poses an opportunity for you to do the same.
- Present yourself at local and regional meetings, seminars, and workshops. Attendees invariably hold responsible positions and frequently need someone possessing your capabilities and assets. Your presentation poses an opportunity for you to display these and for them to see you in action.

- Share your ideas and insights with others by writing an article. Whether the article is written for a business journal or a popular magazine, it will expose you to a wider audience. This avenue poses an opportunity for you to share your experiences and accomplishments with others, as well as for potential employers to gain invaluable insight into your values and principles.

- Attend and participate in local networking sessions. While such events may seem "artificial" to you, they do provide an effective forum for your developing a new or expanding an existing network. This avenue poses an opportunity for you to quickly and efficiently meet tens or hundreds of people, as well as for perhaps tens or hundreds of people (who potentially are aware of existing or emerging opportunities) to instantly know you and possess your business card and a copy of your résumé.

- Attend and actively participate in seminars and workshops designed specifically for individuals in transition. Attendees invariably discuss their target industry, as well as their experiences and accomplishments. This poses an opportunity for you to obtain (and share) information on: different professions and occupations; companies, firms, and institutions; and job search strategies and techniques.

Entry fees into a formal networking session may be $50–$100. Sponsors therefore take steps to ensure an effective event. The key to successful networking sessions, however, is not the process you follow or activities you participate in while at the session, but rather the willingness of the attendees to follow up with one another after the session ends.

Search Firms

Search firms are extremely valuable. They serve as the "linking pin" between you and job opportunities; their representatives are extremely knowledgeable of positions currently available, by industry and by location. Search firms:

- Will—if they find you to be a promising candidate—work with you to refine your résumé and give you invaluable career planning advice; and

- May initially serve as your advocate or sponsor and ultimately arrange for you to meet with potential employers.

When initially contacted by an executive search firm, you will probably be asked to participate in a "pre-qualification" interview. This interview, sometimes taking the form of a written survey rather than an interview and occasionally conducted by an analyst rather than the recruiter, helps the search firm decide whether it will showcase you in a current or future search. To qualify for such premier treatment, you must answer questions such as:

- What unique knowledge, skills, and abilities do you possess?
- In your current or most recent positions, to whom did you report?
- What have you accomplished that required you to function with uncertainty and ambiguity?
- What is your management style?
- What distinguishes you from others pursuing this (type of) position?
- What is your biggest weakness or limitation?
- What are you searching for in an ideal position?
- What have been your greatest challenges and accomplishments?
- What would your least preferred colleague say about you?
- How did you handle your biggest obstacle or failure?
- What is the most important project you have ever led?
- What is the greatest number of people you have ever managed?
- What aspect of managing others do you enjoy the most?

The pre-qualification interview also gives you an opportunity to solicit information from the search firm. At a minimum, seek answers to the following questions:

- What companies and organizations do you typically represent?
- About how many individuals possessing my particular capabilities and assets do you place each year?
- How do you judge the success of your placements?
- Based on the answer to the previous question, how successful are you?

We encourage you to obtain as much information from the recruiter as possible, and attempt to verify the information you attain via additional research and inquiry.

Bear in mind how search firms work when dealing with them. In some cases, employers hire the search firms to find a candidate to fill a particular position. In that case, the search firm is not your agent working for you. It is the agent of the employer and will not necessarily lobby for you. The search firm hired by an employer may not be as aggressive marketing you to the employer as you may have been led to expect. In other cases, the search firm may specialize in certain types of placements, such as executives, computer specialists, attorneys, and so on. You should discuss your relationship with the search firm when you decide on whether to use their services.

Here are some of the leading executive search firms:

- Spencer Stuart at http://www.spencerstuart.com

- Heidrick & Struggles at http://www.heidrick.com
- AT Kearney at http://www.atkearney.com
- Witt/Kieffer & Associates at http://www.wittkieffer.com
- Systems Research Inc. at http://www.systemsresearch.com
- Egon Zehnder at http://www.zehnder.com
- DHR International at http://www.dhrintl.net
- Kanzer Associates, Inc. at http://www.kanzer.com
- David Gomez and Associates at http://www.dgai.com
- M. Wood Company at http://www.mwoodco.com
- Battalia Winston at http://www.battaliawinston.com
- Boyden at http://www.boyden.com

Electronic mail can shorten the time it takes you to communicate with search firms. When e-mailing a search firm, be sure to use an e-mail address that includes your first and last name. Also, be sure to:

- Keep the e-mail short and to the point;
- Identify the position or type of position you are interested in; and
- State whether or not you are willing to relocate.

When using e-mail to communicate with a search firm, make sure the recipient perceives your e-mail to be an asset rather than a hindrance. Include contact information in the e-mail and résumé, send one (rather than multiple) attachments, and use your name (last name first, then first name) as your résumé's file name.

Investment Firms

Contacting investment firms will not benefit a majority of job hunters. However, if you possess executive-level skills and are searching for senior-level management opportunities, these firms may know of executive positions available in their "member" service, manufacturing, industrial, or technology organizations.

To benefit from working with an investment firm, you must be willing to form a trusted relationship and reap the benefits over time.

Global investment firms can be found in almost every major metropolitan area. For example, here are several in the Chicago area:

- Cardwell Enterprises at http://www.cardwell.com
- Sunbelt Business Brokers at http://www.sunbeltnetwork.com
- Open Prairie Ventures at http://www.openprairie.com

- Wind Point Partners at http://www.wppartners.com

Be prudent when deciding whether or not to contact an investment firm as part of your job-hunting strategy. Prior to contacting a firm, we recommend that you review its Web site to determine whether or not: its primary focus and/or "member" organizations are compatible with your field of expertise; it is currently searching for senior-level executives; it is likely to be interested in speaking to someone having your particular skills and abilities.

Potential Employers

Contacting potential employers is an important component of any career transition strategy. However, this action will undoubtedly fail (or be extremely inefficient) if you do not plan prior to moving forward. Preplanning includes your targeting potential employers. In using the term "target," we suggest you contact selected companies, firms, and institutions—not all of them, not all of them in a particular industry or profession, not all of them that happen to be in your (or a particular) location. For this pathway to be meaningful, you must contact only those firms likely to be searching for someone possessing your capabilities and assets, your experiences and accomplishments, your insight and wisdom. We recommend against mass-produced and mass-distributed mailings. Such an approach may yield job offers; our concern is that too much time and effort is spent on an exercise unlikely to yield high quality job offers. Your better approach is to find a person in the organization who has something in common with you. Perhaps you belong to the same trade groups, went to the same school, transacted business together in the past, or even have children in the same school. Find connections and use them.

To increase the likelihood of direct mailings ultimately yielding quality job offers, we recommend that you:

- Create a letter that makes a positive first impression;
- Mail the letter to a person rather than to a "Sir" or "Madam";
- Use correct addresses, titles, and spellings of first and last names throughout the letter;
- Incorporate knowledge of the recipient's industry and organization into the letter;
- Customize information contained in the letter so that it is relevant to the recipient and his or her industry or organization;
- Magnify interest by describing in the letter how you can help the recipient's firm, company, or institution deliver on its value proposition to its customers or clients; and

- Include your mailing address, e-mail address, and telephone numbers in the letter.

To be effective, the direct mailing must immediately interest the recipient. As one associate describes it, "you must simply jump off of the page." You are likely to generate such interest only if your letter is the product of extensive research about the prospective employer and is the result of a focused, "customized" effort. Again, mass-produced and distributed mailings are significantly less likely to be effective.

Alumni Associations and Programs

Most of us, as graduates of colleges and universities, are familiar with alumni associations. They support the graduate by offering or sponsoring alumni directories, résumé writing workshops, special interest groups, e-mail addresses, and insurance programs. Your college or university alumni association can be helpful, regardless of whether you graduated last year or two decades ago. Obtain a recent alumni directory and identify potential employers. Then direct your résumé to your fellow alum and personalize your cover letter.

Several corporations and professional services firms have recently recognized an important fact: their employees, once they leave the organization, frequently enter into relatively influential positions. Individuals in such positions often can decide or influence the decision regarding who will serve as their (new) organization's supplier or consulting firm of choice. Recognizing this fact, several corporations and firms have established alumni programs.

Corporate- and firm-sponsored programs mirror their academic counterparts, in that they typically offer or sponsor alumni directories, résumé writing workshops, special interest groups, e-mail addresses, and insurance programs. However, corporate- and firm-sponsored programs frequently offer:

- Buying programs, enabling alumni to purchase items at discounted prices or rent items at a discounted rate;
- Access to the organization's knowledge base or thought leadership, allowing alumni to access white papers and research reports;
- Links to on-line workshops and seminars, enabling alumni to access information relating to résumé preparation and interviewing techniques;
- Preferred customer programs, allowing alumni to attend vendor-sponsored seminars and workshops at a discounted price; and
- Referral services, enabling employed alumni to list job opportunities in their organization and allowing alumni in transition to post their résumés.

The power of such corporate- and firm-sponsored programs does not come from the technology they use or the benefits they offer. Each person (both inside and outside the sponsoring organization) using such a program, at a minimum, shares a common bond—they were once hired after going through a similar selection process, they once worked together to accomplish the same mission and goals, they once faced the same challenges and opportunities. The power of these programs comes from a sense of trust that occurs when individuals share in such a communal experience. Such trust allows all parties to move forward while assuming that each has the other's best interest in mind.

Do not underestimate the value of being able to operate under such an assumption of mutual trust. For example, it at a minimum allows you to shorten the "courting" process, the time both parties normally spend learning about each other's values, principles, intentions, and personal capabilities. On the other hand, companies and firms must not overestimate the damage that occurs to their alumni programs when they mistreat individuals being laid off. We have said it before and we will say it again, "You must treat your employees with dignity and respect, throughout the entire process."

Career Fairs

Participating in career fairs may not benefit all job hunters. However, if you possess transferable skills and are considering changing professions or occupations, these events may prove useful. To gain the most benefit, pre-planning and research must influence your overall approach to the career fair and how you focus your time while on site. Regarding pre-planning, we recommend you carefully review all information available about the career fair. For example, you need to ascertain:

- Industries that will be participating in the event;
- Companies, firms, and institutions that will be participating in the fair;
- Whether organizations will be conducting on-site interviews; and
- The exhibit layout or facility floor plan. If hundreds of companies are involved, you may not be able to visit each station, and traveling from one station to another can be time consuming.

As with the other paths, it is important that research influence your overall approach and resulting actions. Once you have obtained and reviewed all relevant information, we recommend that you:

- Target the industries and research the context within which those industries are currently operating. For example, determine whether they are growing or in decay, and whether they are likely to be seeking someone with your skills.

- Target the companies and research their current situation. Determine whether you can help them deliver on their value proposition and whether a high quality job offer is likely to be the result of this initial contact.
- Prioritize stations you plan to visit and create a "road map" to save you time traveling from one station to another.

Career fairs are potentially useful because numerous industries and professions are typically represented and numerous companies are typically in attendance. The challenge you must overcome rests in the numbers—hundreds or thousands of other candidates may also attend, each with the objective of meeting with industry (or profession) and company (firm or institution) representatives. You must differentiate yourself from the masses. We recommend you differentiate yourself by sharing a concisely written résumé that projects a positive image; dressing in a manner that also projects a positive image; incorporating your research findings into your conversation; being prepared to summarize your career aspirations, capabilities, and assets in thirty seconds or less; and being prepared if an organization wishes to conduct an on-site interview, even when such an interview is unexpected.

OUTPLACEMENT SERVICES—AN OASIS RATHER THAN A MIRAGE

Outplacement services are:

Services likely to reduce the organization's costs (reducing the amount of time you receive job continuance pay by helping you quickly enter into a position elsewhere).

Services likely to reduce the organization's risks (reducing the likelihood of your seeking legal remedy by helping you quickly enter into a position elsewhere).

Services that—at no charge to you—are invaluable in helping you land your next position.

Services that—at no charge to you—are invaluable in helping you work through personal change issues.

From Your Employer's Viewpoint

Outplacement services—except under certain circumstances—are not required by law. However, your organization's severance package most likely includes some form of outplacement services. They benefit both you and the organization.

The out-counseling session, as we described in chapter 3, is typically very brief. You leave the session with numerous unanswered questions. You have not yet had an opportunity to ask questions, but you have been assured that answers will be forthcoming.

Such answers may come from the organization's outplacement specialist. The specialist typically is not affiliated with the employer. He or she is a specialist, a "hired gun." Retained by the organization, he or she is there to:

- Help you begin dealing with the fact that you no longer will be affiliated with the organization;
- Help you cope with the immediate emotions of disbelief, surprise, and anger; and
- Answer questions you may have regarding the out-counseling process (but, due to a confidentiality agreement, not about others being laid off).

Again, the objective is for the out-counseling process to conclude as quickly—and as peacefully—as possible. The outplacement specialist is being paid (perhaps as much as $3,000 to $6,500 per person!) to help ensure that it does.

From Your Viewpoint

You left the out-counseling session with the understanding that you would have an opportunity to ask questions at a different time and to a different person. The outplacement specialist is that person. Usually, the outplacement specialist is independent and has no vested interest in protecting the employer. He or she is there to assist you in a smooth transition between jobs.

The specialist will, to the best of his or her ability, answer questions not answered during the out-counseling session. Be sure to ask the outplacement specialist to confirm or verify the following:

- The reason for your layoff. At a minimum, ask him or her whether it was due to your performance;
- The reason he or she was given for your layoff;
- Whom you should contact for answers to future questions; and
- Whether or not he or she has heard anything (from the employer or the out-counselor) or seen anything (in your résumé or employment file) that would indicate you will have problems finding a future position.

The specialist will help you begin thinking about making a career change necessitated by a layoff. The specialist will offer advice about what you should do immediately following the out-counseling session, such as:

- Recognize that the emotions you are feeling are normal and that you should try to manage those feelings;

- Contact members of your support group or informal network (especially if they have experienced a similar event in their careers); and
- Begin preparing to once again be on the job hunt.

The specialist might also recommend against your taking certain actions, such as:

- Contacting the out-counselor to obtain additional information about "why" the layoffs occurred and "why" you were included.
- Immediately begin telephoning or meeting with professional contacts. You want to adequately prepare to do so—both emotionally and psychologically.
- Immediately begin distributing résumés. Again, you need to do so in a planned and purposeful manner.

Services Typically Included in the "Package"

The outplacement specialist will introduce you to a variety of services and programs available to you. These typically fall into two categories: career management and transition management.

Career management services (involving personal counseling or a Web site) are designed to help you re-enter the job market. The services might include some form of:

- Professional Assessment

  This assessment may take the form of a one-on-one discussion or a pen-and-paper inventory. This assessment may, for example, help you examine your personal assets (your knowledge, skills, and abilities).
- Career/Job Assessment

  This assessment may also take the form of a one-on-one discussion or a pen-and-paper inventory. This enables you to assess your personal interests and assets within the context of the current job market.
- Career/Job Management Plan

  This may include your working with others to identify your career objectives or create your résumé, as well as to formulate your letter of introduction or cover letter.

Transition management services (involving personal counseling or a Web site) are designed to help you work through personal change issues. These services might include some form of:

- Personal Assessment

  This assessment may take the form of a one-on-one discussion or a pen-and-paper inventory. This assessment may, for example, help you understand your ability to tolerate risk, uncertainty, and ambiguity.

- Transition Management Plan

  This may include your working with others to identify your current state and define your desired state. Perhaps the most powerful component is your working with others to create a plan that can move you from where you are to where you would like to be/need to be/should be.

In addition, the outplacement specialist will introduce you to workshops and seminars designed to help you work through your personal and career transition.

The following two-day career development workshop is similar to one you may have an opportunity to attend:

Day 1

Morning

Dealing with Personal Transitions

Personal Skills Assessment

Creating Objectives

Developing the Résumé, Cover Letter, and Letter of Introduction

Afternoon

Marketing your Personal Skills

Identifying and Capitalizing on Current Opportunities

Tools and Techniques
- Recruiters
- Executive Search Firms
- Using the Internet in your Job Search

Capitalizing on your Personal Network

Day 2

Morning

Developing Your Skills and Abilities
- Asking Effective Questions
- The Job Interview
- Preparing for the Interview
- Interview Skills Development
- Practice Session
- Videotaping
- Personal Critique
- Personal Development Plan

Afternoon

Setting the Stage for Success
- Asking Effective Questions

- Negotiating Compensation
- Reviewing the Job Offer Letter

In addition to a career development workshop, the outplacement firm may offer some or all of the following support services:

- Industry and company directories;
  - Access to proprietary databases and research results;
  - Job leads from previously established networks;
  - Customized searches by industry, geographic location, or company;
  - On-line use of databases;
  - Access to personal e-mail accounts; and
  - Prepaid cellular telephone service.

Such services may prove to be invaluable as you re-enter the job market.

Outplacement Firms

You may receive outplacement services as part of your severance package. An organization external to your firm or company typically provides these services. Having worked with two leading outplacement firms, we can attest to the value they bring and to the services they provide.

Three firms (together having a total of almost four hundred offices) representative of the outplacement industry are:

- Challenger, Gray, & Christmas
  150 S. Wacker Drive #2700
  Chicago, IL 60606
  http://www.challengergray.com

- Lee Hecht Harrison
  50 Tice Boulevard
  Woodcliff Lake, NJ 07677
  http://www.lhh.com

- Manchester Partners International
  One Independent Drive
  Suite 206
  Jacksonville, FL 32202
  http://www.manchesterus.com

Review each firm's Web site (1) to learn more about the services such firms provide, and (2) to compare your outplacement services to those provided by these three leading firms.

In short, whether or not you consider them to be valuable, outplace-ment services are likely to be part of your severance package. This section has provided information you can take into consideration when assessing such services or when deciding whether or not to use them.

CONCLUSION

We have said it before, we will say it again: when it comes to being laid off, one must act rather than react. However, all resulting action must be planned and purposeful. All action must be equally effective and efficient. This chapter has provided resources that, if used, will enable you to move forward in an expeditious manner. chapter 9 provides additional informa-tion for you to consider and tools for you to apply, as you get "back down to business."

CHAPTER 9

A Prescription for Survival

Anyone can offer medical and legal information, but only licensed physicians and lawyers can give medical and legal advice. Information we provide in this chapter is general. It is not based on your specific set of medical or legal facts—as such, it is meant to serve as helpful information, rather than advice. As we have advised you before, you should contact an attorney or outplacement specialist for advice tailored specifically for you. With that said, the following important information will be useful to you!

We know quite a few folks who have been laid off. Our personal observations reveal that:

- No two took the news the same way;
- No two were prepared for the news emotionally or financially in the same way;
- No two progressed through the personal transition the same way (in terms of intensity or duration);
- No two approached the idea of "starting over" the same way; and
- No two rebounded precisely the same way.

All of us are different and must find the inner strength, in our own way, to deal with the forced transition in our lives. Outplacement will help, but you must be innovative and proactive in making your own progress to recovery.

Due to its very nature, no out-counseling session is routine. At a minimum, it upsets the personal life of the individual being laid off, as well as the lives of his or her family members.

Being laid off places you at risk. Your psychological and emotional make-up, financial situation, and personal support system determine the extent to which your life is disrupted. A clear majority of individuals laid off deal with the adversity and learn from the ordeal. Many eventually admit that being out-counseled is one of the best things that ever happened to their career. However, there are those whose paths back to leading a successful, productive life is not as straightforward. There are those whose personal situation and make-up are not conducive to their having a quick rebound. This chapter is for them.

WHEN TO CONSULT A MEDICAL PROFESSIONAL

A common theme throughout this toolkit has been that being laid off yields psychological and emotional stress. This is normal; you are normal if you feel stress after being laid off. The intensity and duration of that stress is determined in part by your emotional strength and psychological resiliency. Do not be afraid to ask for help. Remember, you are not alone. Thousands have lost their jobs this year. Many of them, feeling the same way you do, have reached out for help.

Your being laid off may be one of the greatest challenges your family has ever faced. Consider this to be an opportunity for your family members to better appreciate each other's strengths and weaknesses. This is when your family members can come together to offer mutual understanding and support. This is when your family may come together to understand—and take care of—individual and mutual needs.

I (B. K. S.) have been guided throughout much of my career by the following saying:

"Prescription, without proper diagnosis—regardless of the profession—is malpractice."

We encourage you to monitor each other's emotions and, if certain symptoms emerge, seek the advice of your family physician or other medical professional.

The National Institute of Mental Health (2001: On-line) and Jefferson and Greist (1998: 2) recommend that you seek the advice of a professional if symptoms emerge, persist over time, or interfere with your daily routine. They report that the following may be symptomatic of severe stress or clinical depression:

• Inability to focus on daily routine;
• Increase or decrease in appetite;
• Increase or decrease in sleep;
• Episodes of rage;

- Feelings of unworthiness;
- Thoughts of committing suicide;
- Thoughts of harming another;
- Changes in personal hygiene;
- Increased consumption of alcohol or drugs; and.
- Lack of interest in the life or activity of others.

If left unused, the value of such a checklist (and our including it in this toolkit) may be marginal. However, significant changes in behavior—like those described above—must be recognized and addressed.

Prescription, without proper diagnosis—regardless of the profession—is malpractice . . . even when the diagnosis is self-administered.

We encourage you to seek medical advice if such change in behavior (like those described above) surfaces—failure to do so is likely to result in a cycle that goes something like this:

Step 1: You are laid off.

Step 2: This results in your being psychologically and emotionally disrupted.

Step 3: The disruption leads to one or more of the symptoms listed above.

Step 4: The symptoms you exhibit hinder your ability to become employed.

Step 5: You recognize your inability to become employed.

Step 6: This results in your being further disrupted.

Step 7: This disruption leads to additional and/or more intense symptoms.

Step 8: These symptoms magnify your inability to gain employment.

Step 9: The cycle repeats itself, increasing in intensity and/or duration.

To prevent such a cycle from causing serious damage to yourself, your career, and your family, we encourage you, with the help of your informal support group, to assess your psychological and emotional state. As needed, seek the advice of your personal physician or medical professional.

Information about relevant resources is provided later in this chapter.

WHEN TO CONSULT AN ATTORNEY

We live in a very complex world. No one can be expected to think of everything, much less know everything. Do not be afraid to seek the help of an expert to uncomplicate your life. Just as you may seek medical help for a physical issue or psychological help for psychological or emotional issues, you should seek legal help for complicated legal issues.

No longer is the world made up of individuals loyal to their organizations and of organizations willing to reduce partner or shareholder value instead of cutting jobs. Similarly, gone are the days where trust or a handshake was sufficient to bind us.

Instead, we find ourselves in a world characterized by employment contracts and severance agreements. Similarly, we find ourselves reading two- and three-page job offer letters that conclude by saying "this written job offer does not constitute a contract."

In such a world—to be prudent—you may need to seek the advice of an attorney when undergoing an involuntary career or job change. Such a suggestion may raise the following questions:

- What if a potential employer finds out I have consulted an attorney?
- What if my previous employer finds out I have retained an attorney?
- What if the attorney says everything looks appropriate? Have I not just wasted $200 to $400?

Our response is simple:

Prescription, without proper diagnosis—regardless of the profession—is malpractice . . . even when the "prescription" is your accepting and adhering to a Separation Agreement without knowing (through "proper diagnosis") whether or not the Agreement is adequate and/or appropriate. Note we did not say "legal" or "legally binding."

Our proposed answers to the questions in the bullet points above are:

- If your previous employer finds out you consulted an attorney, he or she may be relieved. If the Older Workers Benefits Protection Act applies to you, your Severance Agreement, which most likely contains a release, must advise you to seek the advice of an attorney before signing. If the statute does not apply to you, your former employer will not be surprised, shocked, or upset if you consult an attorney, because doing so is protective, not antagonistic. It is more routine than you may think.
- It is unlikely that a potential employer will find out you contacted an attorney, unless you say so. If the employer does find out, do not be concerned. Rest assured the potential employer has contacted an attorney for advice on employment matters (drafting employment agreements, employee handbooks, policy manuals, etc.).

- If the attorney tells you the Severance Agreement looks appropriate, have you wasted the amount you paid for that analysis and opinion? When you feel sick, go to the doctor and find out your symptoms will pass without treatment, have you wasted your money for the doctor's services? Of course not. In many cases, the fee you pay for an expert attorney's opinion is worth the psychological comfort of knowing that your rights are protected. You will undoubtedly second-guess yourself if you preemptively agree to a severance agreement without fully investigating both the facts and the law. Your attorney is trained to do that for you.

In response to concerns about how other people may view your contacting an attorney, we encourage you to shift your viewpoint so the following questions seem more appropriate:

- Is it not in everyone's (your and your family's) best interest for someone to review and provide counsel on severance stipulations and conditions? Of course it is!
  - Is this not true, especially when a job offer letter or employment contract is involved?
- Did your employer obtain legal counsel before crafting its Separation Agreement and conducting its layoff? Of course it did!
  - If so, should you not also be allowed to seek the advice of an attorney?
  - If not, is it not that much more important for an attorney to review the Agreement for adequacy and appropriateness? An uninformed employer may inadvertently induce you to waive rights to compensation or benefits.
- Should you not make an informed decision? Of course you should.
  - At a minimum, will not the investment of $200 to $400 help ensure that you are making an informed decision about whether to accept or reject the Separation Agreement?

Although it may be prudent for anyone being laid off to seek legal advice, many will not wish to do so because of personal, financial, or ethical reasons. Others will not wish to do so unless there is an obvious, compelling reason. If this is your viewpoint, consider seeking legal advice if your agreement does not include information about the following:

- Provision of outplacement services;
- When you will receive your final paycheck;
- Length of salary continuance or amount of severance pay;
- Your eligibility for accrued and unused vacation time;
- Continuance of your group insurance;
- COBRA benefits and unemployment insurance;
- Forgiveness of sign-on bonus or relocation and educational assistance;
- Your eligibility for previously earned performance bonuses or commissions;
- Your eligibility for vested portion of the organization's pension program; and
- Provisions for stipulations outlined in your job offer letter.

Your seeking legal advice extends far beyond your finding out about whether or not your Separation Agreement is legal or legally binding—it involves your being able to make informed decisions about the adequacy and appropriateness of its stipulations.

For more detailed information, refer to relevant resources (including American Bar Association publications) cited in the next section.

Prescription, without proper diagnosis—regardless of the profession—is malpractice.

USEFUL RESOURCES

In addition to the resources we introduce elsewhere in this book, we strongly encourage you to access the following ones, should the need arise. Prudence dictates your considering these additional resources; the need for a well-balanced career transition necessitates incorporating these resources into your career transition Action Plan.

Mental Health Agencies

If you, alone or with the help of others, feel you need information on depression and other stress disorders, contact your personal physician or one of the following organizations:

- National Institute of Mental Health
  6001 Executive Blvd., Room 8184, MSC 9663
  Bethesda, MD 20892–9663
  1–800–421–4211
  http://www.nimh.nih.gov

- National Mental Health Association
  1021 Prince Street
  Alexandria, VA 22314–2971
  1–800–969-NMHA
  http://www.nmha.org

- National Alliance for the Mentally Ill
  Colonial Place Three
  2107 Wilson Blvd., Suite 300
  Arlington, VA 22201–3042
  1–800–950-NAMI
  http://www.nami.org

- Depression/Awareness, Recognition and Treatment
  National Institute of Mental Health
  5600 Fishers Lane
  Rockville, MD 20857
  1–800–421–4211

These organizations can give you more detailed information about depression and other stress disorders. Your physician can also diagnose symptoms, prescribe solutions, or refer you to more appropriate resources.

We strongly encourage you to learn more about depression and stress, and what you can do about them. Obtain information from your physician, your local mental health clinic or center, or from the organizations listed above. In the meantime, Mitchell Halper, M.D., a psychiatrist recognized throughout the Chicago area, has a few ideas for you to consider. Here are the results of an interview with Dr. Halper, presented in the form of questions and answers.

1. Various companies and firms, because of the downturn in the economy, have recently laid off scores of employees. As a result of these job losses, have you experienced an increase in clients?

   I have not experienced an increase in clients. It may be due to the fact that many prospective clients are currently pursuing job opportunities or have already attained other jobs. The issue is what will occur if the economy does not rebound: six or nine months from now, will those still without jobs get through this economic downturn relatively unscathed?

   I do have several patients who have been laid off. Unfortunately, it is taking them a long time to enter into new positions. They appear to be effectively managing their job loss—they are reconnecting with family members, thinking about next steps regarding their careers, and spending more time on various aspects of their lives. Viewing their situation as a positive rather than a negative, and as an opportunity rather than failure, opens them up to a whole new world of possibilities.

2. Based on your experience, how much stress does a job loss typically cause—for example, does it equate to the loss of a family member or to one's getting a divorce?

   Job loss is not the same type of stressor as the loss of a family member or one's getting a divorce. As I previously mentioned, the way you perceive this event will determine the extent to which it impacts your life. Whether you interpret this event as a gain or a loss influences the extent to which it increases your anxiety and stress level.

3. When you initially meet with a client, you invariably determine why he or she decided to seek your assistance. What are some reasons typically cited by individuals experiencing a layoff or other form of job loss?

   Reasons they cite are symptomatic of a post-traumatic stress disorder. They frequently experience sleeplessness, loss of appetite, increased anxiety, fear, and anger. In some cases, they experience periods of withdrawal. While such periods are typically brief and may not be noticeable to the individual, family members and close friends are likely to notice them.

4. Expanding on this answer a bit, what warning signs do individuals typically exhibit that suggest he or she should seek professional help?

The duration and magnitude of the symptoms I just described impact whether they are short-term, anxiety-related, or obvious warning signs. Clearly, when these symptoms negatively impact a person's life, he or she should seek professional help.

An interesting point to make here is that we are talking about people. People are different in the way they act and in how they react. Different people respond differently (psychologically and emotionally) to the news of their being laid off or discharged. For example, as I previously stated, people typically experience sleeplessness and loss of appetite. However, the exact opposite—increased sleep and increased appetite—also frequently occurs!

5. Before seeking the assistance of a professional, you must first realize you need help. When an individual begins exhibiting these warning signs, do they themselves or do their family and friends typically recognize them?

My experience suggests the individual typically recognizes that he or she needs help. They realize they are not sleeping well or that they are not eating properly. If such realization does not occur, family members and close friends typically will eventually notice the results—for example, they will notice increased irritability associated with sleep loss or weight loss associated with loss of appetite.

6. If some of our readers feel a family member should seek professional help, how do you recommend they approach their family member with such advice?

If you feel a family member needs help, you must openly communicate your feelings with that person. You must let him or her know that you are concerned, and what contributed to that concern. You must assure the individual that you are bringing this up not out of ridicule or shame, but out of love and compassion. It is important for you to reassure the individual that at times things occur in life that are beyond anyone's control. It is equally important for you to send the message that this is one of those times and that "we, you and I, will work together to get through this."

If you feel a family member needs help, you must think before acting. You should think about what you will say and the manner in which you will say it. You should think about what you will say, so your words express concern and compassion, rather than insult or ridicule. You should think about how you will approach the individual, so your behavior reflects concern and compassion, rather than aggression or hostility.

7. Once individuals realize they need help, what should their first step be—for example, should they contact their personal physician, report to the nearest emergency room, or refer to the Yellow Pages?

Because a relationship already exists between individuals and their personal physician, I recommend they contact their physician. Not only are physicians skilled in diagnosing symptoms and can refer individuals to mental health specialists, they operate under principles of strict confidentiality. The relationship that exists between patient and physician is built on trust. Individuals exhibiting stress-related symptoms resulting from a job loss should rely on that trust and seek the help of their physician.

Individuals, perhaps afraid of being embarrassed, occasionally will not turn to their physician for help even though it is in their best interest to do so. If you need help and are reluctant to speak with your physician, I encourage you to reconsider. Then, if you are still not willing to speak with your physician, I recommend you contact your local mental health clinic or center. As a final option, I recommend that you refer to your local Yellow Pages.

8. Some companies include Employee Assistance Program (EAP) benefits in their severance packages. Are such benefits helpful, and—from the individual's point of view—to be trusted?

Employee Assistance Programs are extremely valuable. They are typically administered by a third-party provider and therefore ensure absolute confidentiality. Health care professionals associated with such programs are generally extremely knowledgeable, are very committed to their profession, and will diligently work with the individual to address psychological and emotional issues surfacing as a result of a job loss.

If offered EAP benefits as part of a severance package, you should assume the benefits will be helpful and the process can be trusted. I strongly encourage you to seek professional assistance through an EAP program, if such assistance is part of your severance or outplacement package.

9. We are told that—regardless of our current fitness level—exercise and diet significantly contribute to our physical well-being. What can we do to contribute to our general mental well-being?

First, recognize this event for what it is—an event. It will not only pass, it may lead to a higher standard of living. See this as an opportunity to re-establish connections with your family and friends. See this as giving you the time to pursue that long-forgotten hobby. See this as a chance to consider other professions or occupations. At the same time, be open with your emotions! Openly discuss your situation, your job search, and your feelings about both. Throughout it all, keep in the back of your mind that you may end up in a position that is much more fulfilling than your previous one. That frequently is the case, at least for a clear majority of my patients.

Second, try to avoid "harshness" in all its forms. Limit your caffeine and sugar intake. Watch your diet—do not eat foods likely to make you feel bad. Limit your alcohol intake, for exactly the same reason. Try to get plenty of fresh air and (something that is too frequently overlooked) sunshine! Of course, exercise. Exercise, in all its forms, truly is an anti-depressant.

Finally, reach out to your family and friends. Remain connected, openly and frequently communicate with them. They have been there during the good times; rely on them to be there for you (and with you) during the challenging times.

10. While organizations such as the National Institute of Mental Health and the National Mental Health Association provide useful information on the topic of mental health, how else might an individual obtain information of a general nature?

NIMH and NMHA provide very useful information. In addition to information, however, an individual experiencing a job loss needs support. That support frequently is in the form of family and friends. Extend that support network to include members of the local mental health community, such as counselors at the local mental health clinic or center. In addition, check the telephone directory to see if NAMI (the National Alliance for the Mentally Ill) has a local chapter in your area. This is a top-notch organization; it provides a lot of support and personal attention to those in need.

11. This book has several audiences: employees, employers, and academia. As a mental health professional, what one message would you like to share with each of these audiences?

To employees: at times, things beyond our control occur. These occurrences make us feel bad. They frighten us, they anger us. At a minimum, they make us realize there are things in life we simply do not control. When faced with such a challenge, it is important that we not focus only on the negative. We must be optimistic, rather than pessimistic. We must move forward, one day at a time, knowing that this event will lead to something better. We must move forward with the belief that this will ultimately yield a higher quality of life, in terms of our focus, our attitude, and our relationship with family and friends. We must also realize that at times we may become frightened and angry. When this occurs, we must be willing to share these feelings with our family. If we can't get beyond such feelings, we must accept the fact that it is OK to seek the help of a personal physician or a mental health professional.

To employers: you must keep in mind you are dealing with people and not machines, computers, or numbers. Again, keep in mind that you are dealing with people! People whom, until hours or days ago, were your colleagues, associates, and friends. You must realize job loss is significant; it impacts individuals in many ways. No two people are likely to accept "bad" news in exactly the same way. You, the bearer of this particular news, must realize that one's emotional reaction is not only natural, it is to be expected. You must also realize that strong emotions associated with feelings of loss of control are normal. You must let the individual experience these emotions and work through them. Only then can true healing begin. By allowing the individual to work through such emotions, you treat the individual in the manner in which he or she deserves to be treated—with respect and dignity. All too often I read where individuals being laid off or discharged are given the news by telephone or, worse yet, are immediately escorted (sometimes by armed guards) out the door. As the employer, you must help change this business reality—such incidents should no longer occur!

To academia: change is continuous, it is inevitable. You must prepare your students for events and situations reflective of such change. Whether they are the employer or employee, they must become sensitive to issues surrounding layoffs and discharges. If they are being laid off or discharged, they must attempt to shift their focus and consider the event to be an opportunity for self-improvement. If they are performing the layoff or discharge, they must attempt to do so in a manner that allows the employee to perceive it as an opportunity for personal growth. Regardless of the role the student plays, he or she must willingly seek—and offer—personal support.

12. A final question: as a mental health professional, what one message would you like to share with those individuals who have been, are about to be, or who are at the risk of experiencing a job loss?

You will survive a job loss. You might even thrive in a job loss. If it looks like it may happen, prepare yourself mentally and emotionally (and of course, financially). If it does happen to you, try to maintain a healthy, positive perspective. If it has already happened to you, see this as a time for personal growth. Reconnect with family and friends. In terms of this particular life event and its many implications—think about it, talk about it, and be open to its countless possibilities. Life is a journey consisting of many straight-aways and turns. In terms of this portion of your journey, know that you will come out the other side (in all likelihood) a much more complete and compassionate person.

Legal Resources

The most useful legal resource you will find is your own attorney. When faced with having to find an attorney, most do not know where to turn. Maybe we hired an attorney to handle the real estate closing when we bought our house, or we hired an attorney to prepare our taxes or will, but is he or she qualified to advise me in employment law matters? A good place to start a search for the right attorney is friends and colleagues. Ask whether any of them knows of an attorney specializing in employment law. Another resource is the local (city, county, or state) bar association. Most bar associations have attorney referral services, some of which are accessible by telephone. Attorneys designate their areas of specialty to the bar association, which will provide referrals based on the legal need of the caller.

Once you get the names of attorneys who specialize in your area of need, interview them by telephone and meet them in person. Some attorneys do not charge for an initial consultation, but most will charge a modest consultation fee for matters like employment law issues.

Choosing an attorney is a very personal issue. You should feel comfortable enough with your attorney to tell him or her uncomfortable facts about your situation. An attorney can represent you zealously and competently only if you arm him or her with all of the facts, "warts" and all. Keep in mind that all states honor the attorney-client privilege. Anything you disclose to your attorney in connection with seeking legal advice (with some inapplicable exceptions such as your plan to commit a crime), and anything your attorney tells you in the nature of advice, is privileged and cannot be disclosed without your consent. Feel comfortable telling all.

When selecting an attorney, your priorities should be to choose someone who is competent and whom you trust. While an initial one-hour meeting may seem inadequate for this purpose, after the meeting, ask yourself:

• Did the attorney ask me to describe the facts in sufficient detail or were we rushed?
• Did the attorney ask questions that showed his or her understanding of the issues?
• Did the attorney identify issues needing research or investigation?
• Did the attorney identify an action plan?
• Did you like the attorney?
• Did you feel like the attorney understood you?

The attorney-client relationship is very personal. Remember, attorneys are both legal technicians and counselors. The most suitable attorney for you is the person with whom you feel the most trust and confidence. As technician, your attorney will work behind the scenes for you to research, investigate, and implement a legal strategy. As counselor, the attorney has to be there for you—and you must feel comfortable relying on your attorney.

Some people and self-help resource providers (usually at their profit) suggest you can represent yourself in simple legal matters. Maybe— maybe not. Rarely should you feel capable of representing yourself. Attorneys have a cliché: "An attorney who represents himself has a fool for a client." Rarely should you represent yourself.

This is not to say, however, that you should not educate yourself as to the issues facing you. Means to identify those issues and to obtain a basic understanding of them (which may assist you in communicating your issues of concern to your attorney) are available over the Internet. Even attorneys subscribe to Internet resources to conduct current-up-to-the-second legal research. Do not, however, rely on Internet sources for legal advice. The generic information they provide may be useful in identifying issues for you, but only an attorney familiar with you, your facts, and your state's laws can give you competent and applicable legal advice.

Due to the changing nature of the law, the authors of this book are not responsible for information, advice, or services provided by any Internet site, even those to which we refer here. Although we list several Web sites and organizations, we do not endorse any particular site or service and are affiliated with none of them (except the American Bar Association, of which M. D. M is a long-time member).

With that said, here are several commercial Web sites you may find useful:

- http://www.findlaw.com
- http://www.freeadvice.com
- http://www.gottrouble.com
- http://www.lawstreet.com
- http://www.lawyers.com
- http://www.legal.net

These and similar sites may give you valuable information. Just keep in mind they may also attempt to sell you books or legal forms. Certain sites may also attempt to induce you to hire an attorney who is listed on the site.

Since many laws are state-specific, we encourage you to obtain needed information from your local bar association or your state's Supreme Court.

Excellent information, including when you might need to hire an attorney, is available in several American Bar Association publications (ABA 2001: On-line). The ABA, consisting of more than 400,000 members, is the largest professional association in the world.

Contact the ABA at:

- American Bar Association
  740 15th Street
  Washington, DC 20005–1019

To save time, you may wish to contact the following division:

- ABA Division for Public Education
  541 N. Fairbanks Court, 15.3
  Chicago, IL 60611–3314

Three ABA books may provide useful information:

- *The ABA Family Legal Guide*
  752 pages
  Available through the publisher at 800–726–0600 (ISBN 0–8129–2361–8)
  Available through the ABA at 800–285–2221 (order number 235–0024)

- *The ABA Guide to Workplace Law*
  196 pages
  Available through the publisher at 800–726–0600 (ISBN 0–8129–2928–4)
  Available through the ABA at 800–285–2221 (order number 235–0038)

- *The ABA Legal Guide for Older Americans*
  232 pages
  Available through the publisher at 800–726–0600 (ISBN 0–8129–2937–3)
  Available through the ABA at 800–285–2221 (order number 235–0040)

CONCLUSION

In this chapter, we presented information about resources you might find helpful during your career transition. The prescription we recommend is seek the advice of professionals when you need it. The information we provide here is not legal or medical advice, but a means to help you know when you need it. We recommend using mental health and legal resources available over the Internet and within easy reach by telephone and through the mail to help you identify your need for professional advice and then to reach out in person to obtain it.

The next chapter ("Loading and Using Your Toolkit") describes how to apply the information we have provided. The appendix presents tools, along with information about their appropriate use, that you may wish to use during your transition. These tools, introduced and applied in previous chapters, are reproduced as templates to ensure ease of use.

CHAPTER 10

Loading and Using Your Toolkit

Throughout this book we have used the metaphor of using our toolkit to help ensure a successful career transition after being laid off or discharged. How you approach the process is in many ways as important as the tools you use. Maintain the right frame of mind and attitude despite your ordeal. Use your skills and abilities, and our tools, constructively toward achieving your goal of advancing your career. In this chapter, we will guide you through this process.

WHAT MUST I DO IMMEDIATELY?

You have left the out-counseling session at which you were told you would no longer be employed after a two-week transition period (or even at 5:00 P.M. today!). You are at a loss as to what to do. What to do certainly is important. That is the point of using the tools we propose in this book. How you do it, however, is equally important.

Your mind-set and behavioral control can be as important in this process as your skill level, which tools you use, and how you use them. We have emphasized many times that employers must treat employees, especially in the layoff process, with dignity and respect. You, too, must act with dignity and treat both yourself and your soon-to-be-former employer with respect.

Maintaining your integrity and your self-respect go hand in hand. Early in my legal career, I (M. D. M.) had the benefit of having as my mentor Michael W. Coffield, voted by his peers in *The American Lawyer* to be among the country's one hundred best trial attorneys. Mike taught me many valuable lessons in life and law early in my career. One memorable lesson was: "As attorneys we have no product to sell—we have only our integrity and ability. If we lose our integrity, we lose everything, because there are thousands of able attorneys out there." These words of wisdom have guided me throughout my career. They should guide you as well during this difficult time.

We safeguard our integrity by acting with the same dignity and respect we expect from our employers. No doubt you will feel indignant when you are laid off. No doubt you will feel that your employer inflicted a personal indignity upon you by laying you off. Nevertheless, we must recognize indignation as a feeling, not a fact—a destructive one at that. We must rise above the indignity. How you react to the trauma of being laid off will determine how quickly and successfully you rebound. In our experience, we have seen many laid-off employees dwell in disbelief and obsess about what has happened to them. They react emotionally and spitefully, not being able to accept the fact of the layoff. "How could they do that to me after all I've done for them?"

This perspective is not productive. In many cases, employees are laid off through no fault of their own. In such cases, there is nothing to be taken personally. If your conduct is driven by spite, instead of striving for your personal career goal, you are destined to lose your focus on the prize— new employment.

By maintaining your dignity and integrity, you also will bolster your self-respect. Your self-respect will be essential in maintaining the positive, constructive attitude you will have to display in your job search. You also will earn the respect of your friends, family, colleagues, former employer, and potential employers. This, of course, also will benefit your job search. A calm, rational, respectful approach always will serve you better than an emotional, impulsive effort to seek retribution. Treat your former employer in the same dignified and respectful manner you expect to be treated. If you defame, bad-mouth, berate, and blame your former employer for your predicament, your integrity and reputation will suffer, not that of your former employer.

By showing respect to your former employer, you may well earn its respect and cooperation in your career transition. Many of your colleagues with your former employer may be your best advocates, references, and sources for job leads. Their respect for you will continue and increase if you take the high road in dealing with your transition. Showing respect for your former employer and its management (whether or not you agree with management decisions) will enhance your self-respect and your reputation and others' inclination to help you.

For example, we urge you to respect your former employer's property and rights just as you demand respect for yours. Just as your employer must not wrongfully discriminate against you, must not violate your contract rights, and must provide you all of the benefits to which you are entitled under any contract, employee handbook, policy manual, or statute, you must not violate your employer's rights.

Your former employer has the right to expect that you respect and maintain the confidentiality of information such as trade secrets, confidential training materials, proprietary production processes, and private sales and marketing information. Your employer has the right to expect you to return all of its property. A common problem employees bring upon themselves intentionally or inadvertently is taking or failing to return property belonging to the employer. For example, many (innocent) employees who occasionally work at home may keep files at home that rightfully belong to the employer. Those documents must be returned. Other (not-so-innocent) employees copy or take confidential information such as customer lists, customer names and addresses, customer account statements, sales histories, work product, or correspondence generated during their former employment hoping to derive a benefit from it in their future employment.

The law takes a very dim view of employees' misappropriating the employer's property or confidential information. Simply because you gathered the information during your employment, or because it was the product of your efforts, does not make it your property. After all, you were paid what you were entitled to for the work; you are not entitled to take the work product, too.

Just as the law takes a dim view of misappropriation, so should you. Engaging in such behavior is not only unlawful, but it also damages your integrity. You cannot afford that. When you lose your integrity, you also lose your self-respect and the respect of others.

The following "war story" demonstrates how devastating misappropriating documents from your employer can be. A client once came to us with a very credible case of both sexual harassment and pregnancy discrimination. She was discharged from her sales position on the basis of allegedly poor sales performance. She had not made her annual quota of sales. She had previously been subjected to sexually harassing conduct and derogatory comments about her appearance because of her pregnancy. She had filed a Charge of Discrimination with the Equal Employment Opportunity Commission, and the employer had filed its response, before she retained us.

She explained to us that after she was told of her discharge, a co-worker friend of hers allowed her to use his password (hers had been canceled) to access the secure portion of the company's Web site, and she downloaded regional sales results showing conclusively that her sales were above the average of her male counterparts. This was evidence that the employer's stated reason for discharging her—poor sales performance—was a pretext for sex and pregnancy discrimination.

She had the proof, all right. Proof that she was a thief! She had a credible case of discrimination under Title VII of the Civil Rights Act of 1964, but she lost it herself because she lost her credibility and integrity by mis-appropriating her employer's confidential information. The sad part of this story is that had she taken the high road and simply contacted an attorney to review her rights, the attorney could have obtained this infor-mation legally simply by issuing a written discovery request, even if the material were allegedly confidential. When you lose your integrity, you lose your self-respect . . . and more.

When faced with the difficult and emotional situation of losing your job, remember always to maintain your dignity, integrity, and self-respect. Most likely, your support network, professional colleagues, and potential employers will notice and respect you even more.

HOW DO I LOAD MY TOOLKIT?

With your reputation, dignity, and self-respect intact, you are ready to move forward. The first question is, "Where do I start?"

At the beginning, naturally. Where do all investigations start? To quote Sergeant Joe Friday of *Dragnet* fame, "Just the facts, ma'am."

Before you can decide your strategy, you must assess the facts con-fronting you. When you accepted the job, you signed many documents and your employer probably gave you several documents. Perhaps you signed an employment agreement; a confidentiality agreement; an inven-tion agreement; an agreement not to compete; or an acknowledgement and receipt together with an employee handbook or employment policy manual. These documents will form the basis of the analysis of your rights and the propriety of your employer's actions in light of your rights. Gath-ering the facts and documents relating to your employment is very impor-tant. It is just the beginning, however, of your homework.

If you kept a journal of your experiences at work, as we suggest, you are an attorney's dream. Most of us, however, have little more than a calendar or perhaps a "chron file." (That is a chronological compilation of corre-spondence you wrote during your employment. Such correspondence belongs to your employer. Leave it where it belongs—with your former employer.) The best you can do is to gather what your employer gave you at the inception of your employment and during your employment. It is important for you to re-create your employment history for your benefit and for your lawyer to review in determining whether you are entitled to compensation of any kind upon the termination of your employment.

The most basic human response to being fired or laid off is to ask, "Why?" You may well have information from which you may glean an answer (if there is one—remember, at-will employees may be let go for no reason). It is unusual, but not unheard of, for employers to provide copies of perfor-mance reviews to employees. Presumably, your performance appraisals will reflect your employer's assessment of your performance. We say presumably, because we often see employees who have been discharged after receiving good or above-average performance reviews. They receive those positive reviews often because the reviewer, a supervisor/colleague, is reluctant to upset the employee or their relationship with a negative rating. This "dishonest" review serves no one. When this happens, the employee is left to wonder why he or she lost the job, only to conclude, because of the positive reviews, "It must have been discrimination." Discussing honesty in the performance appraisal process is beyond the scope of this chapter, but bear in mind what we discussed in chapter 3. We all are at risk. At-will employment is perhaps the riskiest because you may lose it for a good reason, a bad reason, or no reason at all.

After gathering all of the documents that belong to you (note the not-too-subtle reminder not to keep or take any documents belonging to your employer), try to create a timeline of your job history and annotate it with key facts. This will be invaluable when discussing your situation with your attorney. By the way, it also will save you money—attorney's fees—because you will have done much of the background factual work that your attorney will have to review in analyzing your rights.

Other facts and issues you should describe in your timeline are events that preceded, precipitated, or predicted your job loss. For example, your employer may have been experiencing economic difficulties or changes in market conditions, upon which the decision was made. These are issues you will discuss with your attorney when deciding the propriety of your discharge or layoff. They probably will be the stated reasons for your discharge or layoff, to counter any claim of wrongful discharge or discrimination. Your attorney must know these facts.

Finally, while the events are clear in your mind, write in narrative form with as many quotations as possible the story of your final meetings with your employer. Who said what, to whom, and when? These are questions your attorney will ask.

After gathering all of your facts, it is time to formulate a strategy. You may decide to contact an attorney to help you analyze the facts and plan a strategy. In chapter 9 we discussed when to consult an attorney. We should reemphasize the nature of your relationship with your attorney. You probably have heard the term *fiduciary* used in relation to holding funds on behalf of another person. An attorney is in a fiduciary relationship with clients. The word *fiduciary* is derived from the Latin word *fiducia*, which means *trust*. Developing the fiduciary relationship, you and your attorney will develop a close professional relationship based on trust. You must trust your attorney's competence. You have the right to trust and expect his or her diligence and zealous advocacy of your rights.

Your attorney must trust you, too. Your attorney must trust that you will relate the facts concerning your employment accurately and fully so he or she can render accurate and appropriate advice. You will benefit from disclosing all of the facts candidly and completely. Your attorney cannot formulate a winning strategy or give you reliable advice based on incomplete or shaded facts. Tell the truth, the whole truth.

In difficult employment situations, the benefits of hiring an attorney to advise you and act on your behalf may not be obvious to you. Your former employer probably will prefer to discuss your rights and obligations with your attorney, and most likely will prefer to discuss them in writing. Right or wrong, your employer may feel more willing to discuss your situation with "someone who speaks the language" of employment law, rather than directly with you. Your employer's representatives probably have attorneys reviewing your severance arrangements and will not agree to any changes in the severance package or the Severance Agreement without their approval. In the forefront or the background, it is likely that attorneys are making or documenting every decision as to your benefit package.

A second reason your employer may prefer dealing through your attorney instead of with you directly is to avoid doing anything or saying anything that you may use against it in the event litigation ensues. The same holds true for you. Your attorney should handle your negotiations and severance arrangements on your behalf to avoid your saying or doing something to damage your rights.

From your perspective, a valuable benefit of seeking the advice of an attorney is obtaining his or her experience and ability to marshal the facts and apply the facts to the law. That is what attorneys are trained to do. Your initial response to being fired or laid off will be: "They had no right!" An attorney's response will be: "First I have to investigate the facts; then I will research the law; only then can I determine your rights."

This reasoned approach may not seem satisfactory at first. You will want your lawyer to tell you: "You were wronged! We'll sue!" While emotionally satisfying, such a premature response may not satisfy your attorney's fiduciary duty to you. The trust that forms the fiduciary relationship includes your trust in the honesty of your attorney's advice, satisfying or not. This parallels our suggestion that you not let your emotions override your common sense to the detriment of your reputation and integrity. Neither should your attorney give you the easy answer just to please you. Your attorney will look at the situation with more objective eyes. Your attorney's obligation to you is not to be a yes man (or woman), but to be honest with you, even if it means doing nothing or taking what your employer offers.

You and your attorney have much work to do to prepare your position. Many trial attorneys liken their role in the courtroom to that of a teacher. To represent my client competently, I (M. D. M.) must know the facts and the law better than anyone else in the courtroom. That is where you come into play. You provide the facts to your attorney completely and honestly. That is the ammunition your attorney needs to do battle for you.

If I am the teacher in the courtroom, the judge and the jury are my pupils. My job is to marshal all of the evidence, package it, and present it so clearly and so convincingly that only one conclusion follows: my client prevails.

This scenario is certainly the ideal, but again, do not expect your attorney always to give you satisfying answers, much less the answer most profitable to you. Frequently, after a diligent investigation of the facts and legal research, we attorneys determine that although the client feels wronged, no evidence of legally wrongful conduct sufficient to file a lawsuit in good faith exists. Just as you must be forthright and honest with your attorney, your attorney has the ethical and fiduciary obligation to be honest with you. The honest answer may be you do not have a claim.

As we have said repeatedly, at-will employment is inherently risky. There may be no satisfying reason for your employer's actions—nor need there be one. You may disagree with your employer's choices, and you may be able to prove your employer's decision was incorrect. Unfortunately, there is no law against bad business decisions. Likewise, many people do not understand that there is no law against discrimination. Your employer can discriminate against you, as long as the basis of the discrimination is not unlawful (for example, it is unlawful to discriminate on the basis of race, sex, ethnic background, and age). As unfair as it seems to laid-off employees, it is not unlawful for an employer to discriminate against one employee in favor of another for some other reason; for example, in favor of a relative of the owner, a supervisor, a shareholder, or a partner. Our point here is not to endorse or approve discriminatory reasons employers may give to rationalize discharging or laying off an employee. Our point is that not all discrimination is unlawful, not every discharge is wrongful, and not every layoff is inappropriate.

Whether it is in your best interest to litigate or negotiate your rights can be a difficult issue. Judges and mediators often say that any settlement is better than a bad result at trial; and a good settlement is one where both parties walk away pleased that it is over, but not completely satisfied. That is the essence of compromise. Your attorney will explain this to you and discuss the benefits and costs of litigation.

The potential benefits of litigation are more readily apparent than the actual and potential costs. The potential benefits, of course, include compensation and benefits your employer may not have offered initially. The costs, of course, include filing fees and attorney's fees. There are hidden costs, as well.

Another true "war story" will help me (M. D. M.) make this point. A man I know had worked for a large, stable employer for over thirty-five years. From before World War II, through the prosperity of the 1950s, the troubled 1960s, and the stagflation of the 1970s, he had been a dedicated "company man." Through his intelligence, ability, and dedication, he rose through the

ranks from apprentice to journeyman to supervisor to district superinten-
dent. As he approached sixty years of age, the baby boomers were coming
of age, armed with their youth and M.B.A.s. The "old-timers" had experience and years of dedicated service in their favor, but the new economy
valued youth and college degrees. This employer, a utility/monopoly (at
least before the Justice Department induced the break-up of this telecommunications giant), decided it was time for a youth campaign, and this old-
timer, with unparalleled experience but no degree, was given a choice:
early retirement or outright discharge.

In his mid-fifties, he was out of a job. The hurt was deep, for him and his
family. This man is my father. I was fresh out of law school and working
as a law clerk for a federal judge. Full of vim and vigor, I discussed with
my father the possibility of filing an action under the Age Discrimination
in Employment Act. I also discussed the issue with my boss, retired U.S.
District Judge Frank J. McGarr. With many years of experience as a trial
attorney and judge, he provided us an invaluable perspective.

The litigation process is a wonderful means to discover the truth and
redress injustice. Positive results and the vindication of your rights can
turn your life around after a great loss. Reaching that result, however, is
not immediate. Nor is it without emotional costs. First, a claimant must
file a Charge of Discrimination with the Equal Employment Opportunity
Commission. This is a prerequisite to filing an employment discrimination case in federal court. Months later, if no settlement is reached, the
EEOC will issue a Right to Sue Letter, and a lawsuit can be filed. After the
lawsuit is filed, the plaintiff and defendant enter the discovery process,
exchanging documents and taking depositions, a procedure in which
attorneys ask witnesses questions to answer under oath and a court
reporter records the questions and answers. Only after the discovery stage
is concluded can the case go to trial. This process, from the EEOC to trial,
can take several years.

The judge noted that during these years, the litigants often cannot get
on with their lives. They anxiously await vindication of their rights at trial
and defer their recovery, their lives, and their futures until they get "their
day in court." The emotional cost of living daily with the unfortunate fact
of losing your employment and deferring your recovery can be enormous.
A better route to recovery often is negotiating fair severance terms and
diving back into the workforce.

My father listened to the judge's perspective and negotiated his early
retirement. He then used tools we propose in our toolkit, including using
his professional network to explore the market for experienced telecommunications experts. Through his networking efforts, he learned that a
state university system needed someone with his experience. He became
the head of the university's telecommunications department and
remained in that position until he retired—on his timetable.

Our point is not to dissuade you from pursuing litigation. Rather, it is important to weigh the costs and benefits of any strategy you and your attorney determine is available. You may decide that litigation is the best, or only, alternative. If that is the case, do your homework by gathering and investigating the facts in as much detail as possible and then decide whether you should retain an attorney to assist you in formulating and implementing your strategy.

Either way, we recommend moving simultaneously on several fronts. While your attorney is working on a legal strategy, you should be using the tools we suggest and load your own toolkit. Perform your self-assessment, as we outline in chapters 5 and 6; develop your Action Plan, as we suggest in chapter 8; and review our suggestions in chapter 3, "Bulletproofing Your Career," for ideas to get your name out to the employment marketplace. While your attorney is at work for you, you will be at work advancing your career—or developing a new one!

MY TOOLKIT IS LOADED—NOW WHAT?

Your toolkit is now loaded. A few key issues should remain at the forefront of your thinking as you formulate and execute your career transition strategy. Moving forward with these issues in mind will keep you pointed in the right direction, help you keep your priorities in order, and help you maintain a proper perspective as you address the challenge before you. To capture the essence of these issues, we present them in the form of Frequently Asked Questions, along with our proposed answers.

1. Why are so many companies and firms laying off their employees?

   Our turbulent economy, the competitive business environment, and the need for employers to meet the economic expectations of shareholders or partners have created an environment conducive to such action. This change is not necessarily bad, so long as the guiding tenet of the decision makers is to treat employees honestly and with dignity and respect. Research shows that this is not a temporary trend. We must therefore prepare to work within such a business environment throughout the remainder of our careers.

2. I reside in an "at-will" employment state. What exactly does that mean?

   At-will employment means that your employment can be terminated at any time, so long as the reason is not discriminatory. As an at-will employee, you may be discharged for reasons completely unrelated to your performance. Stellar performer or not, you can be discharged without cause and without explanation.

3. Is it true I have no rights as an employee if I am discharged as part of a reduction in force (RIF)?

   Absolutely not! Employment agreements, employment policies, civil service laws, union contracts, and discrimination laws affect your employer's right to reduce its workforce and how such a RIF must occur. If you are facing a RIF, we encourage you (1) to consult your employee handbook, manual, or union contract, and (2) to consider contacting an employment law attorney to determine your rights.

4. The business environment has really changed—it was once rather stable, but now turbulent and uncertain. Do certain skills or abilities allow you to thrive in both environments?

To thrive in any business environment, it is imperative that you possess marketable skills. Such skills enable you to help an organization deliver on its value proposition, whether that proposition involves the creation and distribution of a product or the development and delivery of a service. However, possessing "hot skills" alone is not sufficient; to thrive in both environments, you must also be self-motivated and self-confident.

5. I just read that the economy is about to improve. Does that mean layoffs will soon be a thing of the past?

Unfortunately, no. Many previously assumed that job cuts result only from declining sales or slumps in revenue. However, researchers report (see details in chapter 3) that this is not the case; that even an upturn in the economy does not significantly reduce the number of layoffs.

6. I once read that—regardless of what you are working on—you should always "begin with the end in mind." Is such a perspective appropriate when it comes to career planning?

Not only is such a perspective appropriate, but we also consider it to be absolutely critical! Such a viewpoint helps you recognize factors and events most likely to cause you to begin considering a job change. It therefore sensitizes you to conditions you must recognize when they initially begin to surface. Such a perspective allows you to not only assess conditions contributing to your desire to remain with an organization, but also to be alert and responsive when such conditions begin to change

7. I am not currently being laid off. For that I am extremely thankful. I simply do not think I could handle it! (Although this is not a question, it is an issue worth addressing.)

Your point is well taken. Individuals who have been laid off say they initially felt incapable of surviving the crisis. However, they eventually realized they would get through it, everything would work out, and that this, too, would pass. We are therefore confident, that with the support of your family and friends, you could handle being laid off, if such an event were to ever occur.

8. My family feels I should consider my layoff to be an opportunity rather than a problem. How can I turn such a negative event into a positive force?

It is easier said than done! To capitalize on this life-changing event, you must (among other things): rely on your personal values, reframe your thinking, and reinterpret the situation. Also, while you may disagree with your family on this one issue, we strongly encourage you to continue seeking and relying on the support of your family and friends!

9. I was just severed. The process seemed so cold and distant. Why would my employer of twelve years approach it in such a calculated manner?

Most organizations follow an established and somewhat mechanical process when "severing" employees. It may be that what you experienced was the result of hours or days of special training! You can assume your session was designed to protect the organization, rather than you.

10. Several of my colleagues met with an outplacement specialist moments after being severed. If I am allowed to meet with such a person, what should I ask them?

   At a minimum, ask the outplacement specialist to answer the following three questions: What reasons were you given for my being discharged? Whom should I contact for answers to future questions? Have you heard or read anything that might suggest I will have problems finding a future position?

11. While meeting with the out-counselor or outplacement specialist, should I challenge my dismissal?

   No. You cannot immediately do anything about your dismissal. The decision has already been made, endorsed, and approved by all necessary parties.

12. If I am offered a severance package, should I immediately accept it?

   Here, prudence is the preferred course of action. We recommend that you not simply accept the severance package extended to you. You should first carefully review its conditions and stipulations. You may even need to consider retaining an employment lawyer or an employee benefits specialist to review your severance package. Of course, it is up to you to protect your interests for the future, because your soon-to-be-former employer will not do so.

13. The severance package I am being offered does not include many benefits. I therefore plan to demand more. Is that a good idea?

   We strongly encourage you to proceed cautiously. Keep in mind your employer is not required to provide severance benefits, unless the benefits (1) are required by law (such as civil service benefits); (2) are required in your employment offer, contract, employee handbook, policy manual; or (3) have been agreed upon by your employer and labor union. You must proceed with caution when attempting to negotiate severance benefits. If you reject the severance package, your employer may even withdraw the offer.

14. To receive my severance benefits, I have been asked to sign a "release of claims" form. Is my signing this document simply a legal technicality?

   Proceed with caution! If you sign such a release, you might give up all claims you have against your employer, even wrongful discharge, discrimination or breach of contract claims you do not yet know about! If you prematurely sign such a form, you may give up all rights to benefits to which you were entitled in your job offer letter, your employment agreement, under the employee handbook, and your company's policy manual.

15. I feel my severance was handled poorly. I am therefore concerned about what my employment file contains. I have not been allowed to review my file. Is that proper?

   Not only is it improper, it may be illegal! Most states have laws entitling you or your designee (your attorney) to review your entire employment file. You should ask to review it again. This time, if your employer refuses (which should be unlikely), ask your attorney to make the request. Your request is a valid one. First, your employment file may contain a document providing you rights to severance benefits not available to other employees. Second, a review of your employment file will verify that you did nothing to cause your job loss and that your dismissal was not related to any problems associated with your performance, attitude, commitment, or abilities.

16. What can I do to help ensure that this unplanned career transition ultimately ends in success?

As with anything in life, you must initially decide on your destination and then set an appropriate course. It is therefore critical that you not simply begin searching for another job—you must initially define your objective, determine the path to be taken, and then decide on the steps to be taken along the way. Finally, success requires two main ingredients: an exceptional action plan, along with its effective execution.

17. I have never developed a résumé. Are there two or three key points I should keep in mind while preparing it?

After you have completed your rough draft, review it and ask yourself: Does this résumé present a compelling story? Does it project a professional image? Does it also project commitment and self-confidence?

18. I am preparing to launch a full-scale job search. Is there something I should keep in mind as I prepare?

You will generate, review, and manage a lot of information during the course of your job search. In order for this information to be useful, it must be organized in a manner that allows you quick and easy access. We therefore recommend that you obtain a file cabinet, file cabinet drawers, or a file container to use throughout your job search. Be sure to adopt, and then stick with, a process that you are familiar and comfortable with.

19. I am part of a fairly large family. What can I do to help them help me with my job search?

Our assumption is that each member of your family leads a busy life. To sensitize your family members to potential callers and the messages they need to give them, consider using a family Action Board. This bulletin board should be placed in a location that is central to your family members' lives. For it to be useful, you must update it daily with information about your expected calls, your schedule, and when you are likely to receive and be able to follow up on the caller's message.

20. This is not my first job search. Previously, I simply did not function as efficiently as I could have. What should I do differently this time?

You might mistakenly approach your job search as an isolated event, treating it differently than the other aspects of your life. Rather, you should apply the organization skills you have used throughout your career to your job search. If you normally use a pocket calendar, a desk calendar, a portable day planner, or an electronic planner, continue to do so. To help you focus your actions, you might wish to modify your planner so it contains information relating to your job search. Supplement the tools you have previously used with the ones we provide in chapter 1.

21. What should I include in my résumé?

    We believe effective résumés contain the following five sections: Summary or Profile; Professional Experience and Accomplishments; Specialty Training, Certifications, and Licensures; Awards; Special Recognition. The résumé you produce should not only include these sections, but also must be focused, visually appealing, free of errors, and accurate.

22. When listing my experiences and accomplishments, I appear to include too much information. How can I focus on the most important information?

    Focus only on the key messages you wish to share. Do not include every detail! The detail you do include must be important from the employer's perspective and must be likely to lead to the employer's concluding that you clearly possess the most compelling capabilities and are most likely to succeed in the open position or role.

23. A friend recommends that I not include a cover letter with my résumé. She says my résumé should "stand on its own."

    Your friend is absolutely correct, your résumé should stand on its own. However, keep in mind that your résumé and cover letter serve different purposes. While your résumé provides detailed information, your cover letter presents your overall intention and availability to the prospective employer. The cover letter allows you an initial opportunity to introduce yourself and to begin stating your case. Your cover letter, in essence, establishes the purpose of your contacting the prospective employer, attracts his or her attention, and generates initial interest.

24. Should I use a gimmick, such as colored or oversize paper, to make my cover letter and résumé stand out?

    We recommend that you use a laser printer or a high quality ink jet printer, not a dot matrix printer, to produce a high quality package. Gimmicks do not excite us. We suggest that you print both documents on an off-white, cream, or bright white standard-size (8 1/2 × 11 inch) paper. Mail the cover letter and résumé in an envelope that matches the weight, color, and texture of the paper you are using.

25. You recommend that we "manage" the referral process. Should I not leave this part of the job search up to my references? I trust them!

    Your prospective employer must quickly learn as much as he or she can about you. Your cover letter and résumé will provide some of the needed information. More information is obtained through conversations with individuals who previously worked with you. Through happenstance or in a planned and purposeful manner, professional references influence your chances of being hired. Our advice is to avoid happenstance. We encourage you to influence much of what the prospective employer learns about you from references by managing the referral process.

26. I have a job interview scheduled for next week. How should I prepare?

    Our experience suggests there are certain things you must do to prepare for any interview, whether it is by telephone or face to face with an individual or group. Conduct research or review previous research findings; prepare to answer frequently asked questions; prepare to ask questions; and begin managing your shyness and nervousness now.

27. I am scheduled for an interview tomorrow. What questions might I be asked?

We categorize interview questions into the following five areas: Capabilities (questions relating to your skills and abilities); Experiences (questions relating to experiences which may set you apart from—and above—the other candidates); Accomplishments (questions relating to successes associated with projects, programs, or initiatives); Knowledge of the Industry (or Profession) and Organization (questions to determine your understanding of the position for which you are applying); and Professional Development (questions to determine how previous education and training experiences contributed to your accomplishments).

28. I have been involved in several interviews. When it ends, there seems to be a moment of awkwardness. What can I do to raise my (and the interviewer's) comfort level?

You should conclude every interview on a positive note and with a rather straightforward question. For example, conclude by saying, "I have enjoyed meeting with you, sharing information and ideas with you, and learning more about your organization. I am interested in joining your organization, feel I can contribute to your organization's future success, and am confident I would do well in the position under consideration. What are our next steps?"

29. I have just received a job offer. Are there two or three things I should scrutinize when reviewing the offer?

At a minimum, ensure the salary you are being offered matches industry or profession standards and matches your "market value." Make sure the benefits (insurance coverage, vacation and other forms of leave, retirement, and pension) and bonus structure (including sign-on, relocation, retention, and performance) are also consistent with industry or profession standards.

30. A friend just told me that I must "compare apples to apples, oranges to oranges" when deciding between two job offers. What exactly did she mean?

You may be offered a job that, if accepted, requires you to relocate. When deciding whether or not to accept such a job offer, it is of the utmost importance that you take cost-of-living factors into consideration. For example, you may be inclined to accept a job in another state or city because it offers an attractive salary in comparison with your current salary. However, if you were to relocate, you may quickly discover that costs associated with residing in the new location nullify the salary and bonus increases!

31. I have received a job offer that does not meet my expectations. A friend suggests I "play hardball." Since I am potentially dealing with my future employer, this advice simply does not sound right. What do you recommend?

You have invested a lot of time and energy to get to this point, and you do not want to jeopardize your job offer by inappropriately voicing concerns about a certain option. The organization (potentially your future employer) has also invested a lot of time and energy to get to this point, and in all likelihood will not wish to jeopardize the offer over a trivial point. We encourage you to work out the details and resolve your concern, but do so in an appropriate manner. Approach the employer in a positive, cordial, and professional manner. Make sure your expectations are reasonable, taking into account the capabilities you possess and the environment within which the organization operates. In return, we encourage the prospective employer to listen and be responsive to your concerns.

32. I have been thinking about resigning from my position. I just think I would be happier working elsewhere. Do you think I should resign, or should I reconsider?

Before resigning, we recommend you take some time to reflect. What is causing you to feel unhappy? For example, are you unhappy with your career choice? If that is the case, you should investigate changing careers rather than simply resigning from your current position. After looking inward, we recommend you speak with recruiters, outplacement specialists, and professional colleagues about the job market. The timing may not be right. You may be better off trying to make a bad situation more bearable than losing what you have. Is lack of job satisfaction behind your decision? If so, you might be able to do something proactively, such as initiating a change in your job duties or building a better relationship with your supervisor or coworkers to make your professional life more satisfying.

33. The job market is very tight, but to be candid I see the handwriting on the wall. I have recently been given all of the unfavorable work assignments and just received a very unfavorable (and I believe, an unjustified) performance review. What should I do? What can I do?

Move forward with this in mind: you may eventually have to testify before a jury about how you were treated unfairly or discriminatorily. Plan for that day by preparing to support your subjective feelings with concrete facts to prove your dissatisfaction. We recommend that you immediately begin keeping a journal. Prepare at least one journal page each day. Every day, when you get home, write down what happened that day. Be sure to record names, dates, conversations, events, and witnesses.

34. I just heard that an associate of mine was "constructively discharged." What does that mean?

Under this legal principle, an employer who improperly increases or changes your job duties, working conditions, or work rules has constructively discharged you. Such a discharge potentially entitles you to immediately resign and obtain unemployment compensation as though you were laid off.

35. I have read that you should not "burn bridges" when resigning from a position. I do not like the way I have been treated and intend to speak my mind!

Speaking your mind may satisfy a desire to get back at someone you feel mistreated you, but resist the temptation. Remember, "What you say can and will be used against you." What you say probably will be reported to management and recorded in your personnel file. Inappropriate comments will come back to haunt you. You may well need your former supervisor or manager to provide you a reference. Do not lose the option of asking for a reference by unduly criticizing anyone in the organization. Your former supervisors and coworkers also may become valuable members of the personal network you will use to find another job.

36. I am planning to resign, but do not know how much notice I should give. I do not want to leave too quickly, but am eager to enter the next phase of my life.

How many weeks' notice to give is not always set. Many employment agreements and employee handbooks require a certain notice period, but when none is set (such as for most at-will employees), a reasonable amount of notice should be given. Ten days to two weeks is reasonable. Providing reasonable notice will promote goodwill with your former employer and ease your transition.

37. I am unemployed. My family requires health insurance coverage during this period. What are my options?

One of your options is under the Consolidated Omnibus Budget Reconciliation Act (COBRA). Under COBRA, if your employer has more than twenty employees, it must continue your health insurance under the company's health plan even if you quit. Your employer must notify you of your right to continue coverage within fifteen days of benefits termination. You then have sixty days to notify your employer that you have elected to continue coverage. Continuation coverage will last eighteen months, but it is costly. You must pay the entire cost of the coverage. Your former employer no longer has to make an employer contribution to the total cost of the premium. In addition, your employer may add an administrative charge of 2 percent to the cost, to cover its expenses in administrating your COBRA benefits.

38. A prospective employer has stated that I am subject to a thorough background investigation. I have nothing to hide, why would a company spend money on such an investigation?

The question is not whether a company can afford to conduct background investigations. The question is whether it can afford not to! An employer owes a duty to its workforce and to the public to ascertain the qualifications and competence of the employees it hires, especially when the employees are engaged in occupations that may be hazardous to the safety of others. An employer may be liable for negligent hiring if it hires an incompetent or unfit employee whom it knows, or by the exercise of reasonable care should have known, was incompetent or unfit.

39. A prospective employer just informed me that, as part of a background check, it will solicit information from my previous employer. What information is my previous employer allowed to share?

When the prospective employer contacts your former employer, your former employer may disclose any truthful information about your employment. Fearing a claim of defamation or breach of confidentiality, most employers provide only the dates of employment, final salary, and job title. That most likely will be the case with your previous employer.

40. In addition to the background investigation, the prospective employer has asked me to submit to a variety of "skills" tests. Is this unusual?

Such a request (or requirement) is quite common. In addition to a background check, many employers now require job applicants to submit to a drug test, a job skills test, or a personality or psychological exam. Drug testing may be regulated or prohibited at the application stage by state law. Tests of jobs skills, such as typing, mathematics, writing, and physical agility, also may be administered if they are job related.

41. Employers now focus on policies and procedures, with many developing and distributing voluminous employee handbooks. Why the sudden focus?

We are a society founded on law. We agree to conform our conduct to the rules and regulations enacted by our elected officials. In the workplace, employers and employees each agree to conform their conduct to the legitimate expectations of the other. This can be achieved only by having an agreed system of laws—employment policies governing the employer-employee relationship.

42. In a recent speech, a recruiter proudly stated that his company enforces a progressive discipline policy. What is it, and is it a good thing to have?

Perhaps the most important policy employers must have to enforce their rights, and to avoid being accused of wrongful, selective, or discriminatory enforcement of its policies, is a discipline policy. A common discipline policy provides for gradually increasing penalties for rules infractions of different severity. This is commonly called a progressive discipline policy. Such a policy is invaluable to the employee, because it ensures that discipline is consistently applied. Such consistent application is invaluable to the company, because it reduces accusations of wrongful, selective, or discriminatory enforcement of its policies.

43. I feel I have been discriminated against. How can I prove it?

One way is to show that your employer made a discriminatory comment or specifically told you (or others) that an adverse employment action (such as a suspension, demotion, layoff, or discharge) was because of your race, sex, ethnic background, age, or other federally protected classification. Although such direct proof of discrimination occurs occasionally, it is rare for such blatant, direct proof of discrimination to exist.

44. How else might I prove that I was discriminated against?

The other way is to show that: (1) you are a member of a federally protected class, (2) you met your employer's legitimate expectations, (3) you suffered an adverse employment action, and (4) other similarly situated employees who were not members of the protected class were treated more favorably. If you prove these factors, your employer must show a legitimate, nondiscriminatory reason for the employment action. You then must show that the employer's stated reason for the employment action was not the true reason, but merely a pretext for discrimination.

45. I am applying for a job with an armored car company. I have been asked to submit to a polygraph test. Can my potential employer ask me to submit to such a test?

As a general rule, an employer may not require an employee to take a polygraph test. Consistent with this general rule, no employee or prospective employee may be disciplined, discharged, or discriminated against in any manner for failing or refusing to submit to a polygraph test. The statute does not apply to local, state, or federal governmental agencies, such as law enforcement agencies, employees in certain businesses such as armored car personnel, or security personnel in facilities having a significant impact on health and safety (nuclear power plant, public water works, toxic waste facilities, etc.). From the limited information we have available, it appears your prospective employer can ask you to submit to a polygraph exam, as long as the test is administered in an appropriate manner.

46. I recently read a book that says you should rely on professional and personal friends to help find your next job. That seems too easy. If that's all there is to it, why doesn't everyone already have a job?

Our sentiments, exactly. While your personal network will undoubtedly contribute to your job search, you should also take advantage of electronic databases, use recruiters and interested employers, work with alumni associations and outplacement firms, and participate in career fairs.

47. It sounds as if personal networks are overrated. Is that the case?

Not quite! Your personal and professional friends can be your most valuable resource. The bottom line is this: the more people you have in your personal network, the more people there are who know about your personal values, your capabilities and assets, and your unique skills. Never underestimate the power of your network. Not only will it help you identify and pursue opportunities, but it will also share ideas with you about how to do so successfully, and then frequently will help bridge the gap between your past and future positions.

48. How do I go about expanding my personal network?

Attend local general business seminars and workshops. If you are comfortable doing so, volunteer to give speeches or to lead discussions at local and regional meetings, seminars, and workshops. Share your ideas with others by writing an article. Attend local networking sessions and participate in seminars designed specifically for individuals in transition.

49. I receive numerous calls from executive recruiters. How likely are search firms to significantly contribute to my job search?

To a mixed degree. In some cases, employers hire a search firm to find a candidate to fill a particular position. In that case, the search firm is not your agent working for you, it is the agent of the employer and will not necessarily serve as your advocate. In other cases, the search firm may specialize in certain types of placements, such as executives or attorneys. Here again, the search firm may not necessarily serve as your advocate. Discuss your relationship with the search firm when deciding on whether to use its services.

50. A colleague recently mailed hundreds of résumés to hundreds of companies. She described it as an "attempt to throw paper against the wall to see what sticks." Should I contact hundreds or thousands of potential employers myself or through one of those Internet résumé mass distributors?

We recommend against it. Rather, we suggest you contact selected companies, firms, and institutions—not all of them you can, not all of them in a particular industry or profession, and not all of them that happen to be in a particular location. For this approach to be truly meaningful, you must contact only those firms likely to be searching for someone possessing your capabilities and assets, your experiences and accomplishments, and your insight and wisdom. Target likely employers and go after them.

51. My firm sponsors an alumni program. Are the services such programs offer typically beneficial?

Absolutely, but not for the reasons you may think. The power of firm-sponsored alumni programs does not come from the technology they use or the benefits they offer. Each person, both inside and outside the sponsoring organization, who uses such a program shares a common bond—he or she was once hired after going through a similar selection process, once worked together to accomplish the same mission and goals, and once faced the same challenges and opportunities. The power of these programs comes from a sense of trust that occurs when individuals share in such an experience. Do not underestimate the value of being able to operate under such an assumption of mutual trust.

52. My company offered outplacement services as part of my severance package. I have not yet looked into it, because I just don't think the services will be helpful. What do you think?

We think you should learn more about the services. For example, outplacement benefits typically include career and transition counseling, as well as provide you access to industry and company directories, proprietary databases and research results, job leads from previously established networks, personal e-mail accounts, and fax machines.

53. How can people say my being laid off will help bring my family together?

We do not know if your layoff will actually bring your family closer together. It will, however, present an excellent opportunity for your family to gain a better understanding of each family member's strengths and limitations and will allow ample opportunities for each family member to provide—and receive—mutual support. The bottom line is this: your job loss will allow your family members to work together to overcome an event and contribute as one to an individual family member's overall success.

54. Why is my being laid off so difficult to deal with? I can't stop thinking about it. I am very angry, and my anger does not seem to be diminishing.

You are not alone. Much of a person's identity is wrapped around his or her career. We go to school, spend years learning a profession, and ultimately identify ourselves as part of that profession. Our employers frequently want us to feel as though our profession is more important than attending family events. Over time, work begins to come first. Life appears to have no true meaning outside our professional life. Many of us buy into that philosophy. To many of us, organizational role and responsibility not only add meaning to life, but it also is our life! Use your layoff as an opportunity to reexamine your priorities in life. You may decide that you should not measure your success in life by your employment.

55. What should I focus on as I work through this career transition?

First, carefully focus on (and celebrate) your previous experiences and accomplishments. Secondly, reflect on the past, within the context of exciting new opportunities. Finally, strive to become more self-aware and able to act on those emerging opportunities. We encourage you to purchase and read William Bridges's books about jobs, careers, and personal transitions (listed in the bibliography).

56. My layoff carries significant financial ramifications. How can I even begin "getting my arms around" this particular aspect of my job loss?

Realize that your layoff presents a financial challenge that you and your family can work together to overcome. It does have financial consequences; however, the event has occurred—you must now take action to mitigate its consequences. Do not overreact. Your layoff presents obstacles similar to the ones you addressed while employed. Your knowledge and tenacity, along with the support of your family and friends, will carry you through this challenging time! In terms of immediate actions: audit your financial situation, conduct an accurate appraisal of your monthly liabilities, take decisive steps to minimize your expenditures, and take advantage of your assets.

57. What role does unemployment insurance play?

Unemployment insurance is designed to compensate you partially for lost wages when you are out of a job or if you work less than full time because work is not available. The program attempts to ensure that you will have income while you search for a job. Unemployment insurance differs from Social Security because in all but a few states the funds used to pay benefits are collected from employers. The unemployment insurance program is administered by the states. Check with your state or local unemployment office for information about your state's program.

58. A family member was recently laid off. He took it more personally, and much more emotionally, than I did when I was discharged several years ago. Why the different response?

We know quite a few folks who have been laid off. Our personal observations reveal that no two people take the news the same way; are equally prepared to emotionally accept the news, progress through the personal transition the same way, or approach the idea of "starting over" the same way.

59. These are very trying times! Are there certain things I should watch for, when it comes to stress or depression?

Several sources suggest that these are symptoms of severe stress or clinical depression: an inability to focus on daily routine, an increase or decrease in appetite or sleep, feelings of unworthiness, marked changes in personal hygiene, and an increased consumption of alcohol or drugs.

60. I really do feel like I need some help. I have a lot going on in my life right now, and I can't seem to be able to get a handle on this. What should I do?

Your asking this question is an excellent first step! It will undoubtedly be one of many. We each live in a very complex world, no one (including you!) is expected to think of everything, much less know everything. The wise person is not afraid to seek the help of an expert to uncomplicate his or her life. We encourage you to seek help. Doing so will not only help you, but your family as well.

CONCLUSION

Our intent throughout this book has been to provide practical, useful information to individuals who have been laid off, are about to be laid off, or are at risk of being laid off. We have also referred you to numerous public source documents, databases and Web sites, and institutions and organizations. The challenge you face is significant. We are confident you will take advantage of these support systems.

Keep the issues stressed in this section at the forefront of your thinking as you formulate and execute your career transition strategy. Doing so will keep you pointed in the right direction, help you keep your priorities in order, and help you maintain a proper perspective.

We have sensitized you to a variety of issues. Now, round out your awareness and understanding by reviewing the detailed information presented throughout this book and accessing the recommended sources of information.

Armed with your toolkit, move forward simultaneously on several fronts. Conduct your self-assessment, develop your Action Plan, and then execute your Action Plan in a planned and purposeful manner. Make this planned or unplanned career change a boost to a higher level.

Appendix

The Hammer and Saw

Throughout this toolkit, you were introduced to various tools in the form of matrices, tables, and charts. These tools are designed to help you identify—and address—issues. Each tool, previously described and applied, is reproduced on the following pages.

Information about when you should use these tools and instructions on how to derive the most benefit from their use is provided elsewhere in this book. Refer to the Transition Tools matrix on the following page.

We encourage you to review the tools, determine their utility, and photocopy and use them.

Transition Tools

Tool	Introduced in Chapter	Introduced as Table
Barrier/Solution Table	4	4.1
Pluses/Minuses Table	5	5.1
Discussion Points Matrix	5	5.2
Separation Agreement Review Table	5	5.3
Emotional State Assessment Table	6	6.1
Emotional Readiness Assessment Table	6	6.3
Start/Stop/Continue Table	6	6.5
Review of Current Assets Matrix	6	6.8
Review of Current Liabilities Matrix	6	6.10
Required vs. Optional Expense Matrix	6	6.11
Action Review Chart	6	6.14
Supplies for Conducting a Job Search	7	7.1
Weekly Calendar	7	7.2
Job Database Log Sheet	7	7.4
Organization Contact Log Sheet	7	7.5
Search Firm Contact Log Sheet	7	7.6
Job Lead Log	7	7.7
Personal Contact Log	7	7.8
Transaction Log	7	7.9
Position Review Form	7	7.11
Position Comparison Form	7	7.12
Location Comparison Form	7	7.13
Dual Location Comparison Form	7	7.14

Barrier/Solution Table

Barrier ___	Potential Solutions

Barrier ___	Potential Solutions

Pluses/Minuses Table

+	-

Discussion Points Matrix

On the positive side . . .	On the other hand . . .

Separation Agreement Review Table

Terms Set Forth in Job Offer, Employee Handbook, Policy Manual	How Addressed in Separation Agreement

Emotional State Assessment

Denial	Shock	Anger	Acceptance

Emotional Readiness Assessment

Action to Be Taken	Unacceptable	Marginal	Prepared
Speak with members of network			
Meet with members of network			
Speak with potential headhunter			
Meet with potential headhunter			
Meet with potential employer			
Participate in job interviews			

Start/Stop/Continue

Start	Stop	Continue

Review of Current Assets

Asset	Amount	Liquid	Contingent

Review of Current Liabilities

Monthly Cost (Description of Item)	Amount ($)	Required	Optional

Required versus Optional Expense

Item Description: _____

Question	If "Yes," Likely a Required Expense	If "No," Likely an Optional Expense
If this purchase is not made, will my/this family's safety be in jeopardy?		
If this purchase is not made, will my/this family's health be in jeopardy?		
If this purchase is not made, will my/this family's welfare be in jeopardy?		

Action Review Chart

Stop/End	Continue/Modify	Initiate/Begin

Supplies for Conducting a Job Search

Item	Possess (P) or Acquire (A)
Pens and pencils	
Notepads of 8 1/2 by 11-inch paper	
Notepads of 4 by 5-inch paper	
Scissors	
Paper clips	
Ink cartridges or typewriter ribbons	
Envelopes	
Tape	
Typing or printing paper	
Stationery	
Stamps	

Weekly Calendar

Day	Meet	Telephone	E-mail	Mail
Monday				
Tuesday				
Wednesday				
Thursday				
Friday				
Weekend				

Job Database Log Sheet

Database	Internet Address	User name and Password	Notes

Organization Contact Log Sheet

Company, Firm, or Institution	Date of Contact	Contact Info (Address, E-mail, Telephone)	Notes	Follow-up Actions

Search Firm Contact Log

Firm	Date of Contact	Contact Info (Address, E-mail, Telephone)	Notes	Follow-up Actions

Job Lead Log

Information	Notes
Lead (Company, Firm, Institution)	
Lead address	
Contact	
Title	
Telephone/E-mail	
I received lead from	
Useful information about lead	
My response	___ Telephone Date: _____ ___ E-mail Date: _____ ___ Meeting Date: _____
Results	

Personal Contact Log

NAME	
Title	
Company	
Telephone	
E-mail	
Fax	
Miscellaneous	
NAME	
Title	
Company	
Telephone	
E-mail	
Fax	
Miscellaneous	

Transaction Log

NAME	
Transaction 1. Date: _____ ___ Telephone ___ E-mail ___ Personal meeting	Summary/Result/Follow-up
Transaction 2. Date: _____ ___ Telephone ___ E-mail ___ Personal meeting	Summary/Result/Follow-up
Transaction 3. Date: _____ ___ Telephone ___ E-mail ___ Personal meeting	Summary/Result/Follow-up

Position Review Form

Item for Review	Information Relating to Job Offer
Base salary	
Sign-on bonus	
Guaranteed annual bonus	
Annual retention bonus	
Other annual bonus opportunity	
Stock options	
Health insurance	
Long-term care insurance	
Disability insurance	
Life insurance	
Dental insurance	
Eye care insurance	
Relocation expense reimbursement	
Retirement program	
Vacation leave	
Sick leave	

Position Comparison Form

Item for Review	Job Offer 1	Job Offer 2
Base salary		
Sign-on bonus		
Subsequent bonus opportunity		
Stock options		
Life insurance		
Health insurance		
Disability insurance		
Relocation reimbursement		
Company automobile		
Vacation leave		
Sick leave		
Retirement program		

Location Comparison Form

Item for Review	Job Offer 1	Job Offer 2
Base salary		
Sign-on bonus		
Subsequent bonus opportunity		
Stock options		
Life insurance		
Health insurance		
Disability insurance		
Relocation reimbursement		
Company automobile		
Vacation leave		
Sick leave		
Retirement program		

Dual Location Comparison Form

Item for Comparison	Job Offer 1	Job Offer 2
Base salary		
Sign-on bonus		
Annual bonus opportunity		
State taxes		
Local taxes		
House payment		
Rent payment		
Utilities		
House insurance		
Apartment insurance		
Automobile expense (gas, insurance)		
Food		
Clothes		

Bibliography

Bridges, William. *Managing Transitions.* Reading, MA: Addison-Wesley, 1991.
———. *Job Shift: How to Prosper in a Workplace without Jobs.* Reading, MA: Perseus Books, 1994.
———. *Creating You & Company: Learn to Think Like the CEO of Your Own Career.* Reading, MA: Addison-Wesley, 1997.
Coddington, R. D. "The Significance of Life Events as Etiologic Factors in the Diseases of Children." I—A Survey of Professional Workers. *Journal of Psychosomatic Research,* 1972, 16 (1), 13–16.
Depression. [On-line]. (2001). Rockville, MD: National Institute of Mental Health. Available: http://www.nimh.gov.
Eisenberg, Daniel. *Paying to Keep Your Job.* [On-line]. 2001, 158 (17). New York: Time.com. Available: http://www.time.com.
The Employment Situation: April 2003. [On-line]. (2003, May 1). Washington, DC: Bureau of Labor Statistics. Available: http://www.bls.gov/news.release/pdf/empsit.pdf.
The Employment Situation: December 2002. [On-line]. (2003, January 10). Washington, DC: Bureau of Labor Statistics. Available: http://www.bls.gov/news.release/archives/empsit_01102003.pdf.
Greist, John H., and Jefferson, James W. (1998). *Depression and Your Family: What You Can Do to Help.* (Pfizer Publication No. TX285Y96). New York: Pfizer.
Grieving Process. [On-line]. (2001). State University of New York at Buffalo SHS Counseling Center. Available: http://www.ub-counseling.buffalo.edu.
Holmes, T., and Rahe, R. "The Social Readjustment Rating Scale." *Journal of Psychosomatic Research,* 1967, 11 (10), 216.
Illinois Department of Employment Security. (2001). *Summary of Services.* (IDES Publication No. 4449). Springfield, IL: Illinois Department of Employment Security.

Jefferson, James W., and Greist, John H. (1998). *Unmasking Depression: Seeing Things in a Different Light*. (Pfizer Publication No. TX280Y96). New York: Pfizer.

Jobless Claims Jump. [On-line]. (2001, September 27). Atlanta, GA: CNNfn. Available: http://www.cnnfn.com.

Labor Laws: Severance Packages. [On-line]. (2001). Studio City, CA: GotTrouble.com. Available: http://www.gottrouble.com.

Money Moves to Make When You Lose Your Job. [On-line]. (2001). New York: iVillage.com/MoneyLife. Available: http://www.ivillage.com.

Pohl, Avis. *25 Easy Ways to Save*. [On-line]. (2001). New York: iVillage.com/MoneyLife. Available: http://www.ivillage.com.

Publications. [On-line]. (2001). Washington, DC: American Bar Association. Available: http://www.abanet.org.

State Unemployment Insurance. [On-line]. (2001). Washington, DC: Department of Labor. Available: http://www.workforcesecurity.doleta.gov.

Strope, Leigh. (2001, September 8). Unemployment is Highest in 6 Years. *Kane County Chronicle*, p. B3.

Summary of Services. [On-line]. (2001). Springfield, IL: Department of Employment Security. Available: http://www.ides.state.il.us.

Tischler, Linda. *10 Hard Truths about Layoffs*. [On-line]. (June 2001). New York: Fast Company. Available: http://www.fastcompany.com.

Unemployment Weekly Claims Report. [On-line]. (2003, May 1). Washington, DC: Department of Labor. Available: http://www.dol.gov/opa/media/press/eta/ui/current.htm.

Index

About the Authors

B. KEITH SIMERSON is a Partner with Tradewinds Consulting.

MICHAEL D. McCORMICK is a Partner with Coman & Anderson.